Community
and
Contention

Britain and America
in the
Twentieth Century

Community
and
Contention

Britain and America
in the
Twentieth Century

Bruce M. Russett

The M. I. T. Press

Cambridge, Massachusetts

1963

To my parents

Preface

This is a book of many colors. Its purposes are to develop a body of theory, stated in rather precise terms, for analyzing factors in the relations between two countries, to examine the present and past state of relations between the United States and Great Britain, and to contribute something to the explanation of why those relations are as they are. It has two sets of functions, each of which can be discussed under the headings of theory, description, and hypothesis-testing.

The first set of functions will be fulfilled more completely than the second, and concerns certain variables which have often been neglected, have hardly ever been discussed with precision, and have never been examined systematically on a full scale. These variables include international communication, attention, and mutual identification. In the area of theory, I shall develop a model emphasizing their role in promoting integration. Under description, I shall study trends in these variables over the past seventy-three years as they have affected Britain and America. In regard to hypothesis-testing, I shall show that many of these variables are, as alleged, important in influencing the behavior of individual decision-makers. They have made a difference, in particular cases, in the degree to which leaders in Britain and America have been responsive to each other's needs.

A second set of functions involves the explanation of trends in mutual responsiveness, and represents a more ambitious undertaking. It requires both more theory and an additional piece of description, with a decision as to whether Britain met the United States' needs more readily and fully in the 1890's or in the 1950's, and vice versa. As we shall see, responsiveness in this general sense is not easy to measure, even in terms of more or less. The difficulty is not insuperable, for the opening chapter rather impressionistically sketches trends in responsiveness, and in Chapter 2 there is an attempt to find "hard" indicators of the variable. Part of the difficulty is definitional, and Chapter 2 presents more precise statements of the concepts employed, including responsiveness and integration. At the very least, this part of the study destroys the case that in the obvious, prima facie sense, Britain and America are in all significant ways "closer" to each other now than a half century ago. It offers substantial evidence that in important ways they are less responsive than they once were. Given this situation, the following chapters can be viewed as an explanation of how it all came about.

The attempt to measure trends in responsiveness itself is preliminary and exploratory, and while that dependent variable remains
imprecisely measured, the effort to explain those trends, on the gross
level, is incomplete. It is a fascinating and important task, but I have
only begun to develop the new body of theory and the required new
tools of measurement. The principal purposes of the study remain
those outlined above — theorizing about a set of neglected variables,
describing Anglo-American trends in them, and proving their rele-
vance to domestic and international politics.

Many people have contributed in various ways to the writing of
this book. I owe a particular debt to the imagination and criticism of
Karl W. Deutsch of Yale University, under whose direction I originally wrote this as a Ph.D. dissertation. Without his support I could
not have done the job. Harold Lasswell and Robert Triffin of Yale
made many invaluable suggestions while they served on the committee
supervising the dissertation. Others, including Gabriel Almond, William Emerson, Paul Hammond, and H. Bradford Westerfield of Yale,
Ithiel de Sola Pool of the Massachusetts Institute of Technology, and
Louis Morton of Dartmouth College, read the manuscript in whole
or in part. I owe much to their knowledge and insights.
    A great many others assisted in the early stages of the project,
either in helping me to formulate the research design or to locate
information. Among them are Geoffrey Barraclough, C. E. Carring-
ton, Richard Coakley, Robert A. Dahl, Fred Greene, F. H. Hinsley,
Paul Horst-Madsen, Albert Imlah, Sir Donald MacDougall, R. T.
McKenzie, W. N. Medlicott, and Warner Schilling. A book of this
sort could not have been written without the generous aid of many
officials of public agencies and private organizations in both the
United States and Great Britain, who put up with my insistent requests for peculiar types of information and often went to great effort to help me obtain it. I cannot list them individually here, but
do offer them collectively my sincere thanks. The Carnegie Corporation generously provided financial support. I have also drawn upon
the resources of the Yale Political Data Program.
    Two other people deserve particular mention. My mother spent
long hours typing a detailed and technical manuscript — truly a labor
of love. My wife contributed far more than simply putting up with
me while I wrote this book, and more than correcting grammar and
proofs. While she certainly did those things as well, her ideas and
the results of her acute criticism of my notions are to be found in
every chapter.

                                                    Bruce Martin Russett

New Haven, Connecticut
September, 1962

Addendum

The storm over America's decision to cancel development of "Skybolt" arose after this manuscript went to press. It is too early to know the eventual outcome of the controversy; perhaps in the long run it will strengthen the Atlantic community. Nevertheless it clearly has imposed serious strains on the alliance, and is indicative of the still imperfect Anglo-American communication and mutual understanding emphasized so often in this book. America's abrupt cancellation of the missile and British rage at the decision, even though the United Kingdom was unwilling to pay development costs itself, illustrate a continuing inability of each to comprehend the other's point of view on some very important matters. Since the agreed compromise—whereby the United States will supply Britain with Polaris missiles for a NATO-controlled force—appears highly unpopular in Great Britain, the controversy cannot yet be considered settled. The redefinition of Britain's role as a world power will require not only tactful diplomacy and sympathetic action, but basic attention on both sides to the roots of the "special relationship."

B.M.R.

December, 1962

Contents

Community
and
Contention

Britain and America
in the
Twentieth Century

1

Anglo-American Diplomacy since 1890

Years of Peace

In contrast with the turbulent epoch to begin soon afterward, the early 1890's were quiet years for the English-speaking world. America grew ever more splendid in her isolation; with her demographic and industrial growth, she became not just a potential world power but an actual one. Most of the wounds of the Civil War were at least covered with scar tissue, and America's wealth, population, and industrial capacity already surpassed that of any nation in Europe. Distance, her new power, and the British fleet protected her from foreign threats. Abetted by a massive influx of British capital, all of America's strength could be concentrated upon her own development. For Britain too this was a period of relative calm. She had not fought a major war since 1855, she too possessed a mighty industrial machine, and she and her colonial empire (one fourth of the world) were guarded by the Royal Navy. There were shadows — Germany's rise threatened the balance of power in Europe, as did Japan's in the Far East — but war still seemed unprofitable, undesirable, unlikely.

Anglo-American relations themselves were comparatively peaceful. In 1861 Secretary of State William Seward, desperate for a way to hold the dissolving Union together, had urged his new Chief Executive to pick a quarrel with England. In 1865 it seemed briefly as if a victorious Union, enraged at alleged British assistance to the fallen Confederacy, might turn a million bayonets toward Canada. This threat vanished finally only with the *Alabama* claims settlement and the Treaty of Washington in 1872. But since then there had been no issue which threatened a serious rupture. A few small matters had, in fact, been settled quite amicably. Two treaties were ratified in February 1890, one an extradition treaty and the other a temporary agreement, with Germany as a third party, about the status of Samoa. The next year Congress passed a new copyright law, to the great gratification of English authors who previously had had their works pirated by unscrupulous American publishers.

The seas were not entirely smooth, of course. A prime source of contention was American tariff policy, epitomized by the highly protectionist McKinley Tariff of 1890, a measure which particularly hit British cutlery, tin plate, and woolen manufacturers. Since the United States was still Britain's greatest foreign customer, taking 12 per cent of her exports in 1890, American protection was keenly resented. The United States government, anxious to prevent extermination of the Pribilof Island seals, seemed to insist that the Bering Sea was a mare clausum. This, said Congress in 1889, gave America the right to seize vessels "trespassing" on her rights there. Her Majesty's government could not accept the contention. Trade and fisheries disputes between the United States and Canada remained alive, as did an argument over the Canadian-Alaskan boundary dating from Seward's purchase of his icebox. Pressure grew in America for the construction of an all-American Isthmian canal to link the Atlantic and the Pacific. Both countries, however, had relinquished the right to exclusive control over such a canal by the Clayton-Bulwer Treaty of 1850, and the British were not yet ready to change their minds. A border dispute between British Guiana and Venezuela, still in its early stages, threatened someday to burst into flame, involving the Monroe Doctrine. And perhaps most irritating of all, though hardly a matter for direct governmental conversation, was the Irish question. Gladstone's Home Rule policy was defeated in 1886, and since then Anglophobia among the sons of the shamrock in North America had become particularly intense. Irish-Americans opposed almost all efforts to solve mutual Anglo-American problems, and many of them would have welcomed a war against the English oppressors.[1] In the 1880's

[1] Another issue which one might have expected to have important divisive effects on Anglo-American relations was the Free Silver versus Gold Standard controversy in the United States. Britain was the principal guardian of the "cross of gold," and some Populists felt that she had deliberately driven spikes into American bodies. Said silver Senator William Stewart of Nevada, "War would be a good thing even if we got whipped, for it would rid us of English bank rule." (Richard Hofstadter, *The Age of Reform,* New York, 1960, p. 89) Yet the effects were not very serious, for the Populists' and Silverites' wrath was directed equally at Wall Street, Eastern capitalists, and the Jews.

To English defenders of the gold standard, American monetary policy seemed of little direct interest. The worst that American adoption of bimetallism might do would be to spur those forces in Britain pushing for the same goal;

and 1890's, says C. S. Campbell, "talk of war was not uncommon." [2]

Many of these problems were settled in the following two decades. Temporary agreements patched up the Bering Sea quarrel until 1892, when the two nations signed a convention referring it to arbitration. The award, made in 1896, rejected all the American contentions, and the United States had to pay a half-million dollars in damages for the seizure of Canadian schooners. The arbitrators, however, laid down regulations to protect the seals. Their action was not sufficient because of Russian and Japanese sealers' activities, which were not curtailed until the signing of a four-power convention in 1911. But by then the issue had long disappeared as a cause of Anglo-American friction.

The Alaskan boundary dispute was not settled quite so easily. It became a serious matter with the Yukon gold rush in 1896, which made acute the danger of border incidents. Theodore Roosevelt, in 1902, sent 800 cavalrymen to the Panhandle to bolster the American claim. Negotiation continued, nevertheless, and in the following January London reluctantly accepted Secretary of State John Hay's proposal for arbitration by a joint tribunal. The American government had no intention of yielding its claims, which were in fact the more firmly based, and both parties recognized that arbitration was to be largely a face-saving means for British acquiescence. In October 1903, the Joint Commission reported, granting substantially all of the United States claim. The three Americans and the British commissioner made up the majority, and the two Canadian members dissented. Meanwhile, negotiations about the Newfoundland fisheries dispute dragged on, and in 1909 they were submitted to the Hague Tribunal. That body, in one of its first important cases, tendered a decision safeguarding the interests of New England fishermen in the area but supporting Newfoundland's claim to domestic jurisdiction over some inlets which America claimed were international waters.

---

at best, it might substantially aid India, with its great silver reserves. *The Times* of London declared in two leading articles: "As outsiders, we can look forward with complacency to the further advance in silver prices which the Bill [the Sherman silver purchase bill] may be expected to cause. It will be a benefit to our great Indian dependency, and it will be a matter of indifference to ourselves." (April 21, 1890, 9:3) "That the United States will flourish none the less and that their prosperity will be used as an argument by currency-managers in this country must be expected as matters of course. The United States Legislature has never yet succeeded in devising schemes which will fully counteract the enormous natural advantages of the country. It has tried its best by protection, and it is to try now by the Silver Bill, but the results will be as incomplete as ever." (June 7, 1890, 13:4)

[2] C. S. Campbell, *Anglo-American Understanding, 1898–1903,* Baltimore, 1957, p. 4.

In 1912 an Anglo-American treaty set up a permanent body to deal with future problems as they arose.

America's desire to build a canal across Central America touched a more fundamental interest. During the second month of the new century the first Hay-Pauncefote Treaty was signed, authorizing the United States to construct and manage a canal, but requiring it to be open to all powers in peace and war, and forbidding the United States to fortify it. When the Senate attached far-reaching qualifications, the British declined to ratify. The next year Hay and Pauncefote tried again, this time permitting American fortifications. Both nations promptly ratified.

Of all the issues in dispute, the Venezuelan boundary controversy was the only one which carried any real danger of war. The border had never been properly delineated, and repeated attempts to negotiate a settlement had been fruitless. In July 1895, President Cleveland, annoyed by Britain's repeated refusal to arbitrate, sent a blistering note to London, a missive prepared by his Secretary of State, Richard Olney, and dubbed "Olney's twenty-inch gun." It accused Britain of violating the Monroe Doctrine and threatened war if she did not stop trying to advance the boundary against a weaker power. Lord Salisbury, the Prime Minister, waited four months before replying; when he did so, he rejected both the accusation and Olney's interpretation of the Monroe Doctrine. Cleveland, incensed, asked Congress to make available the money for a commission to determine the Guianan-Venezuelan frontier — a step that amounted to enforced arbitration by the United States. Congress unanimously appropriated the cash.

After a short outburst of chauvinism, cautionary voices began to speak in both countries. Colonial Secretary Joseph Chamberlain declared, "War between the two nations would be an absurdity as well as a crime." [3] British anxiety to reach agreement was increased by the Kaiser's congratulatory telegram to Paul Kruger, President of the Boer Republic, on his defeat of Jameson's British raiders "without appealing to the help of friendly powers." [4] Faced with an increasing threat from Germany, and without a strong, dependable ally in the world, Britain saw the need of keeping on good terms with the United States. London agreed to arbitration provided that no territory under the exclusive use and occupation of either party for sixty years was the subject of arbitration, thus safeguarding her chief concern. A compromise decision, generally favorable to Venezuela, was reached,

[3] Samuel Flagg Bemis, *A Diplomatic History of the United States,* New York, 1955, p. 421.
[4] *Ibid.,* p. 420.

though the United States had to pressure the Venezuelans to accept. In one author's words, the British "sacrificed their prestige to their belief that war with the United States was unthinkable." [5] The last serious threat of war between the two powers passed. In some ways the danger may have contributed to their future peaceful relations:

> In the end it cleared from the soul of the American public much of the perilous stuff of Anglophobia which weighed upon it, and it brought home to Britons the essential need of assiduously cultivating friendly relations with their great neighbor across the Atlantic.[6]

Thus five outstanding issues were settled over a fairly short period, illustrating the basic underlying strength of Anglo-American relations. Neither government wanted war with the other. In the most serious crisis, once the danger in which their intransigence had put them was apparent, both backed down to allow a peaceful settlement. A very powerful force contributing to the ease of settlement was Britain's fear of the German Empire; thus she felt a need to come to terms with America in case a European war should erupt.

Even in the area of tariffs there was a very mild improvement. President Cleveland in 1894 attempted to modify the McKinley Tariff; though obstructed by a Republican Congress, he was able to reduce the average rate of duty from 49.5 per cent to 39.9 per cent.[7] The new Republican administration of 1897 promptly sponsored the Dingley Tariff, which marked the zenith of American protection to that time, with an average rate of 57 per cent. But in 1909 another Republican president, Taft, was able to achieve a few mild reductions against much opposition, and the Democrats passed a modest reform measure, the Underwood Tariff, in 1913. Of all the major problems at issue in the 1890's only the Irish situation remained unchanged at the beginning of World War I; that would have to wait until 1923.

As they settled the issues between them, the two powers found that in many other areas their interests coincided, or at least could be made compatible. In October 1897, Lord Salisbury assured the United States that British interests in Cuba were purely commercial and that he would favor any steps to restore tranquillity there. When war was imminent the following April, England, though begged by

[5] John Bartlet Brebner, *The North Atlantic Triangle,* New Haven, 1945, p. 251.

[6] H. C. Allen, *Great Britain and the United States,* New York, 1955, p. 540.

[7] *Ibid.,* p. 77. The reader must interpret these figures with extreme caution, because their value in suggesting the *effect* of a tariff is very limited. For example, when shipping and production costs are about equal in a highly competitive market, a 10 per cent duty may be prohibitive; under other conditions a 50 per cent tariff may not seriously handicap an exporter.

Spain to hold the Americans back, refused and only sent a note, in common with other major European powers, expressing hope that peace might be preserved. Throughout the ensuing conflict Britain's behavior was distinctly more friendly than that of other European nations. When Dewey bombarded Manila, British and German fleets were in the bay observing. The Royal Navy forces moved between the American and German fleets in order to get a better view of the bombardment; a legend arose that the British Admiral did this to restrain the Germans from attacking Dewey. Far from restricting American expansion in these areas, in July 1898, London made it clear that Britain favored American annexation of both the Philippine Islands and Hawaii.

In the Far East, both Britain and America soon discovered that they had a stake in maintaining freedom of commerce for all nations. The United States government refused to take any action in concert with the British, but by 1899 it felt the need of some kind of agreement with other powers. Hay sent identical notes to London, Berlin, St. Petersburg, Tokyo, Rome, and Paris, proposing the nonintervention-with-commerce principles known as the Open Door. Though the other powers attached conditions, Britain approved. This was followed, during the Boxer rebellion, by the second Open Door Note. The latter, merely a statement of American policy, required no reply, but again the British approved. America was not yet ready to take more forceful action, but British and American interests ran in the same direction. In Africa, Secretary Hay expressed the same kind of desire for peace and friendly interest in halting the Boer War as Britain had in the Spanish-American War. Administration leaders ignored the Democratic platform's support for the Boers. The Samoan problem was finally settled by the islands' division between Germany and the United States, with Britain receiving compensation elsewhere.

Britain also, in making alliances, was careful not to commit herself to fight the United States. When the Anglo-Japanese Alliance was renewed in 1905, each power bound itself to maintain a force in the Far East superior to that of any *European* power in the area. On its second renewal, it stipulated that neither power was obliged to go to war against any nation with which it had a general treaty of arbitration. When the United States failed to ratify the Anglo-American arbitration treaty then being negotiated, Britain secretly informed Japan that it regarded its 1914 Bryan conciliation treaty with the United States as a treaty of arbitration. An ill-starred draft of a proposed British-German treaty of alliance in 1901 stipulated that neither party was bound "to join in hostilities against the United States of America." The negotiations failed, in part because of what

Lord Lansdowne described as "the risk of entangling ourselves in a policy which might be hostile to America." [8]

In Latin America too, the Lion learned to avoid stepping on the Eagle's talons. Venezuela was again the scene of potential trouble when Britain and Germany, exasperated by the local government's refusal to pay its debts, in 1902 blockaded Venezuelan ports and bombarded Venezuelan fortifications. Though the British government had first cleared the matter with Washington to ensure that the Americans would not take offense, both governments misread the probable public reaction. After considerable outcry in the United States, matched by protests in Britain against the government's indiscretion in risking American friendship, the Lion stepped off. Prime Minister Balfour took rapid action to mend the injury, and the three parties — Britain, Germany, and Venezuela — referred their claims to the Hague Tribunal. Ten years later, in Mexico, the British government restrained oil magnate Lord Cowdray from pushing his entrepreneurial efforts so hard as to alienate the American government. [9]

In 1906, *Jane's Fighting Ships* for the first time listed the United States Navy as the world's second largest. From then on, the British government recognized the immense cost of a war with the United States, or even of trying to keep too far ahead of her in naval armaments. The principle of maintaining a navy equal to the world's two largest gave way, in Sir Edward Grey's terms, to "that of not taking account of the American Navy in calculating the requirements of the British Empire." [10] From the other side, however, the probabilities of peace did not seem so great. The lingering fear of war with Britain (and also the fear of being left alone in the world with a hostile Germany) was represented in the Navy's insistence on building many battleships throughout the first two decades of the century. This policy was not abandoned despite a desperate need for destroyers during the war. Even in June 1916 the Assistant Chief of Naval Operations measured American needs "against all possible contingencies," including a war against the United Kingdom. [11]

But the United States too took steps to improve relations. Congress, in providing for the operation of the new Panama Canal in 1912, had exempted United States coastal shipping from paying tolls,

[8] R. B. Mowat, *The Diplomatic Relations of Great Britain and the United States,* London, 1925, p. 92.

[9] On intergovernmental frictions caused by private investors' activities, see Chapter 4.

[10] Quoted in Allen, *Great Britain and the United States,* p. 748.

[11] Warner R. Schilling, "Civil-Naval Politics in World War I," *World Politics,* VII, 4 (July 1955), pp. 580–581.

a clear violation of the Hay-Pauncefote Treaty. Responding to Foreign Office protests, President Wilson personally asked Congress to repeal the discriminatory clause. After a bitter debate in early 1914, Congress did so. In return, Britain brought its Mexican policy into line with Wilson's by withdrawing support from the dictator Huerta.

Not all was sweetness and light, of course. Repeated failures to negotiate or ratify an effective arbitration treaty illustrate some of the difficulties that remained. But the new closeness of the two English-speaking powers was marked, in April 1914, by the first offical visit of a British Cabinet member — Foreign Minister Balfour — to the United States during his term of office. Both governments, but particularly the British, had worked hard to strengthen the ties. The British especially had sacrificed immediate, short-term interests to the long-run need for American friendship in a world that was becoming increasingly hostile to British security.[12] And in many cases short-term sacrifice was not needed, for both powers often found themselves facing essentially the same way from the beginning. The history of this period illustrates the dangers of trying to gauge the relations between two nations by the number and severity of problems that arise to trouble them. The problems at this time were numerous and severe, but on the whole both governments, very particularly the British, proved extraordinarily adept at perceiving the most important needs and demands of the other, and at meeting them.

World War I and After

A few new issues, such as an American tariff rebate on imports carried in American ships, had arisen by 1913, but they were minor compared with the stresses arising from the opening years of the First World War. One of Britain's chief weapons against a continental power, as had been demonstrated a century before, was economic strangulation. Throughout the war she steadily expanded her restrictions on neutral trade with the Central Powers, relying partly on methods developed during the Napoleonic Wars, on United States practices during its blockade of the South during the Civil War, and on imperfectly agreed-upon international law as discussed at several

[12] A. E. Campbell (*Great Britain and the United States, 1895–1903*, London, 1960, p. 79) declares that the British elite assumed that "Great Britain and the United States could have no real and important differences, if only Britain would ignore the irrelevant irritations. The irritations were irrelevant because not based on real differences of interest. . . . Evidence of congruity of interest was not produced — that congruity of interest was assumed." Needless to say, this same attitude did not prevail toward Germany, a fact Campbell attributes in part to British feeling of racial solidarity with America (p. 149).

world conferences since 1856. As the war progressed, she resorted to increasingly extreme measures, justified, and in some ways rightly so, as retaliation for Germany's submarine warfare. She used an expanded interpretation of "continuous voyage," an immensely inclusive definition of "contraband," and finally, in 1917, a full blockade in all but name. She was careful to push the United States very near the point of exasperation, but never actually to it. As Samuel Flagg Bemis says,

> Great Britain had to feel her way carefully because too confirmed an opposition by the United States to interference with neutral rights might produce a general embargo and deprive the Allies of an indispensable source of raw materials and munitions, without which they could not equip armies to survive the onslaughts of Germany on the continent. . . . Great Britain astutely deferred her blockade measures until the developing war trade of the Allies had stayed the United States from the brink of imminent depression and made its swelling prosperity contingent upon acquiescence, under protest, in the British maritime measures. . . .[13]

As events unfolded, Germany's unrestricted submarine warfare proved far more corrosive than Britain's naval measures. The British were seizing American property, but the Germans, after all, were taking American lives. Submarine warfare; the American cultural affinity with Britain, reinforced by Allied propaganda; the economic importance to American business of its sales to Britain and France, fostered by private loans: all combined eventually, despite Wilson's effort to be neutral in thought as well as in deed, to push the United States into war on the side of the Allies.

The end of battle was foreshadowed by the statement of war aims.[14] Three days before Wilson's Fourteen Points speech Lloyd George made a similar declaration; in fact, the two statements were so much alike that Lloyd George's included all of Wilson's with the principal exception of Freedom of the Seas. This omission, however, was to be expected. Though Wilson had substantially accepted British trade-limiting activities once the United States was a belligerent, he was by no means ready to accept them as a permanent feature of international law. But the British, having once again seen the importance of these measures, had not the least intention of giving them up. After some rather heated discussion prior to the Armistice, the subject was finally dropped and did not come up again at the peace conference. The final chapter, at least for a time, was written in 1927, when a State Department examiner and his British colleague,

[13] *Diplomatic History*, pp. 593–594.
[14] On the nature and extent of co-operation during the war, see Chapter 10.

in considering American claims against British maritime restrictions during the war, eliminated all but 95 out of 2658 of those claims.[15] America, it seemed, did not want to set a strict precedent which might limit its own use of naval power in wartime.

Another naval question was also relevant. Congress had before it a bill for shipbuilding that would have given the United States far more capital ships than any other power, including Great Britain. The motives behind the bill were mixed, but they included a lingering belief, in the Navy Department, in the theory of commercial rivalry as a major cause of war. And if commercial rivalry caused war, surely America's greatest economic competitor was the United Kingdom.[16] Wilson was willing to use the naval bill for his own purposes in promoting the League of Nations. It served as a threat both to the Allies and to Congress — a bitter, expensive naval race as an alternative to his League. After a bargain with the British, whereby recognition of the Monroe Doctrine was incorporated into the Covenant, Wilson asked Congress to shelve the naval bill. The Washington Naval Treaty of 1922 finally settled the question of the relative strength of the British and American fleets. Thanks especially to Secretary Hughes's dramatic offer, the two powers agreed on parity in capital ships and aircraft carriers, with Japan permitted 60 per cent of the tonnage allowed to Britain and to America. The United States, at the time of agreement, had a smaller battleship fleet than did the British, but had she completed all the ships then launched or on the ways, her navy would have been clearly the world's most powerful. The agreement was not extended to cruisers and supporting vessels.

Portions of the public in both countries were unhappy. Britain had for centuries depended upon the Royal Navy to protect herself and her empire, so it was a bitter pill to accept parity with anyone. But she had recognized over a decade earlier that she could not afford a war with America, and the formal surrender of supremacy was accepted with generally good grace.[17] In America, Anglophobic elements denounced the "knuckling under" to the Admiralty, but few Congressmen really were prepared to appropriate the funds for a huge naval race, one in which the British had promised to spend their last guinea. With the termination of the Anglo-Japanese Alliance in 1921, all but a few of the older officers ceased to reckon on a war with Leviathan. The Navy Department continued to include among its war plans one called "Red" — for a conflict with the British fleet

---

[15] Allen, *Great Britain and the United States*, p. 693.
[16] Harold and Margaret Sprout, *Toward a New Order of Sea Power*, Princeton, 1940, pp. 47–84.
[17] See Allen, *Great Britain and the United States*, pp. 700–705, 735–744.

— but this reflected just a determination to be prepared for all possible contingencies, whatever their likelihood.[18]

The British were careful in other ways to keep their ties to America intact. The United States government had never been very happy about the Anglo-Japanese Alliance and was not satisfied even when, in 1920, the British made known the reservation about their Bryan conciliation treaty with the United States. At the Imperial Conference in 1920, Arthur Meighen, Prime Minister of Canada, combined with State Department pressure to persuade the conference to recommend suspension of the alliance. Australia and New Zealand wanted it kept, but Meighen, who was fearful of what would happen to Canada in an Anglo-American war, carried his proposal. Britain, reluctant but recognizing the primary need of good relations with the United States, complied. Two new agreements in 1922, the Four-Power Treaty and the Nine-Power Pact, pledged Japan, Britain, America, and other nations to respect one another's existing rights in the Pacific and to respect "the sovereignty, the independence and the territorial integrity of China." In 1928 all three nations, with twelve others, signed the Kellogg-Briand Peace Pact.

America's prohibition experiment might have caused friction, for Britain was the world's largest exporter of alcoholic beverages. The United Kingdom co-operated fully with American authorities, however. Despite a past insistence on universal observance of the three-mile limit to territorial waters, she did not even object when the Coast Guard apprehended bootleggers twelve miles out at sea.

Thus, by the mid-twenties, a number of vexatious issues had been settled, again in large part owing to Britain's perception of America's interests, and her willingness to accede to those interests in order to keep on good terms with her. Even the Irish problem was removed in 1923, though its solution can hardly be termed an indication of Britain's willingness to meet *American* demands.

But all outstanding problems were not settled, as is indicated by the League of Nations fight in the United States. Among the reservations the Senate attached to the Covenant was one declaring that the United States would not be bound by any action of the League in which a member cast more than one vote — a provision directed at the votes of the five British dominions. And in the end, of course, the Senate rejected the League, and America tried to pull back from the world arena once more.

[18] Walter Millis, Harvey Mansfield, and Harold Stein, *Arms and the State,* New York, 1958, pp. 15–26; and Louis Morton, "Going First: The Basic Concept of Allied Strategy in World War II," in Kent Roberts Greenfield, editor, *Command Decisions,* New York, 1959, pp. 7–11.

The war debt situation illustrates another important failure of understanding. By 1920 the United States government had lent approximately ten billion dollars to the Allies; and Britain, while borrowing about four billion from America, had lent eight billion to the other Allies. War loans of this sort were old hat to Britain; in the Napoleonic Wars she had lent £61 million to her allies, only 4 per cent of which was repaid. As for the debts of the most recent war, she expressed willingness to cancel all her allies' debts to her, if the United States would forget its loans. Though this would mean a paper loss to the United Kingdom, anything less seemed to promise a breakdown of the international economic system, an event that would prove far more costly. But America, without this tradition of pooling wartime resources, insisted on full repayment. Reluctantly the British then began negotiations with their debtors, though they asked repayment of only enough to enable Britain to meet her commitments to America. With the help of German reparations made possible by massive private American loans to Germany, the situation dragged on until the crash of 1931. Britain, however, languished in economic depression throughout the twenties, largely because of her international payments problems, and America's stern insistence on her legal rights greatly embittered their relations.

Furthermore, naval problems were not yet completely settled. The three chief naval powers met at Geneva in 1927 to work out ratios for cruiser and auxiliary vessel strength like those already established for larger ships. They failed because of the Americans' alleged need for a large number of big eight-inch-gun cruisers, while the British insisted on many smaller six-inch cruisers for the protection of their commercial lifelines. Representatives argued fruitlessly for months, but the British refused to accept equality either in the number of ships or the amount of tonnage and insisted on "strategic equality," for which no formula could be reached. The conference failed, with the Americans blaming the British for accepting parity in words but not in fact.[19] The tariff situation, too, was exacerbated. The Fordney-McCumber Tariff of 1922 was the highest enacted up to that time, and Congress replied to the onset of the Great Depression in 1930 by raising duties even higher in the Smoot-Hawley Act. This was in a world where America was the world's greatest creditor nation, with debtors who could repay their loans only by selling more to Americans than they bought from them.

[19] Lord Cecil remarked about "a certain tension in Anglo-American relations which was very undesirable." Henry L. Stimson thought the two nations "were really at each other's throats." (Quoted in Elting Morison, *Turmoil and Tradition,* Boston, 1960, p. 319)

Relations were thus strained throughout the decade. One author declares that the stress of war caused Britain to overestimate the extent of partnership and sense of community between them, while the United States underestimated the community of interest, that is, the importance of Britain's holding the line in Europe. Acute disillusion followed, and the partnership was not close enough for the demands made upon it. Though he puts the point rather too strongly, there is much to be said for his conclusion that there were no violent quarrels during the twenties, little active argument, but just indifference to each other's point of view.[20]

Only one of these matters, the naval question, was entirely put to rest in the next decade. Facilitated by changes of government in both countries, an agreement was reached at the London Naval Conference of 1930. The final formula gave Britain 339,000 tons for cruisers, compared with 327,000 for the United States, but the latter was allowed to build more of the larger ships. The delegations easily agreed on equality in smaller vessels and got the Japanese to accept the same ratios as with capital ships. When the treaty foundered, it was with Japan's renunciation, not any disagreement between Britain and America. In H. C. Allen's words, the conference "ended forever British mistrust of American naval equality. More than that, it virtually terminated British jealousy of American naval power, so that by 1938 Britain had come to agree with Cecil that America should be free to build as big a navy as she pleased, 'and more power to it.' " [21]

The Great Depression

With the collapse of the European economy in 1931, America's debtors could no longer meet their obligations. President Hoover proposed a one-year all-round moratorium on international debts, but this was only a stopgap measure. In December of the following year, France and five other nations defaulted outright, but Britain paid in full. The London Economic Conference, called to discuss broad aspects of international relations, was almost a total failure. With President Roosevelt's agreement, Britain made token payments of $10 million in June and December 1933, about 10 per cent of the amount actually due. The next April, Congress passed the Johnson Act, providing that no private individual or corporation could lend money to a government that was in default of a debt to the United States government. The Attorney General then ruled that a token

[20] William Clark, *Less Than Kin*, New York, 1957, pp. 129–130.
[21] *Great Britain and the United States*, p. 750.

payment was not enough to avoid default. Unable to do better, Britain and every other debtor except Finland (the only country of the lot to have a large favorable trade balance with the United States) defaulted completely, and not another cent was ever paid. Since the annual payment due from Britain in 1932 was equivalent to four times British exports to the United States in that year, it is hardly surprising that she could not meet the bill. Possibly more surprising is the complete failure to explore other possible ways of paying the debt. In the nineteenth century a debtor might have met his obligation by transfer of territory; with persuasion, the United States might have been willing to settle for some of the British West Indies. (Denmark had sold her West Indies to America only fifteen years before.) But this solution seems not to have occurred to anyone, perhaps indicating the bitterness on both sides. Also in response to international economic developments, Britain, in 1931 and 1932, made her first major departures from free trade, erecting both tariffs and a system of Imperial Preference which discriminated heavily against American goods.[22]

The two powers were driven still further apart by the events following the Nye Committee's investigation in 1934. That body reported close links between munitions manufacturers and political decision-makers. From this it drew the wholly unwarranted conclusion that America had been dragged into World War I by the financial interests, and there arose a demand for legislation to prevent anything like it from happening in the future. In August 1935, Congress passed the Neutrality Act, forbidding the sale of arms and munitions to belligerents, and giving the President discretionary authority to prohibit American citizens from traveling on belligerents' vessels. This "temporary" measure was renewed the following spring in almost exactly the same form, with an additional provision that prohibited banks from lending money to warring governments. And in May 1937 it was renewed once again, after Congress rejected provisions designed to make the act more flexible. Again a new section was added, this time providing for an embargo on certain additional materials useful for war if the President thought fit to impose it. This section expired in May 1939.

Though these measures were intended primarily to keep America out of a future war, their effect of course threatened to discriminate severely against Great Britain. As in World War I, it was almost a certainty that in any war the British fought, only they and their allies would be able to maintain their commerce with North America. The Administration made one more effort, as war loomed nearer in 1939,

[22] On trade discrimination, see Chapter 5.

to ease the neutrality legislation. Insisting that fighting was imminent, Roosevelt asked Congress to restore his flexibility so as not to assure the European dictators that the democracies would be unable to use the great American arsenal. But with Senator William Borah asserting that his sources promised him there would be no war, Congress adjourned without taking action.

Earlier there had been one other significant case of disagreement on what constituted their vital interests. In January 1932, after Japan attacked Manchuria, Secretary of State Henry L. Stimson declared that the United States would recognize no territorial changes resulting from war. Britain was consulted but made no move to associate herself with Stimson's effort to keep the Open Door open. A year later Stimson asked Britain to join him in invoking the Nine-Power Treaty against Japan; again she refused, preferring to work only through the League of Nations. As happened again more than two decades later, Britain did not feel her interests in the Far East were important enough to take the kind of firm action that might lead to war. Though Stimson was bitter, not even President Hoover was prepared to back his Secretary's policy with sanctions.[23]

In January 1938, Roosevelt had made a halting step toward lining up his country with Britain in Europe. Faced with the deteriorating political situation there, in a highly confidential note to Prime Minister Chamberlain he offered to sponsor a meeting of European heads of government in Washington. Sir Ronald Lindsay, British Ambassador to the United States, forwarded the message, urging very careful attention to it. He said, in effect, that if Britain withheld support, "the progress which has been made in Anglo-American co-operation . . . would be destroyed."[24] Without consulting his Foreign Secretary, Anthony Eden, Chamberlain rebuffed Roosevelt. Eden resigned within a month. Publicly his reason was Chamberlain's persistence in negotiating with Italy before receiving certain fundamental guarantees; privately his chief's treatment of the American offer was a key factor. He could not, of course, mention it in Commons without seriously embarrassing the President.[25]

A chronology in Appendix A shows how, once World War I was past, the two countries began to drift apart. American indifference to British needs, manifested largely in tariff and war debt policy, caused bitterness but had no crippling effects on the British economy as long as the world remained prosperous. But after the crash, that

[23] Charles A. Beard, *American Foreign Policy in the Making*, New Haven, 1946, pp. 134–136.

[24] Winston S. Churchill, *The Second World War*, New York, 1948, I, pp. 251–252.

[25] *Ibid.*, pp. 252–254.

bitterness became more severe and had new opportunities to come
into the open. Its effects were not limited to economic affairs but
spilled over into a resistance to American Far Eastern policy. The
United States replied, in 1935, with the Johnson Act and the Neutrality Act. While British hostility was hardly the sole cause of the
latter, the sequence seems more than a coincidence. Again a failure
of responsiveness in one country was followed by unforeseen failures
in the other, and not just in the area where the original lapse occurred.
Though many of these policies were adopted primarily for domestic
reasons, their harmful effects on the other partner were ignored.

As the threat of war loomed larger from 1938 onward, both governments sought the basis for a new *modus vivendi*. The most important step was the signing, late in 1938, of reciprocal trade agreements between the United States and Britain, and the United States
and Canada. These agreements mitigated the discriminatory effects of
Imperial Preference and tore down some of the barriers to trade
erected by the Smoot-Hawley Tariff. As before World War I, fear of
Germany was a powerful force in making Britain more responsive to
America's wishes.

World War Again

When England went to war once again, few Americans had much
intention of remaining neutral in thought. President Roosevelt's
Neutrality Proclamation declared, "The laws and treaties of the United
States, without interfering with the free expression of opinion and
sympathy, nevertheless impose . . . the duty of an impartial neutrality. . . ." As the war continued, he was responsible for a number of policies which were unneutral in deed as well. In October 1939
he persuaded Congress to amend the Neutrality Act, permitting
warring nations to buy arms, supplies, and munitions if they paid
cash and carried the material in their own ships. International lawyers
declared that it was a violation of neutrality to change the rules in
mid-war, but Hitler valued American neutrality, however biased, too
much to do more than protest. The following May, restrictions on the
sale of obsolete military equipment were removed. In September, the
President announced the famous destroyers-for-bases barter. And on
December 17, 1940, he first suggested the Lend-Lease program.
Congress passed the bill, HR 1776, the next March, to the immense
gratification of the British. In June 1941, Roosevelt froze all German
and Italian assets in the United States, and by fall American naval
vessels were actively engaged in convoy work and had fought a
number of battles with German submarines.

Roosevelt clearly felt it was essential to America that Britain should not fall, though it is not certain whether he felt the United States could never stand alone against the dictators, or whether he merely felt it would require the creation of an odious "garrison state" to do so. In any case, the issue was substantially taken out of the 1940 Presidential election by the Republican nomination of Wendell Willkie, who held views essentially like Roosevelt's.

The Argentia meeting, from which the Atlantic Charter was issued in August 1941, indicated the basic agreement between Roosevelt and Churchill, as well as the limitations to that agreement. One phrase of the Charter referred to "the final destruction of Nazi tyranny." Yet the President could make no commitment to enter the war, even if Japan attacked British or Dutch possessions in the Far East. And though both might agree that Hitler had to be stopped, many of the old divisive issues remained. The statement on international trade merely read, "Fourth, they [the United States and Britain] will endeavor, with due respect for their existing obligations, to further the enjoyment of all states . . . of access on equal terms to the trade and to the raw materials of the world. . . ." There was no promise either to lower tariffs or to eliminate the British discriminatory system. In addition, F.D.R. and many other American officials had little sympathy for British colonial policy and began at this time to press increasingly for self-government in Empire territories. They raised both these issues repeatedly throughout the war.

When the United States entered the war in December 1941, the two nations embarked on a military program which represented, by earlier standards of international conduct, a strikingly close co-operation and co-ordination of effort. In military matters, particularly strategic ones, each side on occasion deferred to the demands of the other — especially later in the war, when the British could not, by themselves, implement Churchill's principles of "Grand Strategy." [26] But during the period many issues, some of them only distantly related to military affairs, arose and were solved, if at all, only with difficulty. The Americans were much more favorably inclined toward Vichy and hostile to De Gaulle's leadership of the Free French than was London. More serious was the American antipathy to the monarchists of Greece and Italy, and Churchill's clear preference for them over their left-wing democratic opponents. When these two countries were liberated, the differences became open, and the rift continued through most of 1944 and 1945, amid heated and sometimes public controversy. To some extent the argument over Greece was a part of the

[26] See Chapter 10.

much larger and better-known disagreement over how to handle the Russians. Roosevelt hoped to pacify Stalin; Churchill long fought for a military campaign in East-Central Europe (of doubtful practicality) to contain the Russians. Their divergence led to argument over such additional matters as the provisional German boundary and the Polish government. While this was not basically an argument over national interest — safeguarding postwar peace and security — it was a disagreement over the best means of ensuring that interest.

The end of World War II hardly brought an end to Anglo-American differences; on the contrary, it permitted the rekindling of controversies formerly kept damped in the interest of the common war effort. Palestine proved a most painful irritant. Britain, encouraging Arab nationalism as a means of driving the French out of Syria, had since 1939 severely restricted Jewish immigration to Palestine. Many American Jews, however, incensed at the trials of their coreligionists to find a haven, demanded free admission of Jews to the "holy land" and establishment of a Jewish state. President Truman was acutely conscious of the needs of American politics and asked the new British Prime Minister, Clement Attlee, to allow the admission of 100,000 Jewish refugees. Attlee refused but suggested a joint Anglo-American Commission to investigate the problem. The commission's report pleased neither Jews nor Arabs. Truman endorsed only the parts the Zionists deemed acceptable, and repeated his demand for the 100,000's admission. Attlee insisted on treating the report as a whole or not at all. The controversy continued into 1947, each month more deeply involving it in political bidding between Truman and New York's Governor Dewey. All parties rejected a final British compromise plan in February 1947, and Britain resolved to get out from under by submitting the whole affair to the United Nations. In May 1948 the issue was "settled" by the establishment of the state of Israel, which was immediately accorded *de facto* recognition by the American government. British recognition did not follow until the next January.

It must be remembered that in February 1947 the British government had notified the United States that it could no longer continue its aid to Greece and Turkey. When America responded with the Truman Doctrine a month later, the United States moved into the most expensive and politically exposed areas of the Near East — at Britain's invitation. Once involved in the area, when the exigencies of American politics demanded a different Palestine policy from Britain's, President Truman had to oppose British plans. His Majesty's government seems not to have expected this of its invitation. It forgot that it might not like the tune when someone else was paying the piper.[27]

If President Truman showed an amazing lack of responsiveness to British needs when he cut off Lend-Lease immediately following the end of the Pacific war in September 1945, the British Loan of 1946, the Marshall Plan, and the Mutual Security Act more than made up for his lapse. The $3¾ billion British Loan, to be repaid at 2 per cent annual interest, represented a bit of hard bargaining on the Americans' part, but it was immensely more generous than the financial terms which came out of World War I — of course Britain's need this time was immensely greater, and immensely easier to demonstrate. The British negotiators, particularly Lord Keynes, had strongly hoped for an interest-free loan. In addition to the interest payments, their American counterparts demanded and got reluctant British pledges to move toward nondiscrimination in trade and to make sterling freely convertible. On July 15, 1947, they did make sterling convertible; the resulting drain on London reserves was so severe that convertibility had to be suspended on August 20. Though there have been a number of significant moves in the direction of convertibility since, it has not even yet been fully restored. The American government, despite appreciable annoyance, accepted the need for some British currency control, quota discrimination, and Imperial Preferences. Only with the gold drain in 1959 did American demands for the elimination of discriminatory measures become imperious, and then they were largely met. From the other side, United States tariffs, shipping subsidies, and the "Buy American" Law have hampered Britain's export drive and caused considerable irritation. But taken as a whole, the economic measures of the postwar period indicated a generally sufficient understanding of the other's problems, and willingness to take the necessary action to meet them. While the actions were sometimes no more than just adequate, they were at least that. Broad measures like the Marshall Plan particularly illustrate American responsiveness.

The extent of Anglo-American co-operation since the war is well

[27] C. M. Woodhouse, former Director General of the Royal Institute of International Affairs, notes that Britain wanted "to involve the U.S.A. in greater responsibility in some areas of the world, for instance Southeastern Europe and Southeast Asia, but at the same time to preserve other areas as British spheres of influence, especially the Middle East." (*British Foreign Policy Since the Second World War,* London, 1961, p. 125) British and American aims in the Middle East were essentially contradictory. Britain's prime interest was economic — the protection of her oil investments and the Suez Canal. America's was strategic — containing the Soviet Union, which often meant supporting local nationalists. (*Ibid.,* pp. 134–135)

known. In June 1948 the British immediately acceded to the American government's request for bases for B-29 bombers; it was implicit that those bombers would be carrying atomic weapons. Since then, many United States military bases have been established in the British Isles. In March 1949 the North Atlantic Treaty was signed, and America entered into her first peacetime alliance with European powers. Britain and America co-operated closely on a common policy in West Germany and Berlin during the blockade, they fought together in Korea, and they generally voted together in the United Nations. Despite appreciable domestic opposition, the British government acceded to West German rearmament. All this is common knowledge and must not be forgotten in discussing the differences which have also arisen.

And differences there have been, for though both nations have a common interest in preventing Soviet aggression, there are many problems in which common defense plays a small enough role that differences of apparent interest come to the fore. On matters of economic policy, for instance, the Communist threat is not immediate enough to ensure agreement in detail; both parties, though wishing to maintain their common strength, do not necessarily see eye to eye on who should get the larger share of increments to that strength. Unless one defines it so broadly as to be meaningless, no nation pursues just one goal at a time. It is one thing for two countries to have similar or identical major interests; the ability to come to agreement on other, conflicting interests can be quite another matter.

By analogy, a family has a certain income available for consumption. All members may agree that the basic needs of each must be met, but there may not be agreement on how the available "luxury" should be divided. If the income is low enough and understanding among the members is poor enough, it is possible that someone's basic needs may be neglected because of that member's inability to convince the others that the needs really are basic, and not just demands for "luxuries." It is even possible that quarrels over the division of luxuries could develop to the point where the family's common interest is temporarily forgotten in the bitterness. The familial tie is no talisman against this sort of difference.

Certainly there have been quarrels over the distribution of luxuries in the Anglo-American family. At other times the members, though agreeing at a higher level, have been at odds over the immediate means of securing common goals. They have never quite agreed on a common policy toward the neutralist nations, or on the desirability of summit conferences. Despite NATO and the often quite close military collaboration manifested, the United States refused until the revision of the Atomic Energy Act in 1958 to give Britain any information about building a hydrogen bomb. When the British finally succeeded and started to build an independent nuclear capacity of their own, the Americans were distinctly unenamored with the idea. The whole British H-bomb effort — at a cost of a half-billion dollars — was, in fact, a symptom of the United Kingdom's basic distrust of American judgment and intentions. More recently the two nations have disagreed over the Congo, Western policy in Berlin, and the amount of inspection necessary to enforce a ban on nuclear testing.

Most serious, perhaps, has been the whole range of problems classifiable as Far Eastern affairs. In response to the North Korean attack in 1950, President Truman authorized the use of American ground forces, and Britain followed; but their co-operation has been marred by numerous disagreements. Britain accorded *de jure* (not just *de facto*) recognition to the government of Communist China in January 1950; the United States, of course, never followed. In recent years the British government has regularly voted to seat Communist China in the United Nations. On September 11, 1950, the Soviet Union moved, in the Security Council, to hear complaints from Communist China that American planes had violated her territory. The United States opposed the motion; Britain favored it. That November, Britain refused a request to allow American planes to pursue attacking Communist fighters over the Manchurian border. Just afterward President Truman implied at a press conference that General MacArthur might be allowed to use the atomic bomb in Korea; Prime Minister Attlee felt compelled to fly to Washington immediately.

Four years later a basic disagreement arose again. Admiral Radford and Secretary of State Dulles pressed for Allied intervention in the Indochinese war. Much to Dulles's anger, Foreign Secretary Eden refused. The American government has never made it clear whether or not it would fight Communist China if she attacked the offshore islands of Quemoy and Matsu. Britain, on the other hand, has issued explicit statements that she would not become embroiled in a Far Eastern war for those stakes. Though she might fight in the Middle East, Southeast Asia is not important enough to Britain for her to risk a major war there.

United States officials have long looked on British colonial policy with something less than full sympathy. In particular areas the American government has explicitly opposed British attempts to take direct action in support of her economic investments. When Iran nationalized British oil interests in 1952, the two powers disagreed as to what should be done. It was necessary in July to send Averell Harriman to Teheran to mediate between Britain and Iran, thus publicly exposing our differences. When a settlement was finally reached in 1954, a number of Conservative Members of Parliament insisted that American oil interests had driven Britain out of what had once been her preserve. As American oil companies, formerly excluded from Iran, had an equal share with the British firms in the new Anglo-Iranian Oil Company, the Tories had at least some grounds for their suspicion.[28] Egypt's feud with Britain over her big military base at Suez developed concurrently. In January 1952, Prime Minister Churchill asked that token American forces be stationed in the area to help the British maintain their position. Washington refused, and urged the British to evacuate the base.[29] Finally, in 1954, Britain was unable to do otherwise, and again there was grumbling about the lack of support from the United States. Eden declares in his memoirs that both the Iranians and the Egyptians were able to exploit Anglo-American differences of opinion.[30]

Suez was to be the scene of a far more obvious and serious Anglo-American schism. In July 1956 the United States government, piqued at Colonel Nasser's increasingly close ties with the Soviet bloc, withdrew its offer of financial assistance for the Aswan high dam. Loans from Britain and the World Bank, contingent upon Egypt's getting American aid, were withdrawn immediately thereafter. Within the week, Nasser nationalized the Suez Canal, proclaiming that he would use the revenues to build his dam. Britain, the United States, and other Western powers negotiated for months on possible ways either of forcing Nasser to give back the canal, or of ensuring that it would always be open to all nations. Though he occasionally equivocated, Dulles generally refused to use sanctions; he first proposed the creation of a Users' Club to which dues for canal passage would be paid, and then would not put teeth into the plan. Britain became increasingly desperate and prepared to retake the canal by force. On October 29, Israel invaded Egypt. The United States government expected Britain and France to join it in urging calm, but instead they presented the combatants with an ultimatum calling for withdrawal from the canal area. When Egypt refused, they attacked. While the United States government sympathized with their plight, it could not tolerate this act, and it joined with almost the entire membership of the General Assembly to condemn Britain, France, and Israel and to force them to pull out.

The Suez crisis merely illustrates in a particularly flagrant manner

[28] John Biggs-Davison, *The Uncertain Ally*, London, 1957, pp. 182–183, polemicizes this view. See Chapter 4 for further discussion.
[29] Allen, *Great Britain and the United States*, p. 928.
[30] Anthony Eden, *Full Circle*, London, 1960, pp. 198, 257.

the complaint that many British commentators have been making for some time. American and British interests are not, in detail, necessarily identical, and the United States has shown a frequent disinclination to pay attention to Britain's interests as defined by her government. Geoffrey Barraclough observed:

> The first fact, as it appears from London, is that American policy has been based on a well-meant illusion — the illusion of a real Anglo-American community of interests. That view was sound enough, from the American point of view, in the post-war years, when the issue was to put new life into Western Europe and halt the imminent spread of communism to the shores of the Atlantic. It has become ever less valid as the European countries have got onto their own legs and rediscovered their own (supposed) "interests." [31]

Drew Middleton stated the British complaint in stronger terms:

> For whatever the alliance means to Americans, to Britons it has meant a special relationship between the two countries under which the United Kingdom is entitled to more consideration than she often receives. It was the realization that the United States did not recognize this special relationship that touched off the wave of criticism and doubt during the Suez crisis. . . . The British feel they are treated by the State Department and the Administration not as the most powerful and reliable of allies, but as just another friendly nation. [32]

Anthony Eden, when he was Foreign Secretary, put the case as forcefully as anyone. On April 16, 1954, he wrote to Sir Roger Makins in Washington about American Far East policy:

> Americans may think the time past when they need consider the feelings or difficulties of their allies. It is the conviction that this tendency becomes more pronounced every week that is creating mounting difficulties for anyone in this country who wants to maintain close Anglo-American relations. [33]

How Close Is the Tie?

To the simple question "Are Britain and the United States closer together now than before World War I?" there is no equally simple answer. It depends on what one means by close. One is struck by the degree to which Britain, faced with the German threat from about 1890 to the beginning of World War I, sacrificed many subordinate interests to cementing her friendship with America. For

---

[31] "What Price Alliance?" *The Nation*, December 1, 1956, p. 474.
[32] Drew Middleton, *The British*, London, 1957, pp. 168–170.
[33] *Full Circle*, p. 99.

all their mutual isolation, in these years Britain and America showed great capacities for resolving their differences and for doing so fairly amicably. When danger reappeared in 1938, the two powers once more made a special effort, though somewhat belatedly, to close ranks. Despite a few lapses, they again showed high responsiveness when the Soviet threat became apparent in the late 1940's and early 1950's. But in less dangerous times there have been numerous failures of responsiveness. These failures were concentrated either just at the end of a period of close co-operation, when old divisive forces re-emerged (1920, 1944–45) or during times when each was directing repeated hostile acts at the other (1930's).

In the 1950's they still exhibited much ability to solve mutual problems and come to each other's aid when necessary. Their experience of joint war efforts and the immediate experience of a common danger resulted in an impressive degree of collaboration in many areas of common concern — far, far more than in 1890. They were especially close in the mutual search for peace and security, a goal which in those years they had to seek together or not at all. But in lesser matters there were a number of dangerous and very obvious lapses, and they were no closer than they were seventy years ago in the ability to perceive what other goals the partner held vital and to help him reach them. Despite their close co-operation, one does not see evidence of sensitivity or sacrifice quite comparable to that of 1890–1913. Particularly in 1954–56, Britain's needs, as interpreted by her government, were either not perceived clearly in Washington or, if seen, were rightly or wrongly not always given high priority. Though they remained allied in a common cause, many Britons were not satisfied that they were getting their money's worth. The Conservative government's efforts to build an independent thermonuclear striking force, so as to be free of complete reliance on American support, stemmed in part from this dissatisfaction. The Labour party's 1960 vote favoring unilateral nuclear disarmament illustrated a different response to a similar feeling in another quarter.[34] American complaints about British nonsupport in the Far East show the other side of the coin.

Since 1958 there appears to have been a significant attempt to revitalize the alliance. American revision of the Atomic Energy Act, British abandonment of efforts to build an entirely independent deterrent, and British relaxation of import restrictions point to this conclusion. Probably the Suez crisis, so revealing of the fissures between them, was responsible for the renewed effort. It remains to be seen, however, whether it marked the beginning of a new trend or was just

[34] On these matters, see Chapter 10.

a temporary response to a new challenge. To discuss this situation in depth, we must have a new framework of analysis, and we must attempt to isolate some of the basic factors which are responsible for one nation's responsiveness to the other.

2

The Basis of Political Community

This review of Anglo-American relations over the past seventy years has not brought us very far; it begs too many questions. How, for example, can we balance the extent of Anglo-American co-operation in 1954 against the wide and serious disagreements that also occurred? Was the net effect one of more, or less, harmonious relations than in 1913, when both co-operation and conflict were not so great?

Loads, Capabilities, and Responsiveness

To treat the problem with more success, we must shift to a different kind of theoretical framework. In this study we shall use a scheme which is basically concerned with the *capabilities* of a political unit or group of units, and the burdens, or *loads,* cast upon it. Two kinds of capabilities are relevant. The first is the capacity to act, dependent upon such factors as military strength, wealth, size, population, natural resources, and administrative abilities. This sort of capacity is often broadly referred to as power and is matched by corresponding loads. Questions about such matters as the global deployment of troops, or the appropriate relative and absolute size of various items in the national budget, are of this order.

The second class of capability is equally important. It includes attention to other units and communication with them to perceive their vital interests and to transmit those perceptions to the points in the unit's decision-making centers where they will be given quick and adequate treatment. The facilities for attention and communication are formal international and supranational institutions for channeling attention, communication, and action; informal practices which do the same; and merely habits and memories of attention.[1] These facilities, in turn, depend on the physical channels for transmitting messages — e.g., the mails, the telegraph, the newspaper press. We are not concerned with these physical channels themselves — though perhaps with some delay the channels are usually adequate to the demands made upon them. That is, if a new telegraph cable is needed to handle increased traffic, it will be laid. We are concerned rather with the messages sent over those channels — i.e., the actual contacts established. What is important is not the mere existence of these physical channels but the frequency of their use. This use, the contacts actually made, is what we mean by the facilities for communication and attention between nations.

An additional facility is covered by the class of attitudes described, in Karl W. Deutsch's terms, as at least partial identification in terms of self-images and interests, mutual sympathy and loyalties, "we-feeling," trust, mutual consideration, and willingness to treat the other's requests sympathetically.[2] This set of variables, which we shall refer to simply as "mutual identification," is as important as the factors of communication and attention. It cannot exist without the other two factors, but communication and attention need not, by themselves, produce mutual identification. The United States and the Soviet Union today devote a high proportion of time and space in the mass media to each other, certainly a higher proportion than they did thirty or forty years ago.[3] Yet the sense of mutual identification is certainly not as high, whether relative to the earlier period or as compared with that felt for other nations at present. Mapping communication flows or attention patterns is no substitute for examining this other variable. We shall do so in Chapter 8, under the nature and effects of political socialization.

All these facilities — attention, communication, and mutual identification — we shall call "capabilities for responsiveness." They must carry the demands which each country makes on the other. These capabilities for responsiveness may overlap with capabilities for action, but it still is useful to distinguish the two conceptually. Without capabilities for action, those for responsiveness become merely a matter of intention which cannot be made effective. But Deutsch et al. found

---

[1] K. W. Deutsch et al., Political Community and the North Atlantic Area, Princeton, 1957, pp. 40–41. For further discussion of loads and capabilities, see Deutsch, "Toward an Inventory of Basic Trends and Patterns in Comparative and International Politics," American Political Science Review, LIV, 1 (March 1960), pp. 34–57.

[2] North Atlantic Area, p. 36. See also K. W. Deutsch, Political Community at the International Level, Princeton, 1954, pp. 33–64.

[3] Ithiel de Sola Pool, Symbols of Internationalism, Stanford, 1951, p. 67.

that in the cases of integration they studied, capabilities for responsiveness were more likely to be lacking than capabilities for action.
"Once a moderate measure of power had been achieved, the capabilities relating to the responsiveness of a political unit and its rulers
seemed to be of crucial importance to the success or failure of
integration." [4]

The loads, or demands on capabilities for responsiveness, can become very heavy. Facilities for transmitting messages may be overloaded, like a telephone cable or switchboard, or the capacities for
decision-making may be faced with more demands than they can
meet at any one time. "It is a burden upon the attention-giving, in-
formation-processing, and decision-making capabilities of administra-
tors, political elites, legislators, or electoral majorities." [5] It is possible,
for instance, that the Berlin blockade, the Soviet-Yugoslav rupture,
the Palestine crisis, and the Presidential election of 1948 so over-
burdened the attention and decision-making capacities of the American government that insufficient regard was paid to the deterioration
of the Nationalist position in China until too late. The watchman had
too many doors to watch, and lost his primary charge. Similarly, many
Administration officials felt that the Korean crisis of 1950 was created
to divert us from our affairs in Europe. They feared not only a dilution of our military forces on the Continent but also an inattention to
European events.

Success in this kind of diversion may seem highly unlikely to the
reader; after all, the physical facilities for watching Europe in 1950
still existed, and men permanently assigned to European affairs
probably remained at their desks. True, but in order to meet a crisis
in one area, reserves are brought forward and put to work; flexibility
for dealing with new problems in another area is lost. Some men are
transferred from attending to matters that at the moment seem quiet;
they cannot watch their old concerns to be sure the quiet continues.
"Basic research" may be neglected in favor of the immediate problem.
Growing problems may be neglected until the optimal moment for
dealing with them is past. Perhaps most important, those men in the
highest positions and with the greatest talent have only a limited
amount of time and energy to put into their work; they live but twenty-
four hours a day. The simultaneous pressures of several major concerns may nearly exhaust the human capacities on this key level.
Given time, the number of "high officials" can be multiplied, but
eventually difficulties of co-ordination result in diminishing returns.

Let us think in terms of a ratio or balance of capabilities and loads.

[4] *North Atlantic Area*, p. 40.
[5] *Ibid.*, p. 41.

In the numerator are the facilities for responsiveness; in the denominator are the loads, the demands for attention made on the system. In regard to problems of relations between two nations we shall be concerned with those facilities directed toward each other, and the demands made on each by the other. These demands need not, of course, be "demands" in the sense of formal communications from one government to the other. They would include informal requests, pleas made by private individuals or agencies either to the government or to other private individuals, and merely "situations" that need attention, whether or not an explicit request is ever made. The Russian diplomat who made arrangements to have a critically ill Egyptian child flown to a Moscow hospital was demonstrating his country's capabilities for responsiveness, even though he was never specifically asked to make the arrangements. Loads must be distinguished in three dimensions: their *number,* their *weight* (that is, the importance they assume to the party making the "request"), and their *direction,* or the degree to which they are complementary or contradictory to other demands being made on the decision center. British demands in 1890 for a lower American tariff were particularly burdensome because they ran counter to the demands of American business pressure groups, and to the sentiments of the politically powerful Irish.

The responsiveness of A to B is thus largely a function of the ratio of the capabilities for responsiveness which A directs toward B over the loads coming from B to A at any given time. Actually, the process is not so mechanical as this formulation may make it appear. Capabilities are not that specific, even in the short run. If the demands from one's partner are, at any point, especially numerous or weighty, a certain amount of capacity can be shifted from less important concerns. Government employees can change tasks, and high officials can spend more time on B's problems. But their freedom to do this depends to a large extent on the other loads which are being put on the national decision-making system. In the above formula, the denominator would have to be adjusted for the severity of the total loads on the system.

Obviously, this theoretical formulation is still incomplete, for the state of affairs in the international arena is also an extremely important variable. An external threat to both parties may, without affecting attention or communication facilities, produce greater responsiveness. Each is more dependent on the other and accords its needs a higher priority than they would otherwise receive. We shall discuss this influence, and its limitations, in a later chapter. At present the capabilities/loads ratio is in a simplified form to point up the importance of factors frequently overlooked. Quite a number of other neglected factors will be examined in the conclusion.

We must distinguish between responsiveness and the response to a particular demand. Merely because integration is low does not mean that a particular problem will be poorly handled. The chances are that it will not be met adequately, but in the short term one problem may be expedited and another botched. Formally, responsiveness is the *probability* that the demands of one party will be met with indulgence rather than with deprivation by the other party. Responsiveness is a general term giving us, in the specific case, only a probability statement.

In deciding whether, in a particular instance, a demand has been met, questions of amount and of timing enter in. A response that is "too little and too late" cannot be considered an indulgence. In the discussion throughout the rest of the study, we shall apply the term "responsiveness" to two different types of actors. First, there is responsiveness by governments, at the level of official action. But there also is the responsiveness of individuals — the probability that an individual, whether an authoritative decision-maker or merely an elector or member of an interest group, will react favorably to the other country's requests.

Responsiveness, it should be noted, actually combines two variables, attention and indulgence. Deprivation may be either the result of inattention (a failure to be aware that a request was made) or the result of a deliberate decision not to meet a demand one has heard. In practice, it is extremely difficult to decide which variable was the most important; most cases undoubtedly result from a combination of the two. The instances of deprivation examined in this study include some where each was probably predominant. For analytical symmetry, note that indulgence also can be deliberate or it can occur "accidentally" despite a failure of attention. Domestic or other international pressures may result in a decision which indulges the other partner, even though no request from the partner was perceived. Barring very detailed study, these factors cannot be separated empirically, but their operation should be remembered.

Finally, responsiveness may apply in situations other than a direct request of one government to the other. A situation calling for indulgence may arise from the relations of one party with a third power. That is, A may demonstrate responsiveness by helping B to achieve his goals vis-à-vis C. Strengthening a military alliance against an external threat consists in indulgence; coercing one's partner to submit to the nationalization of his investments is a case of deprivation, even though it is not administered directly. In game-theoretic terms, this is a co-ordination game, where both players can, by co-operating, gain at the expense either of "nature" or of a third player.[6] Many instances of this type of behavior, or of its visible absence, are included in the study.

Several kinds of data are available for tracing trends in capabilities. Attention can be measured by the proportion of space devoted to the other country in elite newspapers, the proportion of references in scholarly research to work done in the other country, and the amount of attention given another nation in a state's educational system. Students of group behavior have long scrutinized communication patterns to identify subgroups in a population. Communication indices used in this study identify trends in mail flows, trade in goods and services, telephone and telegraph communication, student exchange, travel for business and pleasure, various kinds of contacts among members of the elites, magazines and motion picture exchange, and migration.[7] While we can keep clear conceptually the distinction among the variables, we may not always be able to do so empirically. Thus all of the indicators of communication are also relevant to attention patterns. Many — particularly movies and migration — are in addition useful as partial measures of mutual identification. They tell us the extent to which the two sets of nationals like the same kind of pictures, and the degree to which the nationals of one country feel they have enough in common with those of the other country to make their homes there. Other indicators of mutual identification are the amount of approval expressed in the elite papers and in mass opinion as measured by survey data. There are perhaps other possible measures, but these are the most important ones for which adequate comparative data are available.

Insofar as possible we shall test the degree to which, in the case of individual members of the legislative elites in Britain and America, these capabilities have contributed to their readiness to respond to the needs of the other country. Because we are particularly interested in maintaining the health of the Anglo-American alliance, we shall, in a final chapter, examine the role of capabilities for military co-operation.

Some of these measures of capability may in fact also be indicators

[6] See Thomas C. Schelling, *The Strategy of Conflict,* Cambridge, Mass., 1960, esp. ch. 4.

[7] Quincy Wright ("Modern Technology and the World Order," in W. F. Ogburn, editor, *Technology and International Relations,* Chicago, 1949, pp. 174–198) also suggests the measurement of communication flows, though he seems to see them exclusively as factors promoting integration, a view not held here. For some examples and further references, see Bruce M. Russett, "Cause, Surprise, and No Escape," *Journal of Politics,* XXIV, 1 (February 1962), pp. 3-22.

of loads, of opportunities for quarrels and conflict.[8] If migrants cannot be assimilated into the society of their new country, or if they are thought to lower wage rates and thus help impoverish workers in the receiving country, they may contribute heavily to the burdens of an international relationship. Oriental migration to California surely did not improve American relations with China and Japan. If trade is highly unstable in volume or value, it may bankrupt exporters. If the price of imports is kept high by a monopoly, an oligopoly, or even a government price-support scheme, the importing country may seethe under the "exploitation." We shall discuss these and other problems when we present the data. We shall consider both the ways in which a particular item contributes to or measures capabilities, and the degree to which it may also contribute to loads.

No one set of data of the kind proposed is, of course, sufficient for measuring trends in even one variable. For the attention variable we shall look at newspapers, research, and education, and we shall have even more indices of communication. Only if they showed substantially the same pattern should we be satisfied that we were measuring something of significance. Different people are exposed to different media; the various media have different effects on their viewers. Extraneous factors, such as a law requiring that a certain percentage of all films exhibited be domestically produced, may distort the trend shown by a particular index. It is essential that communications and transactions be high over a wide range for capabilities to be high. To anticipate one of the major findings of the study, we do indeed find a surprisingly high correlation among the various indices.

Note that this approach avoids a problem that Peter Rohn raised when he asked whether in Deutsch's *Political Community and the North Atlantic Area* all indices should be weighted equally, and if not, which were more important.[9] Attention, communication, and mutual identification are all essential to responsiveness; there can be no weighting of the three. For their measurement, of course, the solution is not quite so simple — no one index is, on its face, a sufficient measure of all attention or all communication. But in insisting that all, or at least a substantial majority, of the indices used point in the same direction before we draw any conclusions from the trend, we

[8] Deutsch's list of variables (*International Level*, pp. 36–63) suffers from the fact that it is not always clear which indices are meant as measures of capability and which of loads.

[9] Peter Rohn, "Testing Deutsch's Indices of Communication," *PROD*, III, 1 (September 1959), p. 9. It seems to me that Rohn misunderstands Deutsch *et al.* For them, two of the variables that Rohn attempted to measure, compatibility of major values and mutual responsiveness, were essential to pluralistic security-communities, the others all merely helpful. The matter of weighting indices is, in this framework, irrelevant.

minimize the problem. When the indices are less than unanimous, we naturally do assume that the minority index or indices do not apply to forces whose importance overbalances the combined majority indices. This much assertion of "weight" seems unavoidable, but beyond it we need not and will not go.

Another difficulty raised by Rohn is what he terms "the chicken-egg question." [10] Some indices, he feels, seem to be largely a cause of community, others effect, and still others both. Most of the aspects of capability that we shall examine are in fact both cause and effect. The messages not only contribute to the development of community but also are themselves promoted by the community's existence, as the two elements are mutually reinforcing. While this phenomenon lacks a certain conceptual simplicity, it is well known to both the physical and the social sciences. [11] Nor is the phenomenon a complete description of what goes on. A trend toward greater community need not spiral on upward indefinitely; it can be and often is reversed by factors outside this mutual reinforcement. In the present study, however, we shall be concerned less with the factors promoting a trend in a particular capability than with what that trend is and its effect on integration.

Finally, we shall not discuss the role of force in integration. Separate units can be brought together by superior power, and a common government created by a superordinate elite. The new unit's cohesion, however, is likely to be in danger as long as a major segment of the populace feels significantly deprived. Eventually, if an effort is made to meet or modify the needs of the subject population and parts of it are included in a broadened elite, the sense of deprivation may lessen, and a stable, integrated unit may result. Superior power thus provides an opportunity for amalgamation and for eventual integration, in the sense that "integration" is used in this book. But such a solution is not relevant to the nations at hand, whose association must be free and dependent upon co-operative problem-solving.

The Procedure

In presenting these data, we shall concentrate on the situation in five particular years, chosen so as to be roughly representative of different periods in the history of Anglo-American relations: 1890, 1913, 1928, 1938, and 1954. Each of these years was chosen because it was a "normal" year — that is, a year in which "normal" patterns

---

[10] *Ibid.*

[11] See the concept of "feedback" as developed by Norbert Wiener, *Cybernetics,* New York and Cambridge, Mass., 1948.

of communication and attention were not violently upset by severe international upheavals like a major depression or world war. Thus 1913 is the last year of peace before a major war, as is 1938. The year 1928 immediately precedes the onset of the Great Depression in the United States. To measure the amount of trade or travel between Britain and America while international commerce and transportation were in near-chaos would give no picture which could reliably be transferred to other years. The year 1890 does not immediately precede any great disruptive event, but it is the earliest year for which a number of essential statistics are available. The most recent year for which certain kinds of useful analyses have been conducted by other researchers is 1954. When it seemed likely that the pattern might have changed since then, figures for 1958 were also included.

Please note that these years are "normal" in this restricted sense only. They certainly are *not* years in which there were few events of interest or importance in Anglo-American relations. And we shall not limit our survey of diplomatic events rigidly to these particular years. As for the degree to which the capabilities for responsiveness in these years "represent" those capabilities in other "normal" years, we find a remarkably consistent pattern from year to year within a given period. The proportion of all exports, or of migration, or of mail, going from one country to another does not change substantially over short periods. The *level* of that traffic may vary in response to such factors as business conditions, but where it is already high, as between Britain and America, the *proportions* are remarkably stable.

In our concern with proportions, where possible we shall use a refinement developed by I. Richard Savage and Karl W. Deutsch.[12] Their scheme for the analysis of transaction flows draws on the use of a "null model," so called because "it is not based on economic or other substantive theory but makes its predictions solely in terms of the observed trade originating and terminating in the countries under observation." As a null model, it is not expected to give good predictions or important substantive content; it is intended only to control for the effect of an important variable.[13]

The model assumes that the destination of a consignment of exports

[12] "A Statistical Model of the Gross Analysis of Transaction Flows," *Econometrica*, XXVIII, 3 (July 1960), pp. 551–572. For a similar but somewhat less useful model, see Georgio Mortara, "Indices of the Intensity of International Trade," *PROD Translations*, III, 6 (February 1960), pp. 14–20.

[13] *Ibid.*, p. 551. Obviously, trade will vary from that "predicted" in the null model because of the effect of many factors, including constants such as distance. Since we shall be interested, however, in changes over time rather than deviations from the null model at any particular moment, the effect of constant factors like distance may be ignored.

is determined purely at random; that is, the chances of the consignment's going to country B depend only on the proportion of total world exports that go to B. It is designed simply to allow for the size of B in the world economy in predicting the proportion of A's exports that will go to B. For instance, it can be misleading to show that in 1938 the United States exported slightly more to Britain than to Canada; Britain was a "big" country taking a far larger proportion of world exports than Canada.

In practice, the model controls for bigness by predicting that the value of A's exports to B will correspond to the proportion of B's imports in all world imports. But since no country is treated as exporting to itself, a further refinement is required, and the prediction must eliminate the total of A's exports from the analysis. Britain takes 18 per cent of all world imports, but if America's imports are excluded from the total, Britain takes 20 per cent of world imports. Therefore we should "expect" her to take about 20 per cent of America's exports. This is essentially the kind of calculation the model makes.[14]

Given the "expected" values, it is possible to compute a ratio of the relation of actual to expected exports, or an Index of Relative Acceptance of one country for another's exports, defined as

$$R.A._{ij} = \frac{A_{ij}}{E_{ij}}$$

In the ratio, A is the actual value of trade, E the expected value, i a subscript for an exporting country, and j a subscript for an importing country. With the $R.A.$'s we can see whether a country receives an especially high or an especially low proportion of another nation's exports. More important for present purposes, we can discover whether that proportion has increased or diminished notably over the years.

Since we are dealing with deviations from a predictive model, the question of statistical significance is relevant. Where the mean consignment size is large and the number of consignments small, a num-

---

[14] Readers interested in the formulas and their derivation are referred to the original article. For some of the calculations I have used a modified form of the Savage-Deutsch formula suggested by Thomas Synott. Synott's formula, best used when one is dealing with data for no more than three political entities, simplifies computation immeasurably and gives almost identical results. Naturally, I have used only one formula, either Synott's or the Savage-Deutsch one, when dealing with any one time-series. The modified formula reads:

$$E_{ij} = \tfrac{1}{2} \left(\frac{A_i.A_{.j}}{A.. - A_{.i}} + \frac{A_{.j}A_i.}{A.. - A_{j.}} \right)$$

ber of essentially random decisions of importers to buy in one country rather than another could affect the *R.A.*'s. But with the United States and the United Kingdom together, constituting as they do about one fourth of total world trade, this is not an important consideration. In regard to data on transactions other than trade, such as those for migration, we shall be dealing with a large number of individuals (or of small groups of individuals) making independent decisions about the country to which they will emigrate. In all these instances the number of "consignments" is so large that the difference between two *R.A.*'s, expressed to just two decimal places, will almost always be significant.

There are certain drawbacks in using the *R.A.* model. It would be desirable to allow for the proportion of a country's economy that is devoted to purely domestic trade, that is, to allow for its self-preoccupation. Unfortunately, this is not practical where the extent of one or both countries' self-preoccupation is great. With the United States, for example, domestic transactions of many kinds outnumber all foreign transactions of the same kind by more than 100 to 1. While the formula could in principle be modified to include domestic transactions, the expected and actual values of any international transaction would be reduced to a tiny fraction of the total transactions. The result would be *R.A.*'s that differed only very slightly over the years despite large changes in the absolute number of messages exchanged between the two countries — proportionately they would amount to so little as to make virtually no impact. As a second-best procedure, we shall, after comparing trends in *R.A.*'s for international transactions only, also look at changes in the ratio of foreign to domestic messages for each country. We thus shall have the benefits of both kinds of analysis.

Another disadvantage inherent in the *R.A.* model is that we must have complete data on transactions. For instance, in dealing with student exchange, we should need the total number of foreign students in both Britain and America, the number of each who come from the partner country, and the total number of British and American students abroad. The first sets of data are readily available, but until after World War II there were no figures on the total number of students of either nationality who went abroad. Unfortunately, there are quite a few instances of incomplete information. In such cases we shall do the next-best thing, which is simply to compare changes in the proportion of students "imported" from each country over the years. This procedure eliminates the possibility of controlling for the weight of the "importing" country in the world market, one of

the chief virtues of the null model, but in most instances this fortunately is not a serious loss.

There is an important theoretical reason for this interest in proportions. Means have been developed by which an individual can take
account of more messages and variables simultaneously. Education
raises the level of mental skills and shortens the time required for
certain processes. Time- and labor-saving devices do the same; elec-
tronic computers performing in seconds the calculations that would
take unaided mathematicians years to do are the most extreme example. In government, administrative science has improved efficiency.
Within limits, the expansion of physical capacities and the number of
people working on a project can increase attention-giving power.
Capabilities can expand to meet heavier loads. But by the same token,
there is little or no satisfactory evidence that capabilities, either individual or group, have grown more rapidly than the demands — in
the form of the immense multiplication of messages — have increased.
There is little evidence that in the 1950's governments were able to
give more thorough attention to the totality of messages reaching them
than they were in the nineteenth century. Thus the proportion of
messages coming from a particular source is crucial; if that proportion
falls, we must conclude that the attention given it, the weight it carries
in decision-making, is likely to fall.

To repeat, we shall be interested in the attention of Britain and
America to each other not only vis-à-vis their attention to other
countries but also relative to their own introspection. As will be seen
in the following chapters, the proportion of domestic to foreign transactions of almost all types has fallen during the past half century.
This applies to trade, to mail, and even to the world of scholarship,
where one finds *proportionately* fewer references to articles in foreign
scientific journals. Thus the mere fact that the volume of certain kinds
of Anglo-American communications has risen is not necessarily the
most significant fact; in most cases that volume will be found to
represent a smaller proportion of the total number of communications, domestic and foreign, being sent. The technological advances
which permit much faster and cheaper communication and transportation have not necessarily made the world more "internationalist" in
its attention.

Here we may discuss an objection like that raised by Stanley Hoffman.[15] How, one may ask, can you assign equal importance to every

[15] Stanley Hoffman, "Vers l'étude systématique des mouvements d'in-
tégration internationale," *Revue française de science politique*, IX, 2 (June
1959), p. 478.

piece of mail, whether addressed to a Cabinet member or to a farmer? Comparing just the number of messages sent may be deceptive. The point is well taken, within sharply defined limits. First, some attempt is made to control this. In the postal analysis we are concerned with first-class mail only; we do not treat an advertising circular as of the same importance as a letter. Second, where possible we examine elite communication patterns separately from those on the mass level. And in the end, as so often in this study, we are interested in probabilities. We assume that, on the average, if the proportion of letters from Britain falls, the proportion addressed to members of the elite will also fall.

In examining data on communication and attention, we are concerned not only with the present inflow of messages but with the probable effect of earlier experiences in shaping individual perspectives. That is, we wish to know the forces which have helped to shape a man's attitudes in the past as well as current pressures on him. This implies the view well stated by David Truman, "The politician-legislator is not equivalent to the steel ball in a pinball game, bumping passively from post to post down an inclined plane." [16] Political figures bring to their jobs a set of attitudes, predispositions, and ways of looking at the world. Britain's request for a massive loan in 1946 was seen quite differently by different Congressmen. For some it was additional proof that a fat imperialist England was trying to get others to foot the bill for her wars. Others saw England as genuinely in need of the aid, but only through her own wastefulness and unwillingness to sacrifice. A Congressman with different predispositions regretted the need for a proud power to beg for aid, and wished to speed the loan to end the embarrassment. Yet another ignored the nature of the entity asking the boon, considering the loan solely as a weapon against communism. All these people put a very different meaning on the same message.

The frame of reference which they apply to situations is a product of their life experiences, including especially those of family, education, friendship, profession, group memberships, and media exposure. Thus we shall examine not only the flow of messages reaching a decision-maker at or just preceding the time when he must make up his mind on a matter of importance to Anglo-American relations but also many of the forces which may have tended, at different points in his life, to shape his attitude toward the other country. The argument of course applies as much to the mass of political participants in a democratic society as to the political elites. When we later present

[16] David Truman, *The Governmental Process*, New York, 1951, p. 332.

data on the trends in various factors presumed in this way to affect individual perceptions, we shall precede the discussion by an examination of available empirical evidence on what that effect may be.

In the analysis we attempt to make ordinal, not cardinal, measurements. The use of numbers may sometimes be deceptive, implying a precision we do not pretend they have. Whatever the quality of the numbers, in general the conclusion we draw from them will be in terms of more or less, not how much more or less. This applies to the measurement of loads even more strongly than to capabilities.

The System Applied

In this study we shall use the term "integration" to refer to the process of building capabilities for responsiveness relative to the loads put on the capabilities. If we say two countries are becoming more integrated, we mean that the growth of capabilities is outpacing the increase in loads. Formally, of course, we might also speak of integration as a process of decreasing the loads, but the load level is not very susceptible of manipulation. Loads may rise or drop with little or no human control over them; the capabilities for dealing with those burdens are more easily governed. Thus integration is a process, and we shall refer to the ratio of capabilities to loads at any time as the state of integration, of which responsiveness is largely a function.

Our definition of "integration" is different from the one that Deutsch *et al.* commonly use: "By INTEGRATION we mean the attainment, within a territory, of a 'sense of community' and of institutions and practices strong enough and widespread enough to assure, for a 'long' time, dependable expectations of 'peaceful change' among its population." [17] In the case of Britain and the United States, integration in this sense has already been achieved. Depending on how one interprets the evidence, the two have been integrated (a security-community has existed) possibly since the *Alabama* settlement in 1871, probably since the general *rapprochement* around the turn of the century, and without any doubt since the Washington Conference of 1922 brought the naval-construction race to a halt. That security-community has become more stable in recent years, but it certainly has existed for some time, and prospects are that it will continue for the foreseeable future. We are concerned with the extent to which mutual problems can be resolved within the security-community. This is a matter of

[17] *North Atlantic Area,* p. 5. We shall neglect a number of variables which Deutsch and others have identified as relevant to broader integration. Our concern is with a set of factors particularly relevant to responsiveness.

no small importance, for it is a crucial element in the strength of the free world.

We can illustrate the scheme by referring to the state of Anglo-American relations in the two periods at the extremes of our time span. In the 1890's capabilities were high; Britain and America were closely linked by numerous ties, as we shall show in following chapters. The loads on the relationship were also fairly high. The American tariff was a matter of great concern. Somewhat less serious were disputes over the Bering Sea, an Isthmian canal, copyrights, the Venezuelan and the Alaskan-Canadian boundaries, trade and fisheries, and the perennial Irish problem. Other loads on the system, however, were not excessive. The United States was occupied with the Populist revolt and demands for free silver, but foreign relations other than those with Britain were of little import. The United Kingdom had its own internal concerns, particularly Ireland, but foreign affairs for it too were relatively trouble-free. Its major problem was Germany's rise to power, an event which, in fact, encouraged Britain to draw closer to America. Thus, though the direct loads were fairly high, capabilities were extremely high and other loads relatively low. By 1903 all the above problems except the first and the last, tariffs and Ireland, were solved. New ones of course replaced them, but both Britain and America showed striking mutual responsiveness.

In the middle 1950's the facilities for attention and communication between the two English-speaking nations were relatively much lower than in 1890. The direct loads remained high, though perhaps not as burdensome as they once had been. If the weight of no one issue was quite as great as that of the tariff, and if the direction of some was perhaps more favorable, there were more issues in contention. The problems of trade — tariffs, Buy-American, convertibility, discriminatory quotas, and Imperial Preference — continued to plague; and later East-West trade was added to the list. The Middle East, with Iranian oil and the Suez base, became a serious irritant. The two countries diverged sharply on how to treat the neutrals and Communist China, and on the need for intervention in the Far East. American attitudes toward colonialism caused periodic friction. Britain was attempting to keep her military independence by making her own nuclear weapons; American bases on her territory provided some irritation. Other loads were very high: race problems in the United States and British difficulties in liquidating a vast colonial empire, to mention only the most salient internal problems. The Soviet Union posed an unprecedented threat to both nations. Thus the lower capabilities were burdened with intra-alliance loads that were still quite high, and the pressure of domestic and other international burdens limited what flexibility the capabilities had.

It is not an easy matter to measure trends in responsiveness, even in terms of more or less. To do so requires deciding how fully a particular need was met and whether in a particular instance a demand was seriously watered down in anticipation that only a very modest request would be met, and it imposes a weighting difficulty. The last is akin to the economists' famous index problem — in this sense whether compliance with military needs is more or less important, and how much more or less important, than noncompliance in, for instance, commercial relations.

These are not insuperable difficulties. The opening chapter, while tracing the history of Anglo-American political relations, attempted to convey an impression of trends in responsiveness. It argued that in many important ways responsiveness certainly did not increase over the seventy-year period, and may well even have declined. Instances of the failure of one partner were, in the mid-fifties, more obvious than at any time since the thirties, despite a substantial amount of co-operation that occurred concurrently. But any such description is bound to be impressionistic, imprecise, and open to argument.

In the search for precision, we might ask about the proportion of treaties and executive agreements which each partner signs with the other. The assumption would be that responsiveness, whether as co-ordination or the ability to settle problems amicably, would be reflected in the signing of agreements. Allies will make frequent agreements, enemies few. The graph in Figure 2.1, which is derived from Appendix Tables 2.1 and 2.2, shows the relative number of agreements with each other signed by the United States and Great Britain in each year since 1890. For example, we give a ratio showing the relationship between the number of agreements the United States made with Britain and the average number of agreements it made with every other individual nation in the world. The higher this ratio, the greater the mutual Anglo-American responsiveness indicated. As a control, the relative number of agreements the United States has reached with Russia is also shown.

To a substantial extent the data agree with what one would expect from a general knowledge of Anglo-American relations. During the period of American isolationism and withdrawal from European affairs — 1919 to 1938 — the ratio of Anglo-American agreements to agreements with other countries is quite low — appreciably lower than during the period of co-operation in World War I. For both parties the ratio rose during the joint effort of World War II. In the later 1950's when, as we suggested, their co-operation was

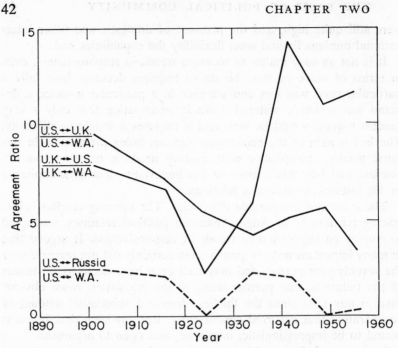

FIGURE 2.1   *Ratio of Agreements Signed with Partner Country to Average Number of Agreements with Every Other Country, 1890–1959 (W.A. stands for World Average.)*

SOURCE: Appendix Tables 2.1, 2.2

limited by a number of conflicts over subsidiary but still serious matters, the index of co-operation was appreciably below the World War II level.

As further proof of the figures' basic validity, note the proportion of American agreements with Russia. Co-operation was fairly high during Czarist days and the First World War, nil in the twenties (when America did not recognize the Soviet Union), much improved in the thirties and early forties, then down again for the late Stalin era, and up slightly for the most recent period. Clearly, a nation does not sign the most treaties with the party with whom it has most to dispute.

Thus the relative number of formal agreements that two countries sign with each other at least roughly corresponds to some common-sense notion of their co-operation. It is still just possible in some cases that two countries might be so close that they do not need formal agreements. The above correlations of "common sense" and agreements cannot entirely disprove this theory, but the high level of Anglo-American agreement-signing during World War II casts doubt on it.

If the results are satisfactory for those periods about which we already have some rather firm notions, what do they tell us about the comparison of periods for which the impressionistic evidence is ambiguous? Specifically, were Britain and America more or less responsive in the fifties than around 1900? Here the indices are contradictory. For the United States, the proportion of Anglo-American treaties was very much higher in the early period, but for Britain it has increased recently.[18] The evidence on responsiveness is ambiguous; two different trends in salience, however, are clearly at work. Though Great Britain has declined in importance as a treaty partner for the United States, America has become ever more important to the United Kingdom.

Another possible source of "hard" data on responsiveness is the *Foreign Office List* or *Foreign Service List* of each country. The relative size of the diplomatic staff of each partner in the other country serves as an indicator of the amount of official attention given that country. Members of the diplomatic corps have many duties, but one of the chief functions of any embassy is intelligence-gathering. In that role we shall discuss embassy staffs in the chapters on elite attention. But this information also provides an indicator of what might be called "propensity to respond," or perhaps better, simply "priority." If the relative size of the American staff in Britain declines, for example, this may indicate that the State Department attaches a relatively lower priority to events and attitudes in Britain, and is less likely to respond favorably even to those requests it perceives. This too is a very tentative hypothesis (an alternative hypothesis is that if two countries are very close, other agencies, formal and informal, take over much of the intelligence function), but it possesses a certain plausibility.

Except for a substantial decline during the depression years, the proportionate size of the British delegation in the United States rose steadily. The size of the American delegation in Britain, however, has declined steadily since 1928 as a proportion of all foreign service officers, and even shows a small *absolute* downturn since 1954. The figures in Table 2.1 indicate for Britain a growing "propensity to

---

[18] We must resist such temptations as to assert that because the Anglo-American percentage of American agreements went down, the United States was less responsive to Britain, but because the Anglo-American percentage of British agreements went up, Britain was more responsive to America. This requires the assumption that in the first case America shows its responsiveness to other countries by signing agreements with them. But if we reverse the assumption (other countries show their responsiveness to American needs by reaching agreements with the United States), then the opposite finding would apply. The figures themselves give us no indication as to which element, if either, is predominant.

TABLE 2.1. Diplomatic Representatives in Partner Country as a Percentage of All Foreign Service and of Total National Government Civilian Employment

	1890	1913	1928	1938	1954	1958
U.S. Percentage of Foreign Service Stationed in Britain	5.7	4.4	5.6	5.5	4.7	4.0
Foreign Service in Britain as Percentage of Gov't Employment	0.00003	0.00003	0.00012	0.00008	0.00006	0.00006
G.B. Percentage of Foreign Service Stationed in America	5.1	6.2	7.5	5.7	8.0	8.7
Foreign Service in America as Percentage of Gov't Employment	n.a.	n.a.	0.00023	0.00015	0.00014	0.00016

SOURCE: Appendix Table 2.3.

respond" to America, but a fall in the United States propensity with regard to the United Kingdom. But since 1928 the embassy staffs of *both* countries have declined relative to the number of all civilians employed by their national governments. Because of the vast expansion of government functions in recent years, one must be wary in assessing the significance of this fact, but it suggests greater responsiveness to domestic interests and less readiness to respond to each other. (Note that this decline occurred in Britain before World War II and the subsequent Labour government.)

Finally, one more set of data promises to be enlightening. Ithiel de Sola Pool and others have identified one newspaper in each major country as an elite newspaper, or a journal which is read by a very high percentage of those in high positions in business and government. In England and America the principal elite papers are *The Times* of London and the *New York Times*. Others, such as the *Guardian* and the New York *Herald Tribune,* are widely read, but neither approaches *The Times* of London or the *New York Times* in elite readership. And not only are these two journals "elite" in their readership, but they tend to parallel rather closely government policy and attitudes. While preserving their independence on particular matters, they generally reflect official policy, especially on foreign affairs, despite changes in the regime.[19]

We shall assume that when either of these papers makes a request of the other government, it is more or less speaking in harmony with the intent of its own government. We thus can classify "request" editorials in three categories. First are those whose requests were

[19] Ithiel de Sola Pool, *The Prestige Papers,* Stanford, 1952, pp. 1–9.

substantially met within a "reasonable" period of time (never more than five years, often much less if the problem was urgent). Second are requests which were substantially ignored or turned down; third and finally are those where a judgment must be contradictory — they were met, but only in part. In addition to these editorials where the writer takes the initiative, there are many others expressing a *post hoc* judgment on a policy of the other country. We can classify them in a similar manner — editorials which approve of a policy or action, those which disapprove of it, and those which express no judgment, all from the viewpoint of the *effects of that policy on the country of the writer*.

TABLE 2.2. Percentage of Newspaper Editorials, in Number and Column Inches, Making Requests of the Other Government Which Were Met, Not Met, and Met Only in Part

	1890		1954	
	No.	Inches	No.	Inches
London *Times* N =	(6)	(142)	(19)	(422)
Request Met	87	80	47	43
Request Met in Part	0	0	16	15
Request Not Met	13	20	37	42
Total	100	100	100	100
New York Times N =	(3)	(66)	(10)	(210)
Request Met	100	100	40	34
Request Met in Part	0	0	20	25
Request Not Met	0	0	40	41
Total	100	100	100	100

The material is scanty, particularly for "request" editorials, but several facts stand out rather noticeably. First, the proportion of requests met was very much higher for both countries in 1890 than in 1954. Second, *post hoc* judgments of each other's policies were much more likely to be favorable in 1954 than in 1890. Finally, both countries considered themselves more closely involved with each other's fate in the later year than in the earlier one, as measured by the percentage of "response" editorials expressing judgments. Not surprisingly, the increase is very much greater for the American paper than for the English one.

As shown in Table 2.3, the second finding (a rise in the proportion of favorable judgments) indicates that the two countries were traveling in more or less parallel directions. Well over 80 per cent of the favorable judgments in both papers were made in the context of

TABLE 2.3. Percentage of Newspaper Editorials, in Number and
Column Inches, Responding Favorably, Unfavorably, and Neutrally
to Actions of the Other Country

	1890		1954	
	No.	Inches	No.	Inches
London *Times* N =	(31)	(860)	(76)	(1488)
Favorable	10	7	20	17
Neutral	71	74	67	72
Unfavorable	19	19	13	11
Total	100	100	100	100
New York Times N =	(75)	(1128)	(82)	(1332)
Favorable	4	3	52	50
Neutral	95	95	39	42
Unfavorable	1	2	9	8
Total	100	100	100	100

the cold war. This kind of approval would be expected of allies. Both
felt the same threat and responded similarly. But the first finding (a
decline in the proportion of "request" editorials receiving favorable
action) suggests that for at least some issues on which the cold war
context did not force a similar viewpoint there were serious failures of
responsiveness. If one power had not already adopted a policy agreeable to the other, that party's request was not likely to cause a change
of heart. For both parties every one of these unmet requests involved
Asian affairs — Communist China, the Colombo Plan, Indochina, or
SEATO. Thus responsiveness, in the sense of a readiness to sacrifice
some of one's own interests to the needs of the other, was not as high
as in 1890.

For certain reasons these conclusions must be tentative. First, they
apply to only two years. Because of the relative rarity of "request"
editorials, one has to read a great many pages to get even as small
a sample as this. A very substantial number of hours must be
spent in reading papers for other years before we can be sure that
we simply have not picked two years when responsiveness was ab-
normally high or low. Second, we ignore the possibility of anticipated
reaction. Perhaps a number of the policies which provoked *post hoc*
favorable comments were adopted just because the other power
wanted them. Thus the event antedated a newspaper "request," and
much actual responsiveness failed to appear in Table 2.2. Although
possible, it seems unlikely that this happened often enough to make
the difference. In 1954 there were fifteen London *Times* editorials
expressing favorable reactions to American policy. Even if we were

to imagine that all fifteen had appeared before the American position was assumed, and thus added them to the "request met" section, the addition would be enough to raise the proportion of "request met" editorials only to 71 per cent — well below the 1890 figure.

In summation, these sets of data give a variety of information. Eight of them (one for each partner on agreements, percentage of foreign service in the other country, foreign service in the other country as a percentage of government employment, and percentage of editorial responses expressing judgments) indicate the salience of each country to the other. Three of these for the United States (all but editorial responses) indicate that Britain has become less salient or "important" to it, but for the United Kingdom the situation is just the reverse. Three of four (all but foreign service as a percentage of government employment) suggest that the United States has become more important to it. There is a much greater sense among Britishers that their fortunes are bound up with the United States, but no development of corresponding strength exists across the water.

Two sets of data indicate more frequent favorable reactions to the other's policy. The *New York Times* is particularly enthusiastic. But on responsiveness, the main purpose for which the data were compiled, the pattern is very different. Eight suggest responsiveness or propensity to respond (one for each partner on agreements, foreign service in the other country, foreign service as a percentage of government employment, and meeting of editorial requests). All but two (British agreements and percentage of foreign service in America) indicate a decline. Though they may protest their affection for each other, they seem somewhat less anxious to take each other's desires into account. (I can't give you anything but love?) Marriage counselors warn that mere declaration of love is worthless unless one is prepared to heed one's partner's wishes fairly often. The contrast between word and deed appears especially strong for America. Its elite paper declares its devotion, but its decision-makers seem less ready to respond.

Since the development of precise measures of responsiveness is still in the exploratory stage, these findings are highly tentative. But coupled with the descriptive treatment of Chapter 1, they destroy the prima facie validity of the argument that Britain and America are unquestionably "closer" to each other now than in the past. Rather, there is important evidence that the two countries have recently been less responsive in areas where their direct interests were not already parallel. Much of their present co-ordination is due to the fact that they both feel external pressure from the same source — the Communist world. Should that threat abate, or seem to abate, or become subordinated to some major crisis from another source, we cannot be confident about the continuation of close co-operation. The evidence is not all in yet, but it gives one grounds for discomfort.

How can responsiveness have declined over the years, given the Anglo-American stakes in mutual preservation? To explore that question is one of the purposes of the following chapters. We shall trace the decline in important capabilities and prove that in individual cases these capabilities are important in promoting responsiveness.

We shall not, in this study, be concerned with the possibilities for a formal merger into a larger unit with a common government. It seems obvious that there is not at this time widespread support for such a project in either country. Successfully amalgamated units have a number of advantages, particularly in the capacity to act quickly and effectively in the common pursuit of individual and common goals. True, we are especially interested in promoting just that kind of action; it is far more our concern than the mere preservation of peace between the two states. Yet successful amalgamation demands a much higher level and wider range of capability than does pluralism, or the maintenance of the member states' separate identity. Particularly in a modern welfare state the demands on a central government are so heavy and diverse that its capacities for attention must be very great if important minorities are not to feel severely deprived.[20] Since we shall emphasize the extent to which Anglo-American capabilities have lagged behind loads, the reasons for not pressing the matter of formal political union at this time should be obvious.

[20] See Deutsch *et al.*, *North Atlantic Area,* ch. 2, on the relative success of the two kinds of security-community in surviving disintegrative forces.

3

Trade in Goods and Services:
The Link of Mutual Interests

Trade and Integration

International trade represents one of the transactions we discussed previously. In this chapter we shall examine some of the evidence on the relation between trade and integration, the circumstances under which commerce encourages responsiveness, and the means by which it does so. We shall also discuss the extent to which trade patterns can serve as indicators of other capabilities, and we shall conclude with evidence on the degree to which commercial transactions have formed a link of declining significance over the last half-century.

Few writers hold that trade necessarily improves relations between two countries, though some have come perilously close. Richard Cobden once told his followers, "I believed Free Trade would have the tendency to unite mankind in the bonds of peace, and it was that, more than any pecuniary consideration, which sustained and actuated me." [1] One finds this sentiment in the most unlikely places. William McKinley, author of the McKinley Tariff, declared, "Good trade insures good will. It should be our settled purpose to open trade wherever we can, making our ships and our commerce messengers of peace and amity." [2] Even Nikita Khrushchev, inverting the economic determinist position, stated, "Trade is like a barometer; it shows the direction of policy." [3]

Most authors, of course, are more moderate. Financial crises and

[1] Richard Cobden, *Speeches on Questions of Public Policy,* John Bright and J. E. T. Rogers, editors, London, 1870, II, p. 421.
[2] Quoted in Margaret Leech, *In the Days of McKinley,* New York, 1959, p. 142.
[3] *New York Times,* September 17, 1959, 18:4.

debt defaults can seriously embitter the relations of two countries, as they did between Britain and America in the first half of the nineteenth century. If two countries are highly interdependent and one of them suffers from severe economic instability, the other is almost certain to share the instability. Depression spreads from its origin by cutting other countries' exports. Irritation may also stem from a circumstance where one nation is the world's major exporter of a particular commodity. Put crudely, the importing state may feel exploited if the supply is controlled by a monopoly or oligopoly. Even government price supports or production controls, though adopted merely to maintain the income of one's own primary producers rather than deliberately to exploit the buyers, may nevertheless arouse hard feelings.

On the whole, there is little evidence that this sort of thing has seriously harassed Anglo-American relations. Britain's exports have consisted almost entirely of manufactured goods, often produced under conditions of sharp competition either among British producers or with foreign manufacturers. The complaint of American protectionists, after all, was not that British goods cost too much, but that they were too cheap.[4] From the other side there has been a little more complaint, including some grumbling about a cotton trust which allegedly kept the price of that commodity inordinately high.[5] Yet most United States agricultural products have been free of this sort of private manipulation, and the fine art of government price supports was not developed until the 1930's. By 1954, Britain had found alternative suppliers for most of these goods. Wheat imports from the United States had been diverted entirely to the Commonwealth, and cotton and tobacco remained the only agricultural goods imported from America in great quantity. Even they faced notable competition, in the first case from India and Egypt, and in the second from Turkey and Britain's African colonies.

If these difficulties are absent, trade becomes a most important connecting link. Deutsch *et al.* insist that a wide range of mutual transactions is essential to the growth of a security-community. These need not be commercial transactions, for strong economic ties are a

[4] British discriminatory practices and the American tariff also contributed to the sum of deprivations stemming from trade, but they are reflected in the absence of commodity trade rather than in its presence. While tariffs and discrimination must be remembered as important irritants, they did not, in any major way, diminish the "capability content" of whatever trade still existed despite them. Our interest here is with the latter problem, the degree to which *existing* trade carries loads rather than capabilities. For the other matter, see Chapter 5.

[5] Ludwell Denny, *America Conquers Britain,* New York, 1930, p. 207. See also the Congressional debate on the Sherman Anti-Trust Act in 1890.

helpful but not an essential condition for integration.[6] But they are important and if not present must be replaced by other transactions. The statement "The helpfulness of economic ties may lie largely in the extent to which they function as a form of communication and as visible sources of reward " [7] hits the crux of the problem.

Economic interests may be important on issues which do not affect them in any immediate sense. Nicholas Roosevelt, writing in 1930 on Anglo-American relations, suggested how this might operate:

> Thanks to the existence of a large body of persons in England whose business has been almost entirely dependent on foreign trade and who have, in consequence, had to inform themselves thoroughly about international conditions . . . a constant watch of world affairs is maintained by influential persons in England with the result that the interdependence of the various parts of the modern world is better understood there than anywhere else. . . .[8]

An exporter is likely to have a general interest in the well-being of his market, an interest that transcends the marketing conditions, narrowly defined, for his product. Furthermore, he may become attuned to the needs of the importing country over a great range of noneconomic matters. Daniel Lerner found that in a sample of French business leaders, support for EDC as opposed to the maintenance of a French national army varied directly with the importance of export trade to the businessman's firm.[9] Only in a few cases could any of these businessmen be said to have a direct "economic interest" in the decision.

Trade thus becomes important as a means of communication. The trader is exposed to a wide variety of messages that would not otherwise reach him; he must listen to viewpoints that he otherwise would never hear. Trade is a capability by which the needs of one country can be made known to another. At present the proposition is no more than a general hypothesis, but in Chapter 9 we shall test it with legislative decision-makers in the United States and the United Kingdom. We shall show that legislators with a tie to some economic interest group trading with the other country tend to be much more responsive to the needs of that country than do legislators without the tie. Trade may also serve as an indirect means of communication for a lawmaker. Though he may not be associated with the interest,

---

[6] K. W. Deutsch et al., *Political Community and the North Atlantic Area,* Princeton, 1957, p. 157.

[7] *Ibid.,* p. 169.

[8] Nicholas Roosevelt, *America and England?,* London, 1930, pp. 204–205.

[9] Daniel Lerner, "French Business Leaders Look at EDC," *Public Opinion Quarterly,* XX, 1 (Spring 1956), p. 220.

the constituents, editors, fellow senators, lobbyists, and others from whom he gets most of his ideas and information may be.

In addition, economic interests tend to bias decisions; an individual may act to further his financial interests. From the other side, persons who are predisposed to particular decisions will try to mobilize available economic interest groups for the support of that decision. That is, economic interests may "determine" political decisions, or they may merely be used to support those decisions. The question of "priority" is for our purposes irrelevant; interdependence, not determination, is the concern of the study.

Subject to later qualifications, it seems plausible that every political interest group has a power base, or power potential, that is roughly proportional to the share of the national income which its members control. As its share in the national income declines, we should expect its *potential* power to fall. Not only would the group become less important as a communicator, but it would have less direct influence over political decision-making.

To repeat, we do not contend that economic strength *determines* political decisions, but like ideology, noneconomic interest groups, and parties, it does constitute a highly relevant variable. Interest groups have numerous ways to influence a legislator. They can contribute to his campaign funds and provide facilities he needs for re-election. They can stimulate the flow of approval, demands, or censure from his constituency. A legislator with limited staff and little time for research may be greatly in need of information on the effects of various events and proposals; an interest group can often supply these data. It may also provide him with legal briefs, or if an amendment to a pending bill seems necessary, it can even provide the amendment all properly drafted. If a legislator is accustomed to relying on an interest group for information, the group has a powerful sanction in the threat, implied or explicit, of withdrawing its advice and assistance. A public campaign, conducted through the mass media, may mold popular opinion or at least mold the legislator's image of that opinion.

One variable affecting an interest group's chance of success is of course its economic base relative to its opponents'; we referred to this above. But it is by no means the only factor. E. E. Schattschneider reported that the amount of activity undertaken by an economic interest group was not related to the size of the interest involved: "equal stakes do not produce equal pressures." [10] Nor is effectiveness highly correlated with size or activity. Some additional

[10] E. E. Schattschneider, *Politics, Pressures, and the Tariff*, New York, 1935, p. 135.

relevant factors include a group's capacity for organization, its previous experience, the degree to which it is concentrated in a few constituencies, and its proximity to the effects of the legislation at issue. Its internal structure may affect the degree to which it can concentrate on behind-the-scenes maneuvering or the amount of public (and often futile) display which its leaders feel is necessary to impress the rank and file with their effort.

But if size and effectiveness are not correlated in any immediate sense, we might expect a change in one to spill over to the other in the long run. A group with a declining economic base would, we should expect, have declining influence over a long span, even though the lag might be substantial. There obviously would be exceptions, and in any case the size and effectiveness of a group are related to its political culture and therefore change slowly. But on the whole, the hypothesis seems reasonable.

It appears most plausible when applied to general rather than specific aims, and when we go beyond the immediate goals of the group. In the ability to maintain a high tariff, or to get the government to bail a foreign investor out of difficulty, the effect of a decline in the group's economic base may be felt only very slowly, or it may be counterbalanced by other variables. But economic interests are relevant to politics in a much wider sense. As previously indicated, commerce is a means of communication, and one participating in it is likely to revise his attitudes on many matters not immediately affecting his self-interest. We should expect a much closer correlation between changes in the size of the interest affected and the speed and direction of changes in its effectiveness as an instrument of international communication promoting responsiveness. A decline in an interest's share in the national income implies a concurrent decline in the proportion of individuals for whom it is a means of transmitting messages.

Not only is trade itself a capability for attention and communication, but it may also contribute to the growth of other capabilities and may even generate forces which tend to keep the trade at a high level. As mentioned in Chapter 2, transactions are likely to be elements of a feedback system in which capabilities and actual integration feed upon each other.

Few markets are completely analogous to the model of perfect competition, as the products of two sellers are seldom completely identical, at least in the mind of the buyer. Customs, habits, traditions, and "myths" about the goods or the seller differentiate two seemingly identical products. A seller who speaks the language and understands the mores of his customers has a great advantage over one who does not. Some sellers can offer more attractive credit terms than others. Past habits may have an effect on the price that can be offered, as goods coming across a much-traveled trade route can be shipped more cheaply than goods sent across one which has not yet developed much traffic.[11] Governments obviously play their part too, not only with quotas, exchange control, and tariff discrimination, but with restrictions such as those on importation into the United States of beef from countries where hoof-and-mouth disease allegedly exists. In general, most of these factors tend to favor the old supplier; unless he manages particularly to annoy his customers, he is likely to keep them in the face of a challenge from a newcomer who can offer only a marginal improvement on his terms. The existence of high capabilities in the present, then, suggests the existence of other important capabilities as well, of high capabilities in the past, and frequently also (though not certainly) of a substantial degree of integration.

It is the very imperfection of these markets, however, particularly insofar as the imperfection is due to conscious manipulation, that requires us to treat them with caution as clues to changes in other capabilities. A shift from a high rate of transaction to a lower one may indicate a decline in mutual approval, or that the transactions had begun to carry an increasingly high load element (that customers or sellers felt the relationship to be bringing substantial deprivations). But it may be due simply to deliberate governmental restriction. Means of diverting trade in commodities are legion. For balance-of-payments reasons the British have severely restricted travel to North America since the war. British authorities have adopted a screening process to ensure that foreign investment coincides with their own plans for the economy and will not put a severe drain on the balance of payments.[12] On the other hand, British and Sterling Area trading restrictions have encouraged American investment in the Commonwealth to produce within the protected market. The United States requirement that half of all foreign-aid shipments be carried in American hulls decreases British earnings from carrying goods from the United States. Thus while it is extremely useful to use transactions data as indicators of attention and communication capabilities, any interpretation of a decline in transactions as necessarily indicating a fall in other capabilities (as mutual approval) can be made only

[11] For example, freight rates are generally cheaper from Kingston, Jamaica, to Britain than from Kingston to Havana, despite the great difference in distance.

[12] See John H. Dunning, *American Investment in British Manufacturing*, London, 1958, pp. 314–318.

with great caution and intimate knowledge of the particular circumstances.

The Pattern of Anglo-American Commerce

In Table 3.1 are figures for exports from Britain and the United States to each other as a proportion of national income and the indices of relative acceptance for exports to each other. With them we shall have a measure of the relative decline of Anglo-American trade since 1890.

TABLE 3.1. Exports to Partner Country as Percentage of National Income and Indices of Relative Acceptance

	1890	1913	1928	1938	1954	1959
U.S. Exports to U.K.						
As Percentage of U.S. Income	4.0	1.9	1.0	0.8	0.2	0.2
Relative Acceptance	.79	.24	−.20	−.21	−.60	−.60
U.K. Exports to U.S.						
As Percentage of U.K. Income	2.3	1.2	1.7	0.6	1.1	2.0
Relative Acceptance	.00	−.43	−.47	−.55	−.64	−.38

SOURCE: Appendix Table 3.1.

Two points emerge clearly. First, the importance of Britain and America as markets for each other has steadily declined relative to the rest of the world. Whereas in 1890 Britain took 80 per cent more than the total of American exports that one would "expect" according to Britain's total trade, by 1959 she took barely two fifths of the amount that one would "expect" from the indifference model. Imperial Preference, various restrictions on dollar trade, and autonomous changes in demand have caused a vast shift away from trade with America (see Chapter 5). This shift was not sudden, but has continued since 1890. A similar but less dramatic shift has occurred in America's position as a market for British goods. In 1890 the United States took just the amount that one would "expect," but by 1959 she took only about one quarter of the "expected" amount.

Second, there was an equally striking decline in Anglo-American trade as a proportion of national income. It was spectacular for the United States, whose exports to Britain dropped from 4.0 per cent of national income to but 0.2 per cent. This was a much sharper drop than occurred in total exports as a proportion of income (from 7.6 per cent to 4.9 per cent). For Britain there was a decline which reached its nadir in 1938. The proportion rose again during Britain's recovery in the 1950's, perhaps because of the modest fall in the American tariff barrier, but remained well beneath that of 1890.[13] Thus groups in each country with a stake in Anglo-American relations had an economic power base which, relative to that of all other groups combined, shrank over the years.[14] In addition, a smaller proportion of businessmen in each country was exposed to communications from the other which came through trade contacts.

More than merchandise trade is relevant. Nations also conduct vast commerce in "invisibles," or services, including income from investments, transportation, foreign travelers in one's own country, and insurance. Investment income, transportation receipts, and travel receipts are by far the most important. Together they accounted for over 85 per cent of all British and American private international income from trade in services in 1954, and their total was over 30 per cent of their income from sales or merchandise.[15] Trade of this magnitude cannot be ignored, particularly as it involves the financial interests of Wall Street and the City which are alleged to be so important in American and British politics.

Analysis of this tie is severely handicapped by a lack of data. Bilateral balance-of-payments figures, necessary to examine trends in the proportion of American "invisible" income derived from Britain and vice versa, are creatures of the post-World War II era and do not exist for previous years. It is possible, nevertheless, to approximate the pattern for the three largest sources of income — investment, travel, and transportation.

Investment is the most significant, accounting for about half of both the United States' and Britain's invisible income in 1954. Like trade, foreign investment does not necessarily add to capabilities. When in the first half of the nineteenth century British investors lost millions of dollars to state governments that defaulted on their bonds, Anglo-American amity hardly was encouraged. An investor whose property had been nationalized would likewise not be happy. Further-

[13] In 1961, British exports to America declined to 1.4 per cent of U.K. national income. U.S. exports to Britain rose to 0.3 per cent of national income, but this was still far below the 1938 mark of 0.8 per cent.

[14] These trends are to some extent peculiar to Anglo-American trade. American exports to other industrialized nations, for example, have not shown nearly as great a drop as have exports to Britain. The index of relative acceptance for American exports to the "Six" of continental Europe was —.43 in 1938 and had actually improved slightly, to —.41, by 1954. Though we are not here immediately concerned with the *cause* of the decline in Anglo-American commerce, any explanation of it must nevertheless offer more than a simple description of forces applying to the whole Atlantic Community.

[15] International Monetary Fund, *Balance of Payments Yearbook, 1953–54*, Washington, 1955, United States, p. 6, and United Kingdom, p. 3.

more, heavy investment by foreign nationals in a particular industry may arouse fears that domestic control of the industry will be lost.[16] Ford Motors' decision to purchase a majority of shares in English Ford provoked just this kind of reaction, as did American acquisition of the Trinidad Oil Company in 1956 and British Aluminum in 1959.[17] A more serious case is probably that of American investment in Cuba. But generally there have been few sources of severe dissatisfaction for British and American lenders in each other's countries in the last seventy years. A recent book estimates that British opposition to American investment in their country was appreciably stronger before the last war than now, and was not great even then.[18] Except possibly for American railroads in 1890 and current developments in British automobile-manufacturing, no major industry in either country has been controlled by foreign investors, and we may safely treat investment as a capability.

We have no information on the volume of investment *income* going in both directions across the Atlantic before World War II, but we do have data on total investment *holdings* in each year (Figure 3.1).

Before World War I, British private investors contributed heavily to the development of the United States. Since then, British holdings in America have dropped sharply, although there was an important flow of capital to the United States during the depression years. American investment in Britain, negligible before 1900, grew substantially after 1913, but increased even more rapidly in the rest of the world. In both instances investment in the other country had fallen as a proportion of total foreign investment. The decline is, of course, much more striking for British investment in America than in the other direction.

We also need information on the provision of transport services. There is no direct data on income, but figures for the tonnage and nationality of ships entering British and American ports can provide the basis for a rough estimate, as shown in Figure 3.2.[19]

For Britain, shipping to and from American ports has declined

[16] See Francis Williams, *The American Invasion,* New York, 1962, ch. 2.

[17] Thomas P. Ronan, "U.S. Capital Held Boon to Britain," *New York Times,* November 30, 1960, 51:1, 55:3–4. See Maurice Edelman, M.P., "Stop the Ford Sell-Out!" *Tribune,* November 23, 1960, p. 1, as an example of some of the more extreme anti-American reactions of the left-wing British press.

[18] Dunning, *American Investment in British Manufacturing,* p. 307.

[19] I am indebted for this suggestion to Paul Horst-Madsen of the International Monetary Fund. Total British shipping entrances to U.K. ports provide a reasonable estimate of total tonnage handled by British ships in a year; similarly, U.S. entrances in American ports give an estimate of total American ships' cargo tonnage.

drastically, as a proportion of all British shipping and even absolutely. Post-World War II British tonnage to the United States has
fallen from about half of all British shipping to about one fifth. Total
British tonnage in American ports has dropped to barely one third
the level of 1928. For the United States the fall is not so drastic, but
nevertheless the trend which, from 1890 to the Second World War,
saw a rising proportion of American shipping to Britain has been
reversed. The mild improvement of 1958 over 1954 was not sufficient
to regain the 1938 peak.

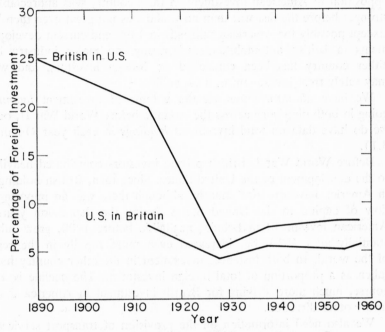

FIGURE 3.1 *Private Investment Holdings in Partner Country as a
Proportion of All Foreign Investment Holdings*
SOURCE: Appendix Table 3.2

The other major category is tourism. In Chapter 6 we shall discuss
trends in tourist exchange, evaluate their significance, and examine
the figures in detail. As with the previous two items we have no
early statistics on the actual earnings from tourism, but we do have
information on the total number of tourists admitted to each country
and the proportion coming from the other partner. The major pattern is a decline in relative earnings (Figure 3.3). For Britain, earnings from American travelers have probably dropped only moderately
as a proportion of all earnings from tourism. For the United States,

on the other hand, recent British tourists represented a much reduced fraction of all incoming visitors — from a peak of 13 per cent in 1938 to 8 per cent in 1958.

Altogether, we have unanimous evidence of a drop in the proportion of Britain's and America's sales of services to each other. We found sharp (over one third) declines from a pre-World War II peak for British investment in the United States, British shipping to America, and British tourists to America. (The former two of course represent British earnings, the latter American income.) Smaller re-

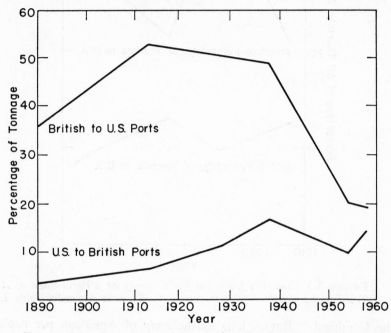

FIGURE 3.2   *Percentage of Total Shipping Tonnage Entering Ports in Partner Country*

SOURCE: Appendix Table 3.3

ductions were evident in the case of American shipping to Great Britain, and American tourists and investment in the United Kingdom.

With a few cautions we may use these figures to estimate actual income from these sources. We shall assume that British earnings from America, and vice versa, are, per investment dollar, per tourist, and per shipping ton, equal to the average earning for all items in the category. This may seem manifestly unrealistic — American tourists almost certainly spend more, apiece, than the average tourist from

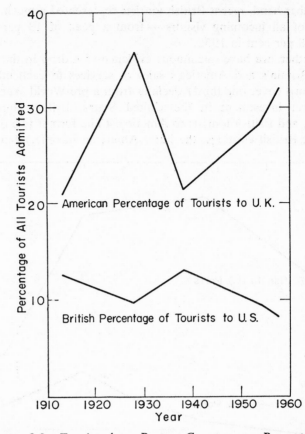

FIGURE 3.3   *Tourists from Partner Country as a Percentage of All Tourists Admitted*   SOURCE: Appendix Table 3.4

the Continent.[20] But as long as the *ratio* of American per capita spending does not change seriously relative to other per capita spending over the years, the effects cannot distort the picture in any major way.[21]

To make the estimates, we need one further bit of information:

[20] This may largely be balanced by the fact that shipping earnings between America and Britain are almost certainly below average. New York is closer to Liverpool than to almost any other non-North American port. Of course England is closer to the Continent and to the Mediterranean than to New York, but Asia, Oceania, South America, and most of Africa are farther.

[21] In the one case where we know the ratio to be changed, the effect of our assumption is to understate, not overstate, the actual decline. The proportion of British investment holdings in the United States was very great in the days when American companies paid relatively high interest rates. Both the proportion of British holdings in the United States and the American interest rates have declined in recent decades; thus the decline in the holdings ratio underestimates the decline in earnings.

the proportion of total earnings which each of these areas — investment, shipping, and travel — accounted for. These data are given in Appendix Table 3.5. We may multiply each of the figures found there by the appropriate percentage in column 3 of Appendix Tables 3.2, 3.3, and 3.4, which give the "British" proportion of American investment holdings, shipping, and incoming tourists, and the American proportion of British holdings, etc.[22] With this procedure we derive an estimate of American and British earnings from the three sources given in Table 3.2.

TABLE 3.2. American and British Earnings from Each Other on Investment, Shipping, and Travel

	1913	1928	1938	1954	1958
U.K. Earnings from U.S.					
Million Pounds	96	n.a.	70	145	168
Percentage of Earnings from all Countries	28.7	n.a.	21.0	17.9	17.1
Percentage of National Income	4.10	n.a.	1.40	0.99	0.92
U.S. Earnings from U.K.					
Million Dollars	19	91	93	269	469
Percentage of Earnings from All Countries	8.6	6.3	9.5	7.2	8.7
Percentage of National Income	0.06	0.11	0.14	0.09	0.13

We repeat: Despite the seeming precision of the percentages, they are rough estimates, based on some assumptions about the rate of earnings in one country being equal to the rate from all countries. But they are sufficiently accurate to indicate whether there has been any notable change in the proportion of British and American earnings from invisibles that the two nations gain from each other.

Clearly, there has been such a change. America has declined, relative to other countries, as a source of invisible income for Britain. Earnings from the United States have fallen even more sharply as a fraction of national income, to less than a quarter of what they were in 1913. For United States earnings a similar trend was partially reversed in 1958. Income from sales to Britain remained smaller, compared with income from other countries, than it had been in 1938, but as a proportion of national income it almost regained the prewar peak. This reflected the modest increase in all invisible earnings as a proportion of national income. For Britain the trend for

[22] That is, for 1958 we know that 5.7 per cent of American foreign-investment holdings were in the United Kingdom, and that total United States earnings from foreign investment were $2922 million. To the product of those two figures ($166 million) we add the equivalent figures for shipping and travel ($1672 million × 14.1% = $236 million and $825 million × 8.1% = $67 million) for a sum of $469 million.

individual items shows up equally clearly in this combined set; for the United States the fall is there but is much less sharp. Britain's invisible earnings from the United States once made a major contribution to her national income (over 4 per cent), though they no longer do so; for the United States, however, where the decline was slight, they have always amounted to much less than 1 per cent of total income.

With trade in goods and services combined, we find that Anglo-American commerce has dropped substantially, relative to national income, in both countries. For the reasons specified earlier in the chapter, we must regard the decline with concern. Despite undoubted lags and exceptions, it implies the weakening of an important bond between the two nations.

4

Investment Rivalry: The Muted Conflict

Foreign Investments and International Hostilities

Economic relationships may become sources of friction rather than links to bind countries more closely. We must now expand the discussion to consider not only direct trade relations between the two Anglo-Saxon powers but situations where nationals of each country may vie for trade or investment opportunities in a third state. Such situations clearly are conducive to instances of friction which might unfavorably affect relations between the two governments.

Investment rivalry has long been identified as a source of conflict between governments. Alarmed by the rise of tariffs in the newly developing industrial regions around the globe, Cecil Rhodes feared that British producers would be shut out of foreign markets. He emphasized the need for a larger market than the British Isles could provide, and urged the acquisition of more colonial territory.[1] Then liberal thinkers like Charles Conant and J. A. Hobson blamed imperial rivalry among the great powers on basic economic forces causing a scramble for markets abroad.[2] Finally the Marxists picked up the argument and added a few embellishments.[3] Lenin was the most famous although hardly the first of the Marxist exponents of

[1] William T. Stead, editor, *The Last Will and Testament of Cecil John Rhodes*, London, 1902.
[2] Charles A. Conant, "The Economic Basis of Imperialism," *North American Review*, September 1898, pp. 326–340, and J. A. Hobson, *Imperialism*, London, 1902.
[3] On the Marxist writers, see William L. Langer, *The Diplomacy of Imperialism*, New York, 1956, pp. 67–69, which has a fuller discussion of thought on the connection of economics with imperialism.

this view.[4] Briefly, the argument is this: Capitalists in the industrial nations, impelled by the falling rate of profit at home, increasingly search for investment opportunities in the underdeveloped areas of the world. As competition for such opportunities becomes keen, rival capitalists enlist the aid of their governments in order to gain exclusive rights to the investment possibilities of particular areas. Repeated and large-scale international conflict over colonies results.

We need not, of course, accept the extreme Leninist view in order to assert that investment rivalry can cause international friction. Such rivalry may fall short of seeking exclusive rights in an area through colonial acquisition, but may result merely in less drastic forms of government intervention on behalf of the prospective lender. Furthermore, the financier may call upon his government to protect his investment once made, or to secure interest payments on the loan. Conflict may result when each of two governments tries to gain preferential treatment for the claims of its own nationals. There is no need to assert that wars or other serious international conflicts always occur this way, but frictions have arisen from this source, as we shall see from a number of examples.

The causal chain by no means always runs *from* investment rivalry *to* intergovernmental conflict. Frequently governments have promoted investment in areas they had designs on for other reasons. Then investment rivalry was at best the immediate rather than the basic cause of conflict. Eugene Staley sums it up this way:

> True enough, private investors abroad have sought to secure diplomatic aid for their projects, and their influence on diplomacy has at times brought conflicts between governments. On the other hand, international friction over private investments has been a good deal more frequent and dangerous where private investments have been pressed into service as instruments, tools, of a larger political purpose which the investments themselves did not originate. Investments used in the quest for national glory, and the like, have been more productive of international friction in the past than investments actuated solely by private profit motives.[5]

In the early 1900's, for example, the British government supported a Six-Power Loan to China on the ground that it was better for the chief powers to work together than to compete for political advantage.[6] The Taft Administration, on the other hand, used diplomatic pressure to force American capital into China when it would not go

[4] Nikolai Lenin, *Imperialism: The Highest Stage of Capitalism,* New Data Edition, New York (no date—first published in 1917).
[5] Eugene Staley, *War and the Private Investor,* Garden City, 1935, pp. xv–xvi.
[6] C. K. Hobson, *The Export of Capital,* London, 1914, p. xxiv.

there of its own accord. Administration leaders wanted a lever to exert political influence in the area and felt that mere trade did not carry the proprietary rights that constituted an opening wedge for that influence. The bankers, however, were never happy with their unprofitable position there, and one of President Wilson's first acts on taking office in 1913 was to withdraw American support from the six-power consortium offering China a reorganization loan. The protests of discontented bankers were not irrelevant to his decision.[7]

A Royal Institute of International Affairs report suggests a number of ways in which governments promote overseas lending.[8] One is the above kind of direct encouragement, sometimes followed by force to protect the investor. Another is investment by the state itself, as in the Anglo-Iranian Oil Company or the Suez and Panama canals. Loans like the Dawes and the Young loans for stabilization may be guaranteed by the government, or guarantees or preferences may be given to issues of colonial securities in order to promote lending in one's overseas territories. Finally, public authorities may, directly or indirectly through some financial mechanism, make low credit rates available to foreign importers.

Thus one cannot deduce from the simultaneous existence of commercial and political rivalry that the former caused the latter. It probably is a mistake to think in simplistic terms like *cause* anyway. One may consider the whole process a feedback cycle, where nothing less than the whole cycle makes the process continue. For example, it may be necessary to have not only investors who are anxious to expand their operations in a particular area but also government officials with some political interest in penetrating the area. Without both factors present there may be neither financial penetration nor overt political rivalry. One factor is possibly more conspicuous than the other in promoting activity (in feedback model terms, one stage of the cycle may be more conspicuous in amplifying changes than the other), yet both may be essential. So Staley's analysis, while highly illuminating in destroying the myth that financial conflicts cause political ones, is still an oversimplification. A more sophisticated conceptual scheme is essential to untangle the driving forces of a complex system of mutually reinforcing relationships.

Regardless of the direction of cause and effect in a particular instance, commercial rivalry is often an *indicator* of political rivalry because of the frequent interdependence of the two. It may be used as

[7] A. Whitney Griswold, *The Far Eastern Policy of the United States,* New York, 1938, pp. 133–175.
[8] *The Problem of International Investment: A Report by a Study Group of Members of the Royal Institute of International Affairs,* New York, 1937, pp. 86–87.

such an indicator if we retain a sense of proportion. In the previous chapter we discussed the rapidly falling share in the national income of both Britain and the United States that was represented by trade between them. From this we deduced that there were in recent years relatively fewer interest groups with a stake in Anglo-American trade, and thus relatively fewer individuals and groups with *this particular kind* of stake in good Anglo-American relations. The obverse of this relationship applies to foreign investment. Investment rivalry implies frictions between nationals of the two countries. These frictions would almost certainly find their way to the governmental level via interest groups or other means of influencing national policy — much the same mechanism as we discussed regarding trade ties. Other things being equal, as the amount of capital engaged in Anglo-American commercial rivalry decreased (or increased) as a proportion of national income, relatively fewer (or more) frictions would arise or reach the level of official policy-making. A decrease in the relative amount of investment in competitive areas would reduce a source of irritation to broader relations.

We therefore must attempt to estimate the severity of commercial rivalry at each of the various periods under examination. Though we shall naturally be extremely interested in cases where economic frictions are transmitted directly to governmental policy, we need not limit ourselves to cases where evidence of that is available. Even though they do not immediately become transmuted into governmental conflict, indirectly they become a source of irritation tending to drive the two governments apart.

Trends: A Rough Assessment

One way of making the estimate is simply to look at the frequency with which various writers mention rivalry. While such an inquiry is not by itself enough, at least it provides a first approximation of the trend.

In 1890 there was little opportunity for conflict over investment. While Britain was easily the world's greatest capital exporter, the amount of foreign lending undertaken by United States entrepreneurs was slight (well under 5 per cent of the British total).[9] There were rather small-scale American investments in Hawaii, Canada, and Central America, but very few if any produced frictions reaching the

---

[9] There are no precise estimates on foreign investment at this time, but see A. K. Cairncross, *Home and Foreign Investment, 1870–1913: Studies in Capital Accumulation,* Cambridge, Eng., 1953, p. 183; and R. W. Dunn, *American Foreign Investment,* New York, 1926, pp. 1–4.

level of Anglo-American governmental discussion. The economic world was Britain's oyster, and American activities were merely the smallest grains of sand. From the American side, however, the situation may have seemed less idyllic. American financiers were taking a growing interest in foreign investment, and they may well have felt themselves shut out of opportunities by the omnipresent Leviathan. The beginnings of conflict already existed.

At the opening of the twentieth century, American financiers rapidly expanded their lending operations abroad, particularly in the Western Hemisphere and Western Europe. During the decade before World War I, the United States government strongly encouraged investment in Central America and the Caribbean, which was treated as a sphere of special interest to the United States. American motives were mixed. The policy was partly an effort to free these countries from real or imagined financial dependence on Europe, which was thought to threaten the Monroe Doctrine. Then too, many members of the Taft Administration believed that the expansion of trade depended upon the establishment of American banks in this area.[10] This era of "Dollar Diplomacy" undoubtedly provided occasions for clashes between the two governments. Private competition for oil was severe in Colombia in 1913 and may also have been a factor in the failure to achieve a co-ordinated Anglo-American policy toward the Mexican dictator Huerta.[11]

About this time the British government took several steps which must have annoyed the United States. In Haiti, Honduras, and Mexico (1910–14) aggressive British officials sought the satisfaction of their compatriots' claims. Haiti was given an ultimatum to compensate a British subject for damage suffered in a revolution. A Royal Navy battleship in 1913 induced Guatemala to restore coffee duties alienated in favor of newer creditors to the service of loans held by British investors.[12] But in Africa, the Liberian government, fearing British domination, requested economic assistance from American financiers and got it in 1913.[13]

Coupled with the events of World War I, the expansion of American lending radically altered the whole structure of international finance. The United Kingdom financed massive overseas purchases of supplies and military equipment by selling about £850 million worth of securi-

---

[10] Charles A. Beard, *The Idea of National Interest,* New York, 1934, pp. 104–112; and *The Problem of International Investment,* pp. 179–180.

[11] Burton J. Hendrick, *The Life and Letters of Walter H. Page,* I, New York, 1922, pp. 185–187.

[12] Herbert Feis, *Europe, the World's Banker,* New Haven, 1930, pp. 109–110.

[13] Cleona Lewis, *America's Stake in International Investments,* Washington, 1938, p. 44.

ties held by its citizens. The war also resulted in some losses to British investors in Germany and Eastern Europe. Concurrently the United States became a major capital exporter. Public and private war loans were floated in this country on an unprecedented scale, and at the same time a great proportion of British and French investors' securities found its way to Wall Street. After the war, American investors went on a massive and often uncritical lending spree, extending funds freely everywhere, especially to the defeated powers and throughout Latin America. Seekers of funds from countries outside the British Empire found interest rates ½ to 1¼ per cent cheaper in New York than on Lombard Street. Even Canada and, to some extent, Australia found lower rates in the United States.

By the end of the 1920's, American investors had nearly elbowed Great Britain out of position as the world's largest capital exporter. Their aggressiveness provided even more opportunities for conflict than in the period immediately preceding the great cataclysm. Ludwell Denny published a revealing book at that time.[14] Though he drew rather extreme conclusions, the mere popularity of a book dealing with Anglo-American commercial rivalry is indicative of the feelings generated. He cited struggles between American oil interests and the British Royal Dutch/Shell organization in Venezuela, Colombia, and even Soviet Russia during the New Economic Policy. The American government allegedly encouraged various investors' attempts to free the United States of dependence on British "monopoly" sources of tin and rubber, as His Majesty's government tried to reduce its reliance on American supplies of copper. Private investors also competed for control of nickel, zinc, and nitrate supplies, although Denny cited no evidence that the governments were involved.[15] Finally, the Greek government in 1929 sought a great loan from the British firm of

[14] Ludwell Denny, *America Conquers Britain*, New York, 1930.

[15] Note the frequent association of rivalry and monopoly. With the decline of free trade and the rise of international cartels, the high profits to be made from monopoly-breaking tended to increase the attractiveness of challenge to rival investors.

See also W. Y. Elliot *et al.*, *International Control in the Non-Ferrous Metals*, New York, 1937, where the tin and copper "monopolies" are discussed, as is the competition for nickel and zinc. While there is evidence that European governments, including the British, encouraged copper production from non-American sources, there is no such evidence offered concerning the United States government and the tin supply. Elliot concludes that on the whole, governments were directly concerned only to secure state revenues or military stockpiles. In fact, the United States government took an extraordinary step in 1931 when it agreed with British and Netherlands authorities on a joint system for *reducing* tin production (in the American case, from United States-owned mines in Bolivia). This is one more piece of evidence for the theme of intergovernmental investment co-operation developed later in the text.

Hambros. The bankers tried to commit the Greeks to take all future loans from them. Greece replied by turning to an American banking firm.[16]

Other writers refer to intervention by the State Department to secure oil concessions in British colonial areas. The first of these, late in the 1920's, concerned attempts by American companies to break the Anglo-French monopoly in Iraq, and was resolved by allowing the American group to buy into the controlling Turkish Petroleum Company.[17] Similarly, United States oil companies wanted to have a go at the rich oil fields of Bahrein and Kuwait. Washington negotiated for its nationals and eventually won a concession in Bahrein equal to Britain's (1930) and a 50 per cent share in the hitherto purely British Kuwait concession (1934).[18]

Following the Great Crash and the widespread default of foreign loans, opportunities for conflict arose less frequently. Many American investors had their fingers burned in Germany and Latin America, and in 1938 they were not anxious to fight their way into the underdeveloped areas of the world. British lenders, through caution and a preference for the safer borrowers of the empire, emerged relatively unscathed. Even in the more industrialized regions, Anglo-American investors often tended to go into industries where they would not compete with each other. By 1934, for example, United Kingdom lenders had put over half again as much money into Canadian railway development as had American financiers. On the other hand, American investments in Canadian industry and government securities were well over twice those of British bankers.[19]

After World War II, instances of friction were still rarer. Again Britain had attempted to finance her desperate war efforts by selling foreign investments — about £1100 million in securities were sold in the early years of the conflict.[20] Finally Lend-Lease came to the United Kingdom's rescue, but the dollar value of many British overseas holdings was again sharply cut by the drastic devaluation of sterling and other nondollar currencies in 1949. Nor have Britons had

[16] Staley, *War and the Private Investor*, pp. 155–156; Lewis, *America's Stake*, p. 229; and Herbert Feis, *The Diplomacy of the Dollar*, Baltimore, 1950, pp. 48–60.

[17] The shares were divided as follows: British, 47½ per cent; U.S., 23¾ per cent; French, 23¾ per cent; and a private claimant, 5 per cent. See Cleona Lewis, *The United States and Foreign Investment Problems*, Washington, 1948, pp. 228–229; and *American Petroleum Interests in Foreign Countries; Hearings before a Special Senate Committee Investigating Petroleum Resources*, 79th Congress, First Session, Washington 1945, pp. 23–24.

[18] By 1954 two American companies had taken over all rights in Bahrein. Kuwait's status was unchanged.

[19] *The Problem of International Investment*, p. 257.

[20] A. R. Conan, *The Sterling Area*, London, 1952, p. 179.

as much foreign exchange available for new overseas investment as
they once did, owing to the smaller export surplus the economy has
provided. By 1954 total United States direct and portfolio investment
abroad was nearly four times that of the United Kingdom.

Because of the vast liquidation of British holdings and the decline
in new lending by British subjects, opportunities for conflict arose less
often. In fact, the two governments frequently worked together. One
author contends that the Iranian crisis was marked by substantial
official co-operation:

> Whatever commercial rivalry may have existed between British
> and American interests, Anglo-American differences of opinion on the
> political level appeared to be confined to matters of timing. . . . There
> was little sign of serious conflict on this point, and there can be no
> doubt that the American unity of view with Britain as regards market-
> ing and transport facilities for the Persian oil, in disappointment of
> the Persian hopes, and its attitude on a loan to Dr. Musaddiq's govern-
> ment were important factors in the final settlement. . . .[21]

This view seems too sanguine. Some Britishers insisted that the
United States had been anxious to displace their companies with its
own. Since American firms, formerly excluded, received a share in
the new concession equal to the British company's, there is some
justification for their view.[22] Still, the tone was largely one of unity
against a common enemy, the nationalizers. Even the old rivalry
between the oil titans, Jersey Standard and Royal Dutch/Shell, has
taken on less of the appearance of British versus American competition. By 1960 almost a quarter of the shares in the Royal Dutch/Shell
"group" were owned by Americans.[23] The 1960's even found the
American government encouraging other nations (especially Germany) to expand their lending to underdeveloped areas. Britain, on
the other hand, was willing to have the United States take over some
of the burdens she no longer could carry alone.

Antipathy or Symbiosis?

Commercial and political conflict are not always associated. Staley
suggests that many more sources of friction arise between a capital-

[21] Coral Bell, *Survey of International Affairs*, London, 1957, pp. 226–227. The
division was: Anglo-Iranian, 40 per cent; five American companies, 8 per cent
each; Royal Dutch/Shell, 14 per cent; and Compagnie Français des Pétroles, 6
per cent.

[22] John Biggs-Davison, *The Uncertain Ally*, London, 1957, pp. 182–183,
polemicizes the view that the United States government was primarily responsible for British petroleum interests' losses.

[23] "Diplomats of Oil," *Time*, May 9, 1960, p. 94.

exporting and a capital-importing country, especially if the latter is weak, than between two rival capital-exporting countries.[24] Instances where two or more lending nations combined to coerce a debtor state are legion.[25] This fact is highly significant for study of the world's two greatest foreign creditors. Furthermore, the Royal Institute study group asserted in 1937 that British and American lending was largely free of political motives and was governed almost entirely by considerations of risk and rate of return.[26] While that statement clearly claims too much, there nevertheless were few instances where investment was blatantly used as an instrument of politics in such a way as to produce serious Anglo-American friction at the official level.

In fact, there have been numerous occasions when, for the sake of harmonious relations between the two nations, a government refused to rescue an investor. Until the end of the nineteenth century, when it began to yield to the increased pressure of highly organized interests, the Foreign Office simply preferred not to be bothered by investors. "Save in exceptional circumstances where some British interest, usually political, seemed to be threatened, there was little wish for formal interference." [27] Although the British government used rather highhanded tactics in Venezuela in 1902, those tactics were met with some indignation in Britain as well as in the United States, and His Majesty's government was thought to have used its discretion unwisely. Though it later interfered against other powers, 1902 marked a kind of watershed in Britain's relations of this sort with the United States. After President Wilson had rattled the Monroe Doctrine in his speech at Mobile in October 1913, Downing Street withdrew support from the English oil magnate, Lord Cowdray, on his projects in Mexico, Colombia, and elsewhere in Latin America. It had previously supported Cowdray, and simultaneously was encouraging oil men in other parts of the world, but it suddenly instructed him to cease trying to extend his concessions by tactics objectionable to the Ameri-

[24] Staley, *War and the Private Investor*, p. 366.

[25] For example, China (1910), Venezuela (1902), and Iran (1954).

[26] *The Problem of International Investment*, p. 21. Actually, the Royal Institute group stated that loans went "to the borrower who could offer the highest return." The rate of return is of course a function of the risks involved; British investors particularly avoided areas where the political risks of domestic instability or foreign intervention were greatest. Before World War I, for example, British investments in Spanish-owned Cuba, Czarist Russia, and the Near East were substantially smaller than French lendings. The French, attracted by the high interest rates offered, suffered accordingly when revolution came. During the same period over two thirds of Britain's investment holdings were in the United States or in the Empire. British investors were, on the whole, remarkably competent in assessing political risks — probably a combination of their native shrewdness and sound Foreign Office advice.

[27] Feis, *Europe*, p. 84.

can government. In July 1914, Sir Edward Grey was urged in Parliament to interfere with a projected Brazilian loan; he refused. Although we have seen cases where it did take action, the Foreign Office often did little for British investors sustaining losses in Latin America.

Corresponding instances of American action can be found. Early in the twentieth century, American financial advisers were forced out of Persia by the English and Russians; American influence in Persia was not considered important to the national interest, and no official steps were taken. In 1927, Abyssinia attempted to escape British, French, and Italian domination by drawing in "neutral" capital. Secretary of State Kellogg refused to encourage American participation in an Abyssinian dam project unless it was agreeable to Britain.[28] Washington was always extremely anxious to prevent European political domination anywhere in the Western Hemisphere and frequently was displeased by the efforts of Old World governments to bail their investors out of difficulty. Yet it was able to avoid conflict and accommodate itself to the situation — the American government itself looked out for the affairs of investors south of the border. In 1905 it established a receivership in the Dominican Republic to assure the repayment of loans to British and French financiers. In 1912 intervention in Nicaragua benefited both British and American lenders. And through American efforts, the 1926 government of Nicaragua agreed with British bondholders to scale down its debt from a nominal $150 million to only $6 million. The British acquiesced despite the size of their loss. Samuel Flagg Bemis calls such actions examples of "preventative diplomacy," designed to remove any justification for intervention by a non-American power.[29]

Note the parallels between the two governments' policies. Each had a rather clear idea of where it would press for its investors and where it would not. The British avoided provocative acts in the Western Hemisphere; the United States was careful in Africa and the Middle East. Two comments by the Assistant Secretary of State under Taft pinpoint this attitude:

> In the encouragement of foreign enterprise, diplomacy must beware of forcing it into spheres where vexatious conflict with special spheres of influence and interest of other countries outweighs all commercial gain to be looked for. Every great power has some "doctrines" that it conceives to be vital to it as the Monroe Doctrine is considered here. Korea and Manchuria, Persia and Siam, come to mind as examples of territory where, while conducting ordinary trade, we

[28] Staley, *War and the Private Investor*, pp. 363–364.
[29] Samuel Flagg Bemis, *The Latin American Policy of the United States,* New York, 1950, pp. 154–159, 164, 209

should be wasting our energies to attempt intensive developments. In return we should gradually crowd out from our own sphere of special interest foreign interests wherever they are predominant to an uncomfortable extent and quite beyond the requirements of an ordinary trade outside the spheres of special interest of the foreign governments concerned. . . .

If he [the American investor] jumped into a pet preserve of Great Britain or France and engaged in enterprises subversive to some policy of "protection, guidance, and control" . . . it is not intended to imply that his government would abandon him to his fate. It would seek equitable damages for him, but probably not specific performance. So it was, in principle, to give an analogous example, when the American advisers were forced out of Persia by Russia and England. American influence in Persia was of no account to our national interest. . . . If, on the other hand, those advisers had been in a country where American influence was of national importance, the American government must have resisted their dismissal and insisted upon specific performance, although the contracts were no more binding in one case than in the other.[30]

In this way Secretary of State Knox's policy of "all proper support to legitimate and beneficial American enterprises in foreign countries" was applied. What was "proper" depended upon what was considered to be in the national interest.

Both the American and British governments exercised conscious control over their foreign investors. The author of the above statement concludes, "Indeed to encourage here, to deter there, in short, more or less to guide foreign investment, is a proper function of government." With the British, the control was no less present, although perhaps more elusive. Subtle and quietly informal, it often depended on the "natural harmony of action" made possible by British habits and the close-knit nature of British official and commercial society. Thus both governments tried hard to avoid conflict with each other and perhaps with France and Japan. There is little evidence that there was ever a formal decision on which areas were considered to be in the other's sphere of influence, but informally the demarcations were rather clear. Particularly, Central America and the Caribbean were the United States' preserve.[31]

[30] Huntington Wilson, "The Relation of Government to Foreign Investment," Annals, LXVIII (November 1916), pp. 302–304.

[31] See what A. E. Campbell (Great Britain and the United States, 1895–1903, London, 1960, p. 79) identifies as a politically inspired article in The Spectator of January 27, 1900: "We want nothing that belongs to America, nor do we claim to interfere with what she considers within her special 'sphere of influence.' Our virtual acceptance of the Monroe doctrine when we agreed to the Venezuelan arbitration has removed the risk of serious quarrel in the future."

Corrective action had to be applied early. A government which wished to avoid conflict with another signaled to its investors before they had established too great a stake in an area. The British government's ability to pull the rug out from under Lord Cowdray illustrates this. He was prevented from extending his concessions, not forced to abandon those already won. Finally, we need not depend entirely on the idea that government officials consciously guided their nationals' lending. Frequently investors could figure out for themselves that financial activity in a particular region would be expensive. Even excluding political factors, rivalry with a foreign investor was certain to be a costly undertaking, thus reducing the return. And investors were sensitive.

> Most freely and in greatest volume it [British capital] moved to countries under the British flag and to the United States — within the circle, that is, of established political friendship. From countries toward which antipathy existed it abstained, quick to detect the beat of the war-drum, no matter how muffled and distant, in the rhythm of relations.[32]

We may speculate on one reason why the two English-speaking states were so successful in subordinating their rivalry to the pursuit of common interests. Both were "have" powers in two senses: Each had a substantial surplus of funds available for lending abroad, and each held sway over large "spheres of influence." Each was willing to grant limited concessions to the other's investors in its own "pet preserve," and, tacitly at least, expected similar treatment in the other's area of dominance. Serious controversies might arise between a power which had a sphere of influence and a "have-not" which was excluded, but not between the two great "haves." Wilson's statement about crowding foreign interests out from our own sphere of special interest was construed rather liberally. The United States in fact helped British lenders in Latin America to collect their debts. In the Middle East, British concessions to American oil interests were fully as notable as the conflicts. The investors of one country could live under the protective umbrella of the other's national power. Symbiosis was as prominent as antipathy.[33] Later, important corporate ties grew up

[32] Feis, *Europe,* p. 88.

[33] Note, however, the gradual change in the nature of this symbiosis. The first United States oil concession in an area of British dominance, Iraq, gave American companies, as well as the French, a share half the size of the British portion. Later agreements in Kuwait, Bahrein, and Iran gave American companies an equal share with the British. Thus the United States rose from junior to full partner in several areas where British investors had formerly been dominant. British influence in American-dominated areas like the Western Hemisphere, however, declined.

to cement the relationship. British and American firms jointly operated concessions in Iraq, Iran, Kuwait, and Bahrein, for example. The interest-group mechanism which might have produced antagonism became instead something of an institutional bond uniting the Anglo-Saxon nations.

Thus investment rivalry has been overrated as an irritant in Anglo-American relations. While our examination of various reports of conflict showed a clear decline in friction, that friction never was too serious anyway.

Trends: A Quantitative Analysis

Nevertheless, it would be useful to have a more precise estimate of trends in at least the *potential* amount of conflict, one not dependent on the selectivity of the writers of secondary analyses and selectivity in the choice of those authorities to be consulted. To assess this conflict *potential,* we shall identify three types of debtor countries: those where the United States is the dominant lender, providing at least three times as much capital as the United Kingdom; those where the United Kingdom is similarly dominant; and those where neither provides as much as three fourths of the Anglo-American total and investors of the two countries must in some crude sense "compete." We might surmise that American lenders to a country where other American financiers provided the great bulk of the loans would not feel particularly threatened by the activities of British lenders in that country, and vice versa. On the other hand, they might feel intensely threatened in countries where neither of the two great lending powers had a clear dominance, or where the rival power was dominant. The use of three fourths as the proportion dividing "dominance" from "competition" is, of course, arbitrary.[34] Nor does it show to what extent British and American investment in a country is, on the particular level, competitive (as when both invest in mining a particular product) or complementary (when one nation's investment is concentrated in mining, the other's in railroads). But when applied to a long time-span, the scheme gives an acceptable measure of financial competition.

In the nineteenth century the United States was very much a debtor nation and exported capital on only a very small scale. Even that much foreign investment was largely confined to North and Central

[34] Some other fraction, such as two thirds or four fifths, might have been used as a dividing line, but a careful examination of the tables will show that the use of a different breaking point would not substantially affect our judgment of the trend.

America. Detailed accounts of the geographical distribution of neither British nor American investment are available, but it would seem likely that only in Canada might United States lending have been on a sufficiently large scale to cause serious competition for British financiers. In fact, even there the British had a nearly clear field. The earliest estimate is for 1899, when United States private long-term investment in Canada amounted to $150 million and British holdings to over $1 billion, or nearly seven times as much.[35] Clearly, Great Britain was "dominant" everywhere with respect to her young rival-to-be. For 1913, 1928, 1938, and 1954, however, we have fairly reliable studies of long-term lending by area, excluding investment in Britain and the United States. For a country-by-country breakdown, the reader is referred to Tables 4.1 to 4.4 in Appendix B.

These tables trace the steps whereby in merely forty years the United States became the dominant foreign lender throughout the Western Hemisphere and in most of Western Europe. Great Britain retains its original dominance only in parts of the Commonwealth and, in a shadowy way, in Eastern Europe and China. (Doubtless, holdings in these two Communist-controlled areas are overvalued in Appendix Table 4.4.) Even in much of the Commonwealth the United States is as important as Britain in providing funds. Many Commonwealth countries, though still dependent on United Kingdom investors for most of their capital needs, have begun to turn to the United States. Since World War II, Australia has repeatedly issued dollar bonds in New York. One study indicates that the United States and Britain provided approximately equal amounts of new investment capital to India in the period 1946–55.[36] Text Table 4.1 summarizes those in Appendix B and gives the proportion of both lenders' total foreign capital invested in each of the three types of country.

United States investors in 1954 were in nearly as advantageous a position as British investors were in 1913. The overwhelming proportion of American investment was in areas where American investors were dominant, and there was almost none where British investors predominated. From the *American* point of view, then, the potentialities for friction must have been greatest in 1913, when American investors had to push their way into areas where British capital predominated, or where substantial competition already existed. But this irritant decreased somewhat after World War I and very much more following World War II.

[35] Jacob Viner, *Canada's Balance of International Indebtedness, 1900–1913*, Cambridge, Mass., 1924.
[36] A. R. Conan, *The Changing Pattern of International Investment in Selected Sterling Countries*, Princeton, 1957, p. 17.

TABLE 4.1. Amount and Percentage of American and British
Capital Invested in Three Types of Country

Lender	Year	Borrowers Where G.B. Dominant		Borrowers Where G.B.-U.S. Compete		Borrowers Where U.S. Dominant		Total
		Amount (in million dollars)	Per-centage	Amount (in million dollars)	Per-centage	Amount (in million dollars)	Per-centage	Amount (in million dollars)
U.S.	1913	1,300	50	1,200	46	105	4	2,605
	1928	643	5	8,535	73	2,557	22	11,735
	1938	1,001	10	7,081	67	2,453	23	10,535
	1954	125	1	3,539	16	18,021	83	21,685
G.B.	1913	13,150	94	770	6	—	—	13,920
	1928	8,249	49	7,833	42	748	4	16,830
	1938	6,620	63	4,957	33	538	4	15,115
	1954	1,376	29	2,099	45	1,227	26	4,702

Because the opportunities for discord had diminished for Americans, however, does not mean that they also receded for the British. In 1913, American attempts to penetrate areas where British capital ruled must have seemed relatively unimportant. Only a small fraction of British investment was in areas where American competition was great. But after the First World War, only about half of British foreign capital was in countries where United Kingdom investors predominated. Thanks to widespread foreign defaults on the more insecure American loans during the depression, this situation was eased in 1938. Yet following World War II, less than one third of Britain's foreign investment was in areas where American loans were not also substantial. Over one quarter, in fact, was to be found where the United States was the dominant lender. One might expect that, from the British point of view, the possibilities for conflict over investment were greater than ever.

Such an analysis would be superficial. Foreign investment was, in 1954, far less important quantitatively to the British economy than it had been for nearly a century. Table 4.2 shows the total foreign investment of each nation, and investment in countries where the lending state was not dominant, as a proportion of annual national income. The percentages in the final column serve as very rough indicators of changes in the degree to which investment rivalry was an irritant to general Anglo-American relations.

Whereas in 1913 Britain's foreign assets represented an amount far greater than her annual national income, the relative size of her foreign

TABLE 4.2. Foreign Investment Holdings as a Proportion of Annual National Income

	Year	Total Foreign Investment Holdings (in million dollars)	Total Investment as Percentage of Annual National Income	Investment in Areas Where Both Compete or Other Investor Is Dominant as Percentage of Income
U.S.	1913	2,605	8	8
	1928	15,170	19	11
	1938	11,491	17	12
	1954	24,365	8	1
G.B.	1913	18,200	158	7
	1928	18,100	90	42
	1938	17,400	69	22
	1954	6,200	15	8

SOURCE OF INCOME DATA: Appendix Table 3.1.

Total investment in this table is larger than the totals of Table 4.1 because these figures also include British investment in the United States and vice versa, and investment in securities not identified geographically.

Note how effectively this table refutes the Leninist notion that foreign investment comes to represent a greater proportion of national income with the passage of time. Relative to the incomes of both countries, the so-called "economic determinants" of international conflict have fallen substantially. This is true for Great Britain and the United States generally, not just vis-à-vis each other.

holdings fell steadily thereafter. Despite the fact that in 1954 a larger proportion of her foreign investment faced American competition than before World War II, that investment made a comparatively small contribution to her national income. Relatively fewer individuals and interest groups were engaged in investment rivalry at that time than at any period since World War I.

Specifically, we should expect that the potentialities for rivalry would be rather slight in 1900 but most seriously irritating to the United States in the years 1913 to 1938, with a peak between the wars. These potentialities were very much less disturbing, however, in 1954. For Britain, the pattern is substantially the same. That is, 1913 would be a year of potentially little conflict, but 1928 one of much greater irritation. Yet that would mark the peak, since by 1938 foreign investment as a whole was less important to the British economy, and a smaller portion of that investment was in areas of competition. Almost certainly, the source of friction was less in 1954, with the sharp diminution in foreign investment relative to income. Therefore we surmise that Anglo-American relations have become less vulnerable to investment rivalries with the passage of time.

Two remaining points, both of which suggest that current rivalry is greater than that indicated by Table 4.2, must be mentioned before closing. First is the possibility that though the liquidation of British foreign investment reduced a source of continuing friction, it may also represent a source of unhappy memories. Investors who once were dominant in an area only to be forced to accommodate American challengers, or who were compelled by economic or political circumstances to sell out, may nourish bitterness and envy for their transatlantic rivals. The apparent reduction in tensions would be deceptive. In place of active competition would be, for one party, the rancor of defeat.

The second argument concerns the importance of foreign investment to Britain's balance of payments. In 1913 the British government had little need for concern over its international accounts, and therefore might not regard investors' problems, affecting only rather narrow interests, very seriously. But since World War II, Britain has had to struggle constantly to earn enough abroad to pay for essential imports, and the income from investments has become vital not merely to the financiers who placed them but to the whole economy. Thus the quantitative reduction in investment competition might be counteracted by a qualitative change making that competition far more salient to government officials than ever before. Foreign investment might remain nearly as great a source of Anglo-American friction as during the interwar years.

These are notable arguments and cannot be dismissed, though it is difficult to evaluate them. The second, about the urgency with which her government must regard anything relevant to Britain's international accounts, loses some force when we see that income from overseas investments contributed less than 8 per cent of her total foreign receipts from goods and services in 1954.[37] While Whitehall can hardly ignore the foreign-investment problem, still it must keep the matter in perspective as only one of many factors influencing Britain's international accounts. Furthermore, the 1940's did not represent the first time that responsible political figures paid much attention to the United Kingdom's international position. On the contrary, Britain's balance of payments deteriorated sharply between the wars, causing much controversy and activity in official circles. Although attention undoubtedly increased still more in the 1940's and 1950's, we must not exaggerate that increase.

But finally, we fall back on what remains an immense reduction in

[37] International Monetary Fund, *Balance of Payments Yearbook, 1954–55,* Washington, 1956, concerning U.K., p. 1. Income from the various items of trade in goods and services is: merchandise, £2816 million; transportation, £402 million; investment, £229; travel, £95 million; other, £353 million.

investment in "competitive" areas. Holdings in countries where British lenders were not dominant fell from 42 per cent of annual national income in 1928 to 8 per cent in 1954. It seems unlikely that the qualitative changes referred to above can compensate entirely for that reduction. On balance, foreign investment has receded as an irritant to Anglo-American relations.[38] Prospects for peace have come to what was never more than a muted conflict.

[38] There may, of course, be a lag between the fact of the decline and its effects. Thus the current generation of British policy-makers may still think in terms of a Britain whose foreign-investment holdings amount to more than a year's national income, instead of the 12 per cent of annual income that they now represent.

5

Trade Discrimination:
Pounds, Quotas, and Preferences

The Development of Discriminatory Practices

Our survey of economic factors in Anglo-American relations is still incomplete. The problem of trade discrimination, especially trade rivalry in third markets, remains. Under the circumstances prevailing before World War I, this kind of rivalry might not be considered a major cause of international friction, except in the ways we discussed under the heading of investment rivalry. Since 1914, however, the environment of world commerce has changed radically, and it has affected no two countries more than the United States and the United Kingdom, the globe's two greatest commercial powers.

These changes were the result of a perennial shortage of foreign exchange, which for much of the time took the form of a dollar shortage. The term "dollar shortage" signified an apparent inability of other nations to combine full employment and a high standard of living with a favorable balance of trade with the United States. In an effort to avoid either domestic deflation or a substantial and continuing trade deficit with the United States — culminating in international bankruptcy and an eventual forced deflation — most of the world outside North America restricted the import of goods from the United States. Only by so doing, it was believed, could these countries keep their imports from America roughly equal to their ability to export to that market. This situation was most acute during World War II and the decade following, but it was already an important element in the interwar period and had its roots in the events of 1914–18. The difficulties of the United States in the last four years emphasize that the dollar shortage was merely one aspect of a general international payments problem.

Not all the world's restrictions on the importation of American goods were due to the dollar shortage. Another event encouraging those measures was the Great Depression of the 1930's, which centered in the United States and had its most disastrous effects there. When the American economy collapsed, many other countries which had not been doing badly suddenly lost their markets, especially for raw materials, in North America. The Smoot-Hawley Tariff of 1930, a misguided attempt to rescue American business, worsened matters, and the circle of catastrophe spread throughout the world. Most countries then determined to insulate themselves from the unstable world market and, for fear of more bad times to come, deliberately reduced their dependence on international trade. They particularly wished to insulate themselves from the colossal and seemingly most unstable American market. In raising their barriers to trade, they soon decided that the effects need not and, in many cases, should not be uniform. Preferential agreements, long extant in the world but employed with relative moderation, were expanded and new ones created. One nation would grant another an exemption from restrictions, or give it special tariff reductions not offered to other states.

The British Empire, while not the most extreme practitioner of such arrangements, was a major one, and because that area had long been the United States' largest foreign market, the burden of British practices on American trade in many ways seemed heaviest. For a long time American businessmen failed to see the need for any of these restrictions on their trade; when they did come to recognize the need for at least some, they believed the restrictions were greater than could possibly be justified. They chafed under Imperial Preference, the Sterling Area, and quota limits on American goods.[1]

Thus American businessmen developed a complaint, or set of complaints, which were at least as serious as those of British businessmen against the American tariff. Faced with a loss of their markets in the British Empire, their frustrations, resentments, and demands for relief filtered up to the national legislature and executive. United States government officials took up the complaint and pressed the British severely for the elimination of trade discrimination both in

[1] To an appreciable extent, the effects of trade restriction were mitigated by both countries' richness in capital exports. Thus an American manufacturer, shut out of the Commonwealth market by import restrictions, could purchase or build a plant in the United Kingdom to produce his goods. American investment holdings in Britain totaled $1257 million in 1954. Assuming a capital output ratio of five to one, the product of that investment was equivalent to about 35 per cent of 1954 United States exports to Britain.

the 1930's and during and after the Second World War. The relaxation of some of the preferential restrictions in the United Kingdom–Canada–United States trade agreements of 1938 was only a preliminary to further American demands. The seriousness of this issue as a divisive factor shows up especially in the inconclusive negotiations on commercial questions which preceded the signing of the Atlantic Charter of 1941.[2] The process whereby the private frustrations of businessmen filter up to the governmental level is the same as that discussed in previous chapters. We now must try to estimate the severity of these antagonisms at each period.

In 1890 there was little possibility of serious rivalry between American and British exporters. Overwhelmingly, United States exports consisted of food and raw materials (manufactured goods accounted for but 16 per cent of total American exports), while the United Kingdom's specialization was precisely opposite. American industry, heavily protected by tariffs, was extremely important within the United States, but was not much of a factor in the world market. In the late 1890's, however, the products of American industry began to displace certain British goods both in Imperial markets and in the United Kingdom itself. This displacement occurred first with tools and light machinery in Australia, musical instruments in New Zealand, carriages and wagons in Cape Colony, and a variety of goods in Canada and the British West Indies.[3]

After 1900 the "invasion" of American manufactured goods grew rapidly in scope and intensity, and American competition became an even more serious threat to British manufacturers after World War I. American goods often seemed better fitted for the needs of such vast young lands as Africa, Australia, and Canada — consumers quickly alleged that American automobiles were superior to British cars for driving long distances over poor roads. From then on, the United States rapidly developed into the world's foremost supplier of capital equipment and other heavy manufactured goods. Manufactures rose from 32 per cent of American exports in 1913 to 45 per cent in 1928, 51 per cent in 1938, and 64 per cent in 1954.

Parallel with this trend, the system of Imperial Preference developed. In 1898, Canada began by applying to British goods only seven

[2] On the strength and persistence of American attempts to end trade discrimination, see especially Richard N. Gardner, *Sterling-Dollar Diplomacy*, Oxford, 1956. All the displeasure was not, of course, on the American side. John Biggs-Davison, in *The Uncertain Ally*, London, 1957, indicates the irritation caused by continued United States protests against a policy which the British considered vital.

[3] Sir John Clapham, *An Economic History of Modern Britain*, III, Cambridge, 1951, pp. 39–44. See also R. H. Heindel, *The American Impact on Great Britain*, Philadelphia, 1940, pp. 138–161.

eighths of the tariff levied on products imported from other countries, and in 1900 it increased this preference so that British goods paid only two thirds of the levy on other nations' products.[4] Imperial Preference was introduced to the Falkland Islands the same year, and to New Zealand and South Africa in 1903. Australia soon followed. Tariffs in these countries, however, were low, and the margins of preference generally not great, so in 1913 the Imperial Preference system could hardly have been a very severe irritant to American exporters.[5] It was somewhat more serious in 1928, following the adoption of Preference by Eire (at independence in 1923) and India (1927). Great Britain was herself a free-trade country until a few small duties were introduced during World War I; after the war a few preferences, especially on automobiles, were granted to Empire countries. But even in 1929, British tariffs generally were so low that the average margin of preference on all imports to the United Kingdom was only 2–3 per cent. While the average margin of preference enjoyed by British goods in Empire markets was higher (about 5 per cent), it was not, in most cases, a major deterrent to American exporters.[6]

In addition to Preference there were other direct means for promoting intra-Empire trade, such as the Empire Marketing Board and the Imperial Economic Committee. British government orders were often placed within the Empire even when there were cheaper supplies outside, and loans were sometimes "earmarked" for the purchase of British export goods. Two of these official credit schemes were the East African Loan Act and the Export Credit Plan.[7] These attempts

[4] Canada's tariff, though not so much its Imperial Preference aspects, was important in Canadian-American relations at this time. See Brebner, *North Atlantic Triangle*.

[5] See S. B. Saul, *Studies in British Overseas Trade, 1870–1914,* Liverpool, 1960, p. 217.

[6] By "margin of preference" we mean the difference between the percentage of duty that an item would pay if it were imported from the United States and the percentage of duty it would pay if imported from the United Kingdom. Estimates of the margin of preference from 1929 onwards are from Donald MacDougall and Rosemary Hutt, "Imperial Preference: A Quantitative Analysis," *Economic Journal,* LXIV, 2 (June 1954), pp. 233–257. On the development of Imperial Preference, see David L. Glickman, "The British Imperial Preference System," *Quarterly Journal of Economics,* LXI, 3 (May 1947), pp. 439–470, and United States Tariff Commission, *Preliminary Survey of the Development and the Present Extent of British Imperial Preference,* Washington, 1934. At all times preferences were greatest in the white dominions, excluding South Africa. See MacDougall and Hutt for the country-by-country breakdown.

[7] United States Tariff Commission, *Preliminary Survey,* pp. 4–5, and Ludwell Denny, *America Conquers Britain,* New York, 1930, p. 132.

to make trade follow the loan undoubtedly frustrated some American exports and were more irritating than anything that existed in 1913, but the net effect of all this trade discrimination was clearly less serious than it was to be in later years.

With the onset of the Great Depression, Britain for the first time instituted high tariffs as part of a general system of protection, and most Empire countries and colonial territories followed. At the Ottawa Conference of July 1932, preferences were widened and extended to many goods, making the whole Preference system much more effective as a force for diverting trade. Many small territories, such as Hong Kong, the Straits Settlements, the Federated Malay States, Ceylon, and Malta, introduced Preference for the first time. This produced demands for modification from the United States, and in 1938 Secretary of State Cordell Hull signed reciprocal trade agreements for the mutual reduction of tariffs with Great Britain (including the colonies) and with Canada. The zenith of Preference was then past, but in 1937, the last full year before the conclusion of those agreements, United Kingdom exporters had an average margin of preference on all goods imported by the Commonwealth of 10–11 per cent. Reciprocally, Commonwealth exporters gained a preference of 10–12 per cent in the United Kingdom. In addition, Britain made preferential agreements with several Latin American countries. By far the most important were with Argentina, and the Roca-Runciman Agreement of 1934 particularly roused American exporters' ire.

By the end of the war the system of Empire (now Commonwealth) Preference had become less effective as a trade-diverting force. Changes in the pattern of trade, and the world rise in prices which sharply reduced the percentage incidence of ad valorem tariffs, brought the over-all margin of preference given to British exports down to about 7 per cent in 1948. The margin given by the United Kingdom to imports from the Commonwealth also came down, to 6–7 per cent. The preferential arrangements with Argentina were dropped. MacDougall and Hutt did not make a detailed survey of the situation in 1954 but estimated that by mid-1953 it had not changed radically. Preference accorded to British exports may have declined to 6–7 per cent and that given by Britain to Commonwealth imports to 6 per cent, but that was all. Even those modifications were due largely to the rise in world prices, and hardly at all to the 1949 and 1951 negotiations under the General Agreement on Tariffs and Trade (GATT). But the result was that Preference was, in 1954, a much less inhibiting factor to American exporters than in 1938.

How much effect did Preference have? Sir Donald MacDougall

attempted to answer this question in another article.[8] He found that between the wars the United States had, on the whole, a comparative disadvantage in the imperfect markets of the world for a number of reasons. Imperial Preference was one, but others included differences in transport costs, greater selling efforts by British exporters, stronger commercial and credit ties between Britain and overseas markets, and quantitative restrictions on dollar goods. To account for all of Britain's advantage in these markets in terms of Preference alone, one would have to assume an elasticity of substitution of at least −11 of American for British goods. That is, a 1 per cent change in price would produce an 11 per cent change in the quantity exported. In fact, such a high elasticity of substitution is virtually impossible; MacDougall estimates, very roughly, that it may actually be in the neighborhood of −3.

Later in the chapter we shall try to assess the effect of lowering the margins between 1937 and 1953 on American trade, but that must be evaluated with at least two other factors. Imperial Preference was not Britain's only response to the changes which swept over the world economy after 1929. In the 1930's the Sterling Area was organized, and in 1938 it included Scandinavia, Portugal, Egypt, Iraq, Thailand, and all of the British Empire except Canada. At that time it was not explicitly a trade-diverting or trade-restricting force, though it did have some such effects. The members agreed to keep a certain proportion of their foreign exchange reserves in sterling and to peg their exchange rates to the price of sterling. There was no formal constitution, and although the members did agree to exercise some restraint in buying goods that had to be paid for in dollars, these restrictions were slight and very informal. While the pre-World War II Sterling Area unquestionably helped Britain to maintain her exports to these countries, there is no reason to believe it discriminated substantially more against the United States than against the rest of the world.

During and after World War II, the Sterling Area system became more formalized and the restrictions more severe. Under Britain's exchange-control system, English law made the Sterling Area a legal entity within which payments could be made freely; to other areas, payments could be made only under varying and carefully specified conditions. There is no definite central control of the Sterling Area, but the various governments co-ordinate their policy to an impressive degree. The central banks of each state maintain close contacts

[8] Donald MacDougall, "British and American Exports: A Study Suggested by the Theory of Comparative Costs; Part II," *Economic Journal*, LXI, 4 (September 1952), pp. 487–521.

with the others — contacts which are tighter because of their common banking tradition. Two standing committees, the Sterling Area Statistical Committee and the Commonwealth Liaison Committee, exist to co-ordinate policy, and restrictions are set out in detail in written agreements. Until recently each member undertook to spend only a certain amount for imports from the Dollar Area, and trade undoubtedly was diverted from the United States to sterling suppliers.

The Sterling Area brings benefits to all its members, and its policies are by no means under the exclusive control of Great Britain. Very few members, if they were on their own, could have afforded to import dollar goods without any limits. But the United Kingdom controls the London capital market and is custodian of the area's foreign-exchange reserves. All members hold large sterling balances and so have an important stake in maintaining their value. Thus Britain has very substantial, if not unlimited, influence over members' policies. Americans who regarded Britain as solely responsible for the loss of their export markets to the Commonwealth took a very much oversimplified view of the matter; nevertheless, Britain does bear no little responsibility.

The principal instruments of trade diversion in the Sterling Area have been quantitative restrictions, or quotas, on the importation of goods, particularly from the Dollar Area. Importers may buy goods from restricted areas only with specific permission, and the quantities of such goods permitted to all importers are strictly controlled. Though by 1954 most goods could be imported from the Sterling Area without restriction, quantitative controls were maintained on most products from the Dollar Area — 81 per cent of all British imports could come from the Sterling Area without specific license, but only 28 per cent of all imports could come from the Dollar Area without license. The controls on most raw material imports were light, but fell heavily on the importation of food, fuels, and manufactures. Appendix Table 5.1 gives a more detailed breakdown of the restrictions' incidence.

Appendix Table 5.1 of course covers only the import restrictions of the United Kingdom itself, but it also serves as an approximation of the controls in the colonies. Nonself-governing areas were strongly urged to adopt the same schedule that Britain had, and exceptions were made only most reluctantly. In fact, the table certainly understates the scope of controls in the colonial territories, where manufactured goods make up a very much higher proportion of total imports. But detailed figures of this sort simply are not available for Commonwealth countries other than the United Kingdom.

In addition, these data indicate merely the *scope* of import control.

We can say nothing nearly as precise about its *effectiveness,* i.e., what imports would otherwise have been. The question of effectiveness would require a very hypothetical sort of inquiry about changes in taste, technology, supply conditions, and the degree to which other aspects of policy would have remained the same in the absence of import controls — that is, how the dollar deficit would have been financed.

The Effects of Discrimination

We must, nevertheless, make at least a comparative estimate of the effect of these various instruments of trade discrimination in each of the years under study. There is no doubt that in 1890 commercial discrimination was for our purposes irrelevant to Anglo-American relations, but in each of the next three years considered — 1913, 1928, 1938 — it represented an increasing source of antagonism. The question, then, is the degree to which the irritation was increased or decreased by the policies of 1954.

First, we know the decline in the amount of preference granted United Kingdom exports: from 10–11 per cent in 1938 to 6–7 per cent by mid-1953. Secondly, we can estimate very roughly the increase in United States exports permitted in 1954 by the reduction. Using the elasticity of substitution of −3 suggested by MacDougall, with all other things being equal, Commonwealth imports from Britain would have been about 12 per cent higher (10–11 minus 6–7 per cent times 3), and imports from America, if the 1937 rates had been in effect in 1954, correspondingly lower in amount. But in terms of the overseas preference area's total imports from the world, this is less than 4 per cent. Given the widespread use of quantitative restrictions considered above, it seems clear that the limitation of dollar imports by those restrictions more than made up the difference. Even when we exclude Canada, which did not have such limits on United States products, the reduction in preference is more than outweighed. This is the conclusion which writers who have tried to compare the two periods have invariably reached.[9] Responsible officials in the State

---

[9] See, for instance, Bank for International Settlements, *The Sterling Area,* Basel, 1953, pp. 64–65, and Philip Bell, *The Sterling Area in the Postwar World,* Oxford, 1926, pp. 326–333. Bell (p. 331) lists the six classes of industrial products in which the United States and Great Britain compete, and which composed 51 per cent of American exports to the Overseas Sterling Area (OSA) in 1934–1938. In four of these classes — iron and steel manufactures, chemicals, cotton manufactures, and synthetic yarn and piece goods (which accounted for 9 per cent of United States exports to the OSA) — the American gain in volume after World War II was greater than the British. In two classes, however — machinery and vehicles (accounting for 42 per cent of United States exports to the OSA in 1934–38) — British exports to this area showed a greater relative postwar gain than did American exports.

Department declare that they have heard many more complaints from American businessmen about quantitative controls than about Imperial Preference.

The same situation applies to exports to the United Kingdom itself, where the effect of quotas far overbalances the decline in preferences. Also, the weight is borne by different exporters. Preference fell overwhelmingly on food and raw materials; quantitative restrictions were most severe on manufactured goods.

We may confirm most of these findings by examining the pattern of trade in each of the three years, as shown in Table 5.1.

TABLE 5.1. American and British Exports to Various Areas in 1928, and Percentage Change in Value of Exports to Each, in Constant Prices

Importing Country or Area	1928 Value (in million dollars)		1938 Percentage Increase or Decrease over 1928, in Constant Prices		1954 Percentage Increase or Decrease over 1938, in Constant Prices	
	U.S.	U.K.	U.S.	U.K.	U.S.	U.K.
United States	—	336	—	−33	—	+79
United Kingdom	848	—	−16	—	−35	—
Canada	924	188	−32	−7	+188	+85
Other Preference Countries, and Members of Sterling Area in Both 1938 and 1954	385	1,470	+6	+18	+55	+93
Sterling Area Members in 1938 Only	177	272	+24	+67	+41	+88
Argentina	179	155	−34	−1	−31	−61
Rest of World	2,614	1,664	−19	−16	+214	+38
Total	5,127	4,085	−18	+2	+136	+69
Total (million dollars, in 1928 prices)	5,127	4,085	4,210	4,163	9,970	7,020
Total (million dollars, in current prices)	5,127	4,085	3,094	2,603	15,115	7,766

SOURCES: For 1928 trade, League of Nations, *The Network of World Trade*, Geneva, 1942, pp. 126, 167. For 1938 and 1954, in current prices, United Nations, Statistical Papers, Series T, IV, 9, *Direction of International Trade*, New York, 1958. Adjusted to export price indices from U.S. Bureau of the Census, *Historical Statistics of the United States, Colonial Times to 1957*, Washington, 1960, p. 537; Board of Trade, *Statistical Abstract of the United Kingdom, 1924 to 1938*, London, 1940, pp. 338–339, and Central Statistical Office of the United Kingdom, *Statistical Abstract of the United Kingdom, 1952*, London, 1953, p. 196, and *Statistical Abstract of the United Kingdom, 1959*, London, 1960, p. 214.

We must recall the arrangements in force in each of the last two years and compare the effects to be expected with those which actually occurred. In 1938, Britain, the Empire, and Argentina had high preferences that did not exist in 1928, and many countries had joined the Sterling Area. American trade with these areas should have diminished more or risen less than the United Kingdom's as a result. This happened as expected. Though America's trade with the rest of the world — which did not discriminate between Britain and the United States — fell slightly more than did Britain's, the difference between America's loss and Britain's was less than anywhere else. And note the changes in the 1938 Sterling Area. Although Britain showed a greater gain than the United States, America's trade nevertheless expanded more there than in any other area, confirming our original statement: The Sterling Area at that time discriminated in favor of its members, but not substantially more against the United States than against other countries.

In 1954 the situation had changed as follows: Preference was much lower throughout the Commonwealth and had been abandoned with Argentina; thus the gain should be greater for the United States than for Britain. But the other Preference and Sterling Area countries and the former Sterling Area countries had introduced rigorous quantitative restrictions on American goods, which would be expected to tip the balance back in Britain's favor despite the decline in Preference. There were also quantitative restrictions in the rest of the world, but, on the whole, they were much less severe. Expectations are again borne out. The United States either gained more than Britain, or lost less, in Canada, Argentina, and the rest of the world, and gained less in the other Preference and past and present Sterling Area nations. The relative gain for Britain in the other Preference and 1954 Sterling Area countries would have been even larger but for two factors. First, the area included Iceland and Iraq, which were Sterling Area but not Preference countries, and where the American gain was particularly great. Second, South Africa in 1954 eliminated discrimination against the Dollar Area. Note the continued decline in the real value of American exports to Great Britain.

There is one other means of showing that the effects of trade discrimination weighed relatively more heavily on the United States in 1954 than in 1938. We can examine the degree to which the exports of the two great trading nations diverged from the pattern one would expect if we used the null model. Where the deviations presented in Tables 5.2 and 5.3 are striking, we may surmise something about the effects of discrimination and the way in which discrimination changed between those years.

TABLE 5.2. British and American Exports to Empire and Sterling Area Countries, 1938; Relative Deficits or Excesses in Percentage above or below Par Level as Predicted from Null Model

Percentage Excess or Deficit in 1938 Export Dollar Volume	British Exports		United States Exports	
	Dependent on U.K.	Sovereign	Dependent on U.K.	Sovereign
+100% or more	Nigeria 491 Ghana 465 Kenya-Uganda 422 S. Rhodesia 317 Cyprus 311 Trinidad 255 Jamaica 252 Sudan 218 N. Rhodesia 123 India 122 Tanganyika 106	Eire 394 New Zealand 264 Union S. Africa 225 Australia 218 Iceland 197 Iraq 169		Canada 326
+30 to 99%	Ceylon 77 Malaya & Singapore 37 Burma 36		Trinidad 95 Jamaica 87 Kenya-Uganda 35	
+0.1 to 29%		Canada 13		Union S. Africa 7 Australia 6
−0.1 to 29%	Hong Kong −14		Hong Kong −13 Cyprus −16 Tanganyika −27 Ghana −28	Eire −2 New Zealand −17 United Kingdom −26
−30 to 59%			Nigeria −47 India −59	Iraq −43
−60 to 100%			S. Rhodesia −63 Sudan −65 N. Rhodesia −73 Burma −77 Malaya & Singapore −79 Ceylon −87	Iceland −88

SOURCE: United Nations, Statistical Papers, Series T, VI, 10, *Direction of International Trade*, New York, 1956, and computations in Karl W. Deutsch and I. Richard Savage, *Regionalism, Trade, and International Community*, forthcoming.

TABLE 5.3. British and American Exports to Commonwealth and Sterling Area Countries, 1954; Relative Deficits or Excesses in Percentage above or below Par Level as Predicted from Null Model

Percentage Excess or Deficit in 1954 U.K. Export Dollar Volume	British Exports		United States Exports	
	Dependent on U.K.	Sovereign	Dependent on U.K.	Sovereign
100% or more	Uganda 606 Kenya 543 Ghana 438 Nigeria 384 Jamaica 355 Tanganyika 346 Cyprus 342 Rhodesia & Nyasaland 275 Trinidad 255 Sudan 241 Br. Persian Gulf Sts. 201	Eire 482 New Zealand 436 Australia 329 Union S. Africa 234 Iraq 219 Pakistan 209 Burma 163 India 126		Canada 276
+30 to 99%	Malaya & Singapore 80	Ceylon 91	Trinidad 95	
+0.1 to 29%	Hong Kong 8	Iceland 13	Jamaica 13	Union S. Africa 0.1
−0.1 to 29%		Canada −13		Iceland 00 Iraq −20
−30 to 59%			Hong Kong −55 Uganda −59	India −32 Australia −37 Pakistan −53
−60 to 100%			Tanganyika −75 Br. Persian Gulf Sts. −77 Nigeria −79 Kenya −82 Malaya & Singapore −82 Rhodesia & Nyasaland −82 Ghana −83 Cyprus −88 Sudan −94	U.K. −60 New Zealand −61 Eire −68 Ceylon −85 Burma −86

The United States was relatively worse off in 1954 than in 1938. Of six Commonwealth countries to which it had exported more than one would expect from the null model (seven if Kenya and Uganda are counted separately), only four remained on the positive side of the line, and three of them had slipped nearer the indifference point. And of those which remained, one (Canada) was in the Dollar Area, two others (Trinidad and Jamaica) were in the Western Hemisphere, and the fourth (South Africa) eliminated dollar-discriminatory import controls that same year. As for the Commonwealth countries and colonies which had previously imported a smaller amount from the United States than the null model would indicate, almost all in 1954 imported still less. The only exceptions, notably enough, were three of the four newly independent Commonwealth nations — Ceylon, India, and Pakistan. Britain's over-all trade with most of these nations, on the other hand, improved moderately.

The change in the ratio of foreign trade to national income in the United States provides a final indication of the increased weight of British discriminatory practices in 1954. Foreign trade was only 7.8 per cent of national income in 1938; by 1954 it was 9.2 per cent, according to the data presented in Chapter 3. Thus there were relatively more exporters, and probably more potential exporters, to feel that weight.

Perhaps this burden was borne with somewhat better spirit in 1954 than earlier. Commonwealth Preference had been in existence for some time and was not the fresh wound it had been in 1938. In 1938 few Americans saw much economic justification for discrimination against their country's exports; in 1954, after the experiences of the dollar shortage and Britain's abortive attempt to go convertible, they were more likely to be understanding. Among economists who look back on the postwar years, there is general agreement that until about 1952 the Sterling Area spent all the dollars it could get. In the absence of discrimination, the Area would have had either to restrict all imports severely or to suffer a drastic deflation sufficient to bring dollar income and outgo into equality. In either case nondiscrimination would not have increased American exports to the Sterling Area significantly. And though Britain was the largest offender, she was hardly the only practitioner of discriminatory policies, and was not entirely responsible even for the policies of the Sterling Area.[10]

[10] It is well to keep this whole matter in perspective by remembering the size of the sums involved. There is no way of estimating the total that American exports would have reached in the absence of all discrimination, but we can at least set an upper limit. Less than $2 billion would have sufficed to bring 1954 American exports to all lagging Sterling Area and Imperial Preference countries up to the "expected" level given by the null

Yet on the other side of the ledger, Americans in 1954 must have been aware that their objections to world-wide discrimination carried somewhat more justice than they had only a year or two before. From 1952 until the end of 1955, Britain and her Sterling Area partners were earning a dollar surplus; had there been no discrimination, they could have bought somewhat more from the United States. And even though nondiscrimination might not have permitted substantially more American imports because of balance-of-payments problems, it would have aroused less antagonism. The products affected would then have been chosen by the economic invisible hand rather than by conscious official design. Thus the conclusion stands — trade discrimination was, over the sixty-five-year period, a steadily growing irritant.

Recent Developments

By way of a postscript, we must mention certain changes in trade controls since 1954, for this factor has undergone a more radical transformation than any other discussed in the whole study. Britain and the Sterling Area found themselves earning more dollars than they were spending. Since the beginning of 1956, they have gradually dismantled the system of quantitative restrictions on dollar imports to the point where the remains are hardly more than vestigial. The study of quantitative restrictions referred to earlier found that by June 1958, 50 per cent of all private imports could come from the Dollar Area without special license, and government importation was almost nil.[11] By the end of 1960, liberalization had progressed so far that only a few minor categories of imports remained restricted.[12] Much the same situation now applies to the dominions and colonies. Some of the newer countries like India maintain heavy import restrictions, yet to a very substantial degree they no longer discriminate against dollar goods but apply restrictions more or less equally to the products of all nations.

Even Imperial Preference declined very slightly as a trade-diverting

model (see Table 5.3). When we recall the threat of deflation and that the failure of these countries to take the "expected" amount of American exports is due to far more than official restriction alone, however broadly defined, it is clear that the trade-diverting effects of discrimination could not have amounted to more than a billion dollars in 1954. While that is a large sum, it is only about 7 per cent of total American exports and less than 0.3 per cent of the GNP.

[11] M. F. W. Hemming, C. M. Miles, and G. F. Ray, "A Statistical Summary of the Extent of Import Control in the United Kingdom since the War," *Review of Economic Studies*, XXVI (2), 70 (February 1959), pp. 104–107.

[12] See the special issue on the Sterling Area, *Bulletin of the Oxford University Institute of Statistics*, XXI, 4 (November 1959).

force. A new study, which used the calculating methods of Mac-
Dougall and Hutt, found that the preference margin accorded by
Britain to imports from the Commonwealth had fallen from 6 per
cent in 1953 to between 5 and 6 per cent in 1957. This study listed
a number of Commonwealth exports which were beneficiaries of
British preferences, and the countries which were their major competi-
tors. The United States was not mentioned in any instance.[13]

Trade discrimination, therefore, in less than five years greatly
receded as an irritant to Anglo-American relations. Because of the
trading contacts built up over the years, its effects will continue for
a long while to give a comparative advantage to many British products, but as an active force it is now less important than at any time
since the beginning of the 1930's.

---

[13] Political and Economic Planning, *Commonwealth Preference in the
United Kingdom,* London, 1960, pp. 9–11. Finally, note that foreign trade as
a proportion of American national income had, by 1959, fallen back to 8.1
per cent.

6

Elite Communication and Attention

Elites and Attentive Public

For the United States and Great Britain to be responsive to each other, they must have channels for continual communication and mutual attention. Later in the study we shall discuss the significance of common memories and their contribution to responsiveness, but by themselves they can never be sufficient. Important as are the memories of America's heritage from England, or of common efforts in war, those memories alone cannot make Americans understand British needs or react favorably to them. There must be some means for communicating current needs and desires.

Furthermore, many Americans do not directly share the heritage of Britain. Advocates of Anglo-American alliance at the turn of the century stressed the Anglo-Saxon cultural tradition. But so many Americans of other than British ethnic stock were so unresponsive that by World War I the Anglophiles were forced to shift their emphasis from race to the bond of the English language.[1] As Mr. Dooley said, "An Anglo-Saxon . . . is a German that's forgot who was his parents." Anyhow, the tie of race has become weaker over the years. In 1890, 14 per cent of all foreign-born Americans were of English, Scots, or Welsh birth; by 1950, the proportion had fallen to 8 per cent.[2]

Nor does the link of a common tongue suffice. Bernard Shaw's

[1] Richard Hofstadter, *Social Darwinism in American Thought*, Boston, 1955, pp. 182–184.
[2] Rowland T. Berthoff, *British Immigrants in Industrial America*, Cambridge, Mass., 1953, p. 7.

remark about two nations divided by a common language is renowned, and it applies not only to the Irish. Two people using the same words may not mean the same thing by those words, and hence may be unable to make effective contact. As one writer remarked, "All who speak the English language expect comprehension and even similarity of each other." [3] A failure to achieve comprehension may thus be particularly disappointing. More generally,

> Language itself, even if exact and precise, is a very limited device for producing common understanding when it has no basis in common experience. The linguists who argue for a world language neglect the fact that basic misunderstandings occur not at the linguistic but at the psychological level.[4]

This common experience depends at least in part on the existence of continuing and varied contacts between the two cultures. The fact of communication does not by itself produce understanding or responsiveness; it may, by expressing grievances or differences of outlook, merely add to loads.

> On the whole it may also be assumed that increasing direct and indirect contacts between peoples may further the ability to understand and appreciate each other's peculiarities and conceivably reduce national chauvinism and racial prejudice; but on the other hand, there is always the possibility that such contacts may work both ways and create frictions and disputes as well.[5]

Yet communication is a necessary if not a sufficient condition for amicable relations between two nations which are affected by the consequences of each other's actions. Even if communication may contribute to loads, it is essential as a capability for responsiveness. Four of Deutsch et al.'s helpful conditions for a pluralistic security-community were related to this matter: unbroken links of social communication, mobility of persons, a multiplicity of ranges of com-

[3] John MacCormac, *America and World Mastery: The Future of the United States, Canada, and the British Empire,* New York, 1942, p. 155.

[4] Daniel Katz, "Psychological Barriers to Communication," *Annals of the American Academy of Political Science,* March, 1947, p. 19, as quoted in Frederick S. Dunn, *War and the Minds of Men,* New York, 1950, p. 75.

[5] Trygve Mathisen, *Methodology in the Study of International Relations,* New York, 1959, p. 91. Reviews of the literature are to be found in Dunn, *War and the Minds of Men;* Eugene Jacobson, Hideye Kumata, and Jeanne E. Gullahorn, "Cross-Cultural Contributions to Attitude Research," *Public Opinion Quarterly,* XXIV, 2 (Summer 1960), pp. 205–233; and Richard W. Van Wagenen, *Research in the International Organization Field,* Princeton, 1952. Though a little outdated, the best bibliographical source is Bruce L. Smith and Chitra M. Smith, *International Communication and Political Opinion,* Princeton, 1956. See also Ithiel de Sola Pool, *Communication and Values in Relation to War and Peace,* New York, 1960.

munications, and a compensation of flows of communications and transactions.[6] To avoid the ambiguous formulation that refuses to say whether in a given case communication is a factor working for or against responsiveness — a formulation which could be used to explain all outcomes, and therefore none — we shall treat communication and attention facilities as capabilities except where we have particular evidence that they are associated with important deprivations. We have already discussed some of those circumstances and shall continue to look for other instances. In Chapter 9, we shall make a limited test of the degree to which communication has added to capabilities at the level of legislative decision-making.

Indices of international communications of all sorts are relevant, but those suggesting the attitudes of a certain type of individual, the member of the elite, are particularly important. Though all citizens have some influence over decision-making, if only in the negative way of failing to vote, influence is not distributed evenly. Properly we should speak of "elites" rather than use the term only in the singular. There is a business elite, a military elite, a communications elite, a political elite or elites, and others. A member of one of these elites may be able to exert particular influence over one type of decision but not over others. There is no need to imply that members of a particular elite, whether by implicit or explicit agreement, operate substantially as a unit, or that they can make all the politically relevant decisions of a society. But a position of influence in certain areas of activity clearly gives an individual some bases of influence to transfer more or less successfully into other areas. A man with wealth often has some formal role in political decision-making. If not, he may be intimate with the powerful. Skill important in his commercial activities may also be useful in the political arena. Or his wealth may enable him to hire the services of the skillful. His influence, whether potential or actual, is limited, but he undoubtedly has some advantages not available to those who lack his resources.

We shall pay special attention to contacts among members of the various elites. Obviously, this category must include the formal elites, men in high executive or legislative positions, but also it consists of men whose wealth or professional position suggests a disproportionate influence in decision-making. Thus we include not only the elites but what Gabriel Almond identifies as the "attentive public" — that 10–15 per cent of the population which is interested in foreign

[6] K. W. Deutsch *et al.*, *Political Community and the North Atlantic Area*, Princeton, 1957, p. 58. George Homans, *The Human Group*, New York, 1950, ch. 5, reports that in small-group experiments there is a strong positive relationship between the frequency of interaction and favorable attitudes towards members of the group.

affairs and is reasonably well informed about them.[7] People in this stratum discuss policy alternatives, and the elites must compete for their approval. First we shall examine ties affecting the attentive public in general, and later focus on the political elites in particular.

Travel

Travel, it is said, is one of the most effective means of acquiring an understanding of other countries' problems and viewpoints. International travel by students may be especially important in this respect. Students are not yet members of the elite but may well move into that stratum. University-trained individuals form a disproportionate segment of the elites, and students who have traveled abroad are particularly likely to end up in influential posts. The caliber of applicants for scholarships to the United States and Britain is usually high, and the prestige of such a scholarship is a distinct advantage in later competition — the words "former Rhodes scholar" become an open-sesame to myriad doors, and Rhodes scholars have their own "old-boy net." We shall, therefore, treat student exchange as an aspect of elite communications, though the effects of that exchange may not become apparent on the decision-making level for a decade or more.

As with international communications in general, there is no consensus on the effectiveness of student exchange between nations. One recent study of Belgian former exchange students found no evidence "that former grantees retain political and social attitudes substantially more pro-American than those of non-grantees." [8] The sample, however, was so small as to prohibit any but a rather large difference in attitude frequency from achieving statistical significance. At least the author does find "a warm friendliness toward individual Americans." Another study, after reviewing a number of inquiries, concludes that foreign students do gain more favorable attitudes toward America than do those who stay at home.[9] The evidence is not conclusive, and in a later chapter we shall examine the apparent effect of education abroad on particular legislators, but for the present, student exchange seems worthy of attention.

[7] Gabriel Almond, *The American People and Foreign Policy*, New Haven, 1950, ch. 8.

[8] O. W. Riegel, "Residual Effects of Exchange of Persons," *Public Opinion Quarterly*, XVII, 3 (Fall 1953), p. 326.

[9] Elmo Wilson, "Evaluating Exchange of Persons Programs," *Public Opinion Quarterly*, XIX, 1 (Spring 1955), pp. 20–30. See also D. E. Eckhart, *The American Impact on Europe through the Influence of Foreign Students in the United States since 1918*, Master's Thesis, University of Wisconsin, Madison, 1950.

In both the United States and Great Britain the first censuses of foreign students were conducted in the late 1920's. The figures for several years are compared in Table 6.1.

TABLE 6.1.　Student Exchange

Students in the United States

Year	British	Other Foreign	British per 10,000 American Students	British Percentage of All Foreign
1929–30	365	9,250	0.33	3.8
1937–38	238	9,443	0.18	2.5
1953–54	877	32,956	0.40	2.6
1957–58	982	42,409	0.23	2.3

Students in the United Kingdom

Year	American	Other Foreign	Americans per 10,000 British Students	American Percentage of All Foreign
1929–30	621	4,865	11.3	11.3
1937–38	558	5,522	9.1	9.2
1953–54	756	7,878	8.6	8.8
1957–58	925	9,891	9.1	8.5

SOURCES: Foreign Students in U.S. — Committee on Friendly Relations Among Foreign Students, *The Unofficial Ambassadors*, New York, 1931, p. 11, and *The Unofficial Ambassadors*, New York, 1938, p. 14; UNESCO, *Study Abroad, 1955–56*, Paris, 1955, pp. 548–551, and *Study Abroad, 1959–60*, Paris, 1959, p. 51. All Students in the U.S. — Bureau of the Census, *Historical Statistics of the United States, Colonial Times to 1957*, Washington, 1960, p. 210; and *Statistical Abstract of the United States*, 1960, p. 123.

Foreign Students in U.K. — T. S. Sterling, editor, *Yearbook of the Universities of the Empire, 1930*, London, 1930, p. 683, and *Yearbook of the Universities of the Empire, 1938*, London, 1938, pp. 1029–1030; Association of Universities of the British Commonwealth, *Commonwealth Universities Yearbook, 1955*, London, 1955, pp. 1765–1767, and *Commonwealth Universities Yearbook, 1959*, London, 1959, pp. 1243–1244. "Foreign students" include Commonwealth students but exclude those from Eire. All students in U.K. — *Annual Abstract of Statistics of the United Kingdom, 1924 to 1938*, p. 50, and *Annual Abstract of Statistics, 1959*, p. 100.

The proportion of American students in relation to all foreign students in Britain has fallen steadily and substantially, and the same is true for British students in the United States. Equally striking is the failure of the total number of Anglo-American exchange students, in either direction, to keep pace with the great increase in the number of individuals attending institutions of higher learning in both countries. Despite a modest increase in the number of students exchanged, the proportion affected by this important Anglo-American link has dropped.

There is even less agreement on the role of temporary travel and residence abroad in generating significant understanding of other countries' needs. Some observers insist that tourists are unlikely to make good ambassadors, that they are on the average more obnoxious and less perceptive than their stay-at-home countrymen. Their impressions are likely to be shallow, and their pleasant associations overwhelmed by primitive English plumbing or twentieth-century American commercialism. Many a voyager has left his country ready to like a foreign land and returned only too glad to have the experience behind him. We have some slight evidence to support this view, but most evidence indicates that whereas in individual cases the effect may be detrimental, on the whole tourism is probably beneficial to the relations of two nations.[10] Again it would seem worthwhile to examine Anglo-American relations in this respect, reserving judgment on its effects for later testing. While all tourists cannot properly be termed members of any elite, practically all of them belong to the attentive public — they show their interest in foreign affairs by going abroad.

We have information about the number and nationality of non-immigrant aliens admitted to the United States and about visitors on business and on holiday admitted to the United Kingdom since 1913. Since we also have data about the number of citizens leaving each country on temporary visits abroad, we are able this time to use the matrix analysis introduced in Chapter 2. The indices of relative acceptance ($R.A.$'s) are as shown in Table 6.2.

During most of the period since 1913, Britain and America have sent a smaller proportion of tourists to each other than would have been "predicted" by the null model. In the case of British tourists this is not surprising, because of the ease and cheapness of travel to the Continent. More surprising is the relative decline in American travel to Britain since 1928. Not only did the proportion of American

[10] Pierre de Bie, "Certain Psychological Aspects of Benelux," *International Social Science Bulletin,* III (Summer 1951), pp. 540–542, suggests that increased contact does not lead to better understanding. Erich Reigrotski and Nels Anderson, "National Stereotypes and Foreign Contacts," *Public Opinion Quarterly,* XXIII, 4 (Winter 1959), pp. 515–528, on the other hand, report that contacts such as travel or having friends and relatives in a foreign country were associated with favorable images of that country's people. Ithiel de Sola Pool, Suzanne Keller, and Raymond A. Bauer, "The Influence of Foreign Travel on Political Attitudes of American Businessmen," *Public Opinion Quarterly,* XX. 1 (Spring 1956), pp. 161–173, find that travel at least tempers the extremes of self-interest. Businessmen with an interest in free trade become more protectionist, and those whose self-interest favored protection become more liberal. Dunn, *War and the Minds of Men,* pp. 100–103, and Van Wagenen, *Research,* pp. 51–52, review the literature and conclude with mild optimism about the benefits of the exchange of persons. Obviously, much depends on the particular circumstances in each case.

TABLE 6.2.   Tourists Admitted from Partner Country, and Indices
of Relative Acceptance (*R.A.*)

	1913	1928	1938	1954	1958
U.S. Tourists to U.K.					
Number	100,000	113,000	77,000	194,000	310,000
R.A.	−.31	.07	−.34	−.41	−.21
U.K. Tourists to U.S.					
Number	29,000	19,000	24,000	54,000	69,000
R.A.	−.80	−.87	−.83	−.84	−.87

SOURCE: Appendix Table 3.4.

tourists go down, but from 1913 to 1954 the number of American
travelers to the United Kingdom did little more than keep ahead of
population increase (67 per cent) in the United States. The immense improvement in transatlantic air and sea transport has not
increased the number of tourists exchanged as vastly as has often
been supposed. Thus 1928 represents the peak, at least for American
travel to Britain, though it is possible that we have substantially underestimated the proportion of American tourists to Britain in 1913
(see Appendix Table 3.4). While 1913 certainly would not surpass
the 1928 peak, conceivably it might well be a match for 1958.

The proportion of British tourists to the United States has fallen
only a little over the years, though the level has always been low.
Perhaps it was especially low in the 1950's because of Britain's dollar shortage and consequent limitation on nonessential travel to North
America.[11] Yet the reason for the small amount of travel is less important than the fact that contact through travel was surprisingly
slight.

Attention

For members of the elite who do not travel abroad, the most important source of information and attitudes on foreign events is
likely to be the newspaper. On September 20, 1912, Henry Adams
remarked disgustedly to his friend Cecil Spring-Rice, "Today's Boston
newspaper, twelve pages, contained not one allusion or item regard-

[11] Organization for European Economic Co-operation, *Liberalization of
Europe's Dollar Trade,* Paris, 1957, p. 173, shows that travel to the United
States was more heavily restricted by the United Kingdom than by many
European countries. But by 1958 the restrictions were eased (any British
traveler could take £100 with him, whereas previously he could not take
any sterling unless his trip was approved on grounds of business or government need). After 1958 they were further relaxed and no longer exerted
an appreciable deterrent to travel to America.

ing the outside world." [12] It would be hard to find an example of such isolation now. Careful analyses indicate that Henry Adams's case was not typical even of the American press in 1912. In a thorough content analysis of the elite papers, *The Times* of London and the *New York Times,* Ithiel de Sola Pool obtained the findings which are summarized in Table 6.3.

TABLE 6.3. British and American Attention to Each Other in Editorials of Elite Papers

Years	Symbols of International Politics as Percentage of All International Symbols		References to Other Country as Percentage of All Geographic Symbols Other than Self-References	
	(1)	*(2)*	*(3)*	*(4)*
	London Times	*New York Times*	*London Times*	*New York Times*
1890–1913	27	24	7.2	18.0
1914–1918	64	49	6.6	11.1
1919–1929	44	41	9.1	16.9
1930–1935	41	35	9.3	19.5
1936–1938	44	33	9.5	17.5
1939–1940	49	49	5.7	19.9
1941–1945	50	53	10.0	22.7
1946–1949	36	41	11.2	17.4

SOURCE: Ithiel de Sola Pool, *Symbols of Internationalism,* Stanford, 1951, p. 67. Periods for the *New York Times* are not quite identical with those given above. The correct periods would be 1900–1913, 1914–1918, 1919–1929, 1930–1932, 1933–1938, 1939–1941, 1942–1945, and 1946–1949.

In both countries the prestige papers have given more editorial attention to international affairs since 1913. If we ignore the wartime periods, in the *New York Times* such attention was greater in the 1940's than during the depression-ridden 1930's — though not, strikingly enough, any greater than during the so-called isolationist 1920's. But *The Times* of London in the late 1940's showed much more national self-preoccupation than at any time since the years before World War I. [13]

[12] Quoted in H. C. Allen, *Great Britain and the United States,* New York, 1955, p. 650.

[13] This latter finding of Pool's is different from that of the *Report of the Royal Commission on the Press, 1947–49,* Cmd. 7700, London, 1949, pp. 250–251. In the Commission's analysis of the proportion of column inches devoted to various classes of news items in 1927, 1937, and 1947, home news was given a constant 51 per cent of nonadvertising space in *The Times.* The difference between these results and Pool's must largely be due to the difference in subject matter — editorials as opposed to all news items. Other factors may include Pool's use of several-year periods rather than single years, a difference in sampling methods, or the difference in analytical method (Pool's symbol count versus the Commission's measurement of inches).

In any case, we find that of all references to foreign countries and areas, relative attention to the United States by *Times* editorials rose substantially and steadily over the various peacetime periods. Even with the decline in attention to all foreign affairs, it would appear that the over-all proportion of attention to the United States did not fall. This need not, however, indicate as much as it seems, since by any standard United States policy had a heavier impact on world events, and on the fate of Britain, in 1947 than it did in 1927. On this ground one would expect attention to rise. But the *New York Times* gave no such increased attention to Leviathan. Of the American paper's attention to foreign doings, Britain occupied no larger place in the late forties than she had at the beginning of the century, and a smaller place, in fact, than she had in the twenties. Given the trend shown in column 2 of Table 6.3, Britain probably did just a little better than hold her own during the whole period.

In *The Times* of London we found that the United States was given increasing attention relative to other foreign countries, and at least a stable amount relative to all news items. We have some evidence that the British academic elite has not matched this performance. A study of footnote references in nine British scientific journals shows a moderate decline in British self-preoccupation (that is, attention to works of British scholarship), a sharper decline in attention to work done in most of the world, but a very notable increase in attention to American scientific findings. Yet these results are deceptive. Certainly anyone would agree that the contribution of American scientists to world knowledge has increased greatly during the past sixty years. Unless British researchers were to be terribly parochial, their attention to American labors would have to increase. Thus we must find some means to control for the greater product of United States scientists, in order to see whether British attention has grown commensurately.

Two possibilities, neither by itself completely satisfactory, are offered. For the first we count the number of Nobel Prizes in physics, chemistry, and medicine and physiology won by Britain, America, and the rest of the world in each of the periods. We can then make an "attention ratio" of the proportion of references to the proportion of Nobel Prizes won. A figure greater than unity indicates greater than "expected" attention. Abstracting journals which print summaries of virtually all books and articles published in a particular field, regardless of country of origin, provide another possible control. Again we make a ratio of the proportion of references in British journals to the proportion of summaries contributed by each nation in the abstracting journals. Neither of these controls is perfect, but

together they give us some means of allowing for the growing product
of American science. Figure 6.1, taken from the data in Appendix
Tables 6.1 and 6.2, shows the pattern.

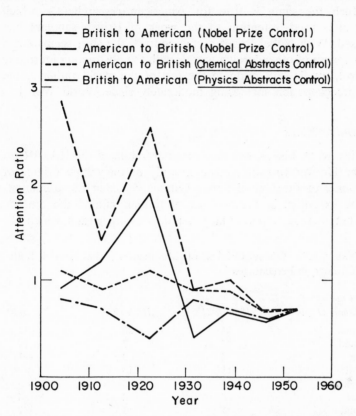

FIGURE 6.1   *Attention in Scientific Journals to Scholarship in Part-*
ner Country, with Nobel Prizes and Abstracting Journals as Controls
SOURCE: Appendix Tables 6.1, 6.2

Though gross British attention to American research has increased
over the period, the picture changes markedly when we obtain measures weighted for the contribution of United States scientists to
world output. Whichever control is used, the trend indicated is one of
a decline in attention to American contributions — a very modest
drop if the abstracting journal is used as the control, or a sharp one
with Nobel Prizes as the control. As an examination of Appendix
Table 6.1 will show, in the first case the decline would seem to be at
the expense of greater self-preoccupation, for attention to non-American foreign work would also appear to have fallen. The second control, Nobel Prizes, would seem to indicate that the attention shift

has been to other foreign efforts, with national self-preoccupation essentially unchanged. But in either case a drop in attention to American work shows up.

Much the same is true for American researchers — whichever control is used, attention to the work of British scholars has decreased. With Nobel Prizes as the control, the shift seems largely at the expense of other foreign works; with the abstracting journal as the control, we find attention to the rest of the world rather stable but self-preoccupation increasing moderately since World War I.

Executive Elites

Richard B. Fisher, in a draft memorandum of the RADIR project at the Hoover Institute, made a study of the ethnic origins of the personnel of the United States Cabinet.[14] Given the dominant role of the executive in the conduct of foreign affairs, the attitudes of Cabinet members, particularly on day-to-day affairs which do not

TABLE 6.4. Ethnic Origins of Members of the United States Cabinet, in Percentages

Country of Ethnic Origin	1889–1921	1922–1953	Net Shift
England	32	20	−12
Scotland	27	7	−20
Wales	4	3	−1
Ireland	11	15	+4
Germany	5	8	+3
France	6	2	−4
Holland	1	3	+2
Unknown	29	50	+21
Total	115	108	−7
Number =	100	133	—

SOURCE: Richard B. Fisher, *The Personnel of the Presidency, Vice-Presidency, and Cabinet since 1889*, Stanford (1954?), mimeo., pp. 49a, 49b, and 63. Totals exceed 100 because a member may trace his ancestry to two or more nationalities. Members who held office during more than one Presidential term are counted twice or three times, as appropriate.

call for Presidential or Congressional intervention, are obviously highly significant. A member's ethnic origin, while certainly not of overwhelming importance, may nevertheless have some influence on

[14] Richard B. Fisher, *The Personnel of the Presidency, the Vice-Presidency, and the Cabinet since 1889*, Stanford (1954?), mimeo.

his sympathies toward foreign nations. Using standard biographical materials as sources, Fisher found the pattern shown in Table 6.4.

The findings are of only limited usefulness because of the large percentage of unknowns, particularly in the later period. Yet on the face of it, the proportion of members of British background has declined sharply. This remains true even if we allot the unknowns in each period in proportion to the origins of those whose background has been identified.

Another draft memorandum, similar to Fisher's of the American Cabinet, also came from the RADIR project.[15] The British Cabinet is important in foreign policy not only by virtue of its explicitly executive functions but because of its very substantial control over debate and the course of legislation, and the requirement that all bills authorizing expenditure must originate with the government. Although most of Summers's and Fisher's material is not divided into separate periods, one table is somewhat instructive (Table 6.5).

TABLE 6.5.   Members of British Cabinet Who Traveled Abroad for Business (Private and Government) Reasons, in Percentages

Destination	1886–1919	1919–1950	Net Shift
United States	13.0	12.1	−0.9
France	14.4	25.8	+11.4
South Africa	10.6	13.3	+2.7
India and Burma	9.7	13.3	+3.6
Canada	4.6	7.0	+2.4
Travel to All Countries	46.8	60.2	+13.4
Number =	(222)	(250)	—

SOURCE: Thomas Summers and Richard Fisher, *The British Cabinet*, Stanford (1954?), mimeo., p. 46. While travel for business reasons gives data on only a portion of all travel, the information is still useful. Any data on pleasure trips would be incomplete, for a member would seem to be bragging if he spoke of his holidays in the short biographies the authors used as sources.

A smaller proportion of Cabinet members journeyed to America in the second period than in the first, even though the percentage going to other countries rose from 33.8 per cent to 48.1 per cent. Here is another index of declining relative communication between the two great English-speaking powers.

Other data on the Cabinet give a somewhat different impression. In connection with a later analysis of attitude patterns in the House of Commons, I investigated the business and personal connections of

[15] Thomas E. Summers and Richard B. Fisher, *The British Cabinet*, Stanford (1954?), mimeo.

British Cabinet members in three of the key years under examination — 1890, 1938, and 1954. Standard biographical sources such
as *Who's Who* provided the basic material, and I looked for the following among Cabinet members: those who were officers or directors
of firms with American subsidiaries, or which were themselves subsidiaries of American firms; those who owned businesses in the
United States; those whose firms imported American goods or exported to the United States; those who were members of banking
firms engaged in foreign banking or with branches in America, merchant bankers, and owners of shipping lines with vessels that sailed to
American ports.

In addition to these economic ties, it seemed essential to identify
as many personal ties as possible. Into this category fall men who
were born or educated in the United States, who worked there for a
while, or who married Americans. There was also a class of personal
ties that seemed intrinsically weaker — ties which should not be included with the others, yet ought not to be ignored. They included
men who had been awarded honorary degrees from American universities or medals for war service in joint causes, or who had worked
on joint Anglo-American agencies during the world wars. While
these influences were unlikely to be as great as those of marriage or
education, because they often took the form of rewards, they might
well predispose the men in question to be responsive. Some other
relevant kinds of information were not mentioned in the short biographical sketches. Parents' birth, ancestry, and business connections
were largely ignored, as was touring.

I examined biographies of both Cabinet members and of ministers
and undersecretaries of state. Note that in each year given in Table
6.6 a Conservative government was in power; changes cannot be
laid primarily to the different make-up of the two parties.

Ties with America clearly have not diminished at the executive
level, and have in some respects become more numerous. The frequency of "strong" ties has remained essentially stable — one man in
each government, though only in the last two governments was he a
Cabinet member. The frequency of "weak" ties has grown remarkably, however, a development made possible by Anglo-American co-
operation in the last war. Two ministers and a Cabinet member
reported holding medals awarded by the American government, and
another, Lord Alexander of Tunis, was Supreme Allied Commander
in the Mediterranean. While these ties obviously were not available
to the 1890 Cabinet and so are not strictly comparable, they are yet
a factor linking the two nations. The others in the Cabinet with
"weak" ties included three with honorary degrees (plus degrees for

TABLE 6.6. Members of the British Cabinet and Ministry with Economic and Personal Ties to the United States

	1890	1938	1954
Percentage with "Strong" Personal Ties to U.S. in Cabinet	0	5	6
Cabinet and Ministers	3	3	3
Percentage with Only "Weak" Personal Ties to U.S. in Cabinet	0	5	33
Cabinet and Ministers	0	3	24
Percentage with Economic Ties to U.S. in Cabinet	18–24*	5	28
Cabinet and Ministers	26–31**	3	26
Total Number of Members in Cabinet	17	21	18
Cabinet and Ministers	39	35	33

* One member was a director of the International Investment Trust, Ltd.; it seems likely that his firm held stocks or bonds in American undertakings. His inclusion would raise the percentage to the upper limit.
** One member was a ship owner, and I cannot be sure of the routes plied by his ships. Inclusion of him and the above member would raise the percentage to the upper limit.

SOURCES and additional methodological notes: Appendix C.

one man with medals), and one was an honorary member of American legal associations.

The proportion with economic ties has remained roughly constant: a slight decline in the proportion in both Cabinet and ministry, a modest increase among Cabinet members alone. The proportion was lowest in 1938, the year when Anglo-American trade was at its nadir. (Note that the percentages are not additive — two 1954 Cabinet members with "weak" personal ties also had economic links to the United States.)

As a final note on the executive, remember the data in Table 2.1 on the diplomatic delegations in each country. The proportion of all Foreign Service or Foreign Office men serving in the partner state is an excellent index of attention in the official foreign-policy-making organs. We found a notable rise in British attention to the United States in recent years, but a steady decline in the State Department's concern for Britain since 1928.

Legislative Elites

The contacts of members of the House of Commons with the United States are also highly significant. Though the government may sometimes seem unhindered in the pursuit of such technical and often esoteric matters as foreign policy, the House retains its role as a brake, setting a limit to the government's freedom of action.

I took a random sample of about 20 per cent of the House of

Commons in each of the three years 1890, 1938, and 1954, with the results shown in Table 6.7.

TABLE 6.7.   Members of the House of Commons with Economic and Personal Ties to the United States

	1890	*1938*	*1954*
Number in Sample =	(134)	(132)	(129)
Percentage with "Strong" Ties to U.S.	3.0	8.3	5.5
Percentage with Only "Weak" Personal Ties to U.S.	0	1.5	3.9
Percentage Who Have Traveled to U.S.	2.2	1.5	1.5
Percentage with Any Personal Ties to U.S.	5.2	11.3	10.9
Percentage with Economic Ties to U.S.	14.2–15.7*	12.1	12.4

* Two members were attached to shipping firms whose trading routes I could not ascertain. Inclusion of those members as having economic ties with America raises the percentage to the upper limit.

SOURCE: Appendix C.

Relatively few members of the House have had ties with the United States in any of the above years. Changes in the proportions with such links are thus small and usually not significant. (To be statistically significant even at the 0.10 level in Table 6.7, any two percentages must be at least 5 per cent apart.) The number with "strong" personal ties to America rose from 1890 to 1938 but seems to have declined since then.[16] The number with weak ties may have increased slightly, although the proportion who temporarily visited the United States appears to have been constant. This last figure, however, is deceptive for reasons which we shall give later.[17] If we

[16] Since 1938 was not the zenith for many of the personal ties — travel, student exchange — mentioned in the aggregate earlier, it may be surprising that it is so here. But the House was, in a sense, living on its capital; there may be a substantial lag between one peak and the other. An M.P. in 1938, for instance, belonged to a generation educated at a time when one was more likely to be educated in America, instead of some other foreign country, than when he was actually in Parliament. Thus it may take decades before a decline in such a link on the aggregate level shows up among decision-makers, and one may even hypothesize a further decline at the formal decision-making level in the future as present trends in travel take effect. Then, too, the changing character of the House of Commons is important. In 1938 the proportion of well-to-do (and thus able to travel) members was higher than in the years after World War II.

[17] Most M.P.'s do not report their travels in the biographies used here as source materials. For the analysis of Members' attitudes done in Chapter 9, it was possible to use other current sources to supplement the meager biographical data, but these materials were not available for the earlier years. For the sake of comparability we must, at this stage, limit ourselves to the *Who's Who* type of biography in each period.

include the somewhat dubious data on travel, we find that the proportion with personal ties of any sort to America has increased since 1890, but has fallen slightly since 1938.

Somewhat surprisingly, considering the change in trade patterns, there has been no significant decline in the number of Members of Parliament with economic links. Part of the explanation, however, can be found in the nature of those bonds. In 1890 three M.P.'s were attached to firms making goods for export to America (woolens and cutlery), three imported goods from the United States (cotton and flour), six to eight were engaged in services (banking and shipping), and eight had ties of investment capital with the growing republic. One man had both a capital and an export tie. But in 1954, the sixteen M.P.'s with ties were distributed this way: Eight had ties of export (books, whisky, woolens), one of import (cigars), only four of services, and six of capital. Three men, publishers, had links of capital or services as well. But of the eight "exporters," six were book publishers. Without the three publishers who had no other tie there would have been a significant decline from 1890. Secondly, there was in the earliest year no volume comparable to the FBI *Register of British Manufacturers,* a very useful means of identifying the kind of product manufactured by a particular firm. Had there been one, I might well have found some additional "exporting" companies.

It is equally important to have such data on the American legislature. Murray G. Lawson has examined information on the birthplaces of members of Congress. In Table 6.8 are the data for the six years under consideration.[18] Despite some ups and downs, the number of British-born members, whether compared with the total number of members or with the other foreign-born, has dropped notably since 1890.

To supplement this information, I made a particular study of the ties of Senators on my own. Because of the Senate's small membership, it was possible to deal with the whole Senate rather than with just samples. It is especially important to study the composition of the Senate since it has a special role in the formation of foreign policy, notably in advising and consenting to major appointments and the ratification of treaties. To illustrate the Senate's importance in this area, the Committee on Foreign Relations has long been a prized assignment, but until recently Congressmen often regarded the House Foreign Affairs Committee as a spot to avoid.

[18] "The Foreign-Born in Congress, 1789–1949; A Statistical Summary," *American Political Science Review,* LI, 4 (December 1957), pp. 1183–1189, and personal communication from the author.

TABLE 6.8. Members of Congress Born in Britain and Other Foreign Countries

	Total *Number of* All Foreign-Born		British-Born *Members as* *Percentage* of All Foreign-Born	
Year	House	Senate	House	Senate
1890	19	4	32	75
1913	19	5	16	20
1928	17	3	24	0
1938	23	3	17	33
1954	4	1	50	0
1958	5	0	20	—

The United States Census, giving data on production of goods by states, provided a kind of information that we lacked in studying the House of Commons. We could count the number of Senators with "constituency ties" as well. This term is applied to a Senator whose home state gained at least 5 per cent of its gross income from a commodity of which at least 5 per cent of total American production was exported to Britain. It was assumed that producers of this commodity would then have a substantial source of influence over their Senators. The cut-off points chosen are arbitrary, but other possible points, such as 2 per cent and 10 per cent, were tried without significantly changing the pattern shown in Table 6.9.

TABLE 6.9. Members of the United States Senate with Economic and Personal Ties to Great Britain

	1890	*1954*
Number in Senate	(84)	(96)
Percentage with Personal Ties to Britain	4.8	4.1
Percentage with Personal Economic Ties	7.1	7.3
Percentage with Constituency Economic Ties	54.8	12.5

SOURCE: Appendix C.

The number of Senators with personal ties to Britain has not fallen since 1890, but the character of the tie has changed somewhat. Three 1890 Senators were born there, and another had lived in England for some time. Of the four with ties in 1954, two (Fulbright and Kennedy) had spent time at English universities, and one (Kefauver) had a British-born wife. The fourth (Knowland) had a "weak" tie — service in England during the war. The proportion with economic ties of a personal nature remained about even, though in 1954 the emphasis was on ties of capital (five Senators — Bush,

Flanders, Lehman, Purtell, and Symington) and banking (two Senators — Ives and Bush); only one member, a cotton exporter (Maybank), had a direct tie to commodity trade. In 1890, however, at least three Senators were linked to products important to Anglo-American commerce. One was a cotton planter, another was in oil-refining, and the third was the European sales representative of Remington Arms Company. The other three had ties of capital. Quite possibly, however, this proportion with economic ties in 1890 is understated. The 1890's were years of huge British capital investment in American railroads, and three other Senators were attached to railroads that issued bonds in Britain. Had they been included in the table, the proportion would have been raised to 10.7 per cent.

The one startling change is, of course, the decline in the importance of constituency ties, which reflects the shriveling of American exports to Britain. (In 1954, British imports from the United States totaled only one and a half times what they were in 1890, despite an eleven-fold increase in British national income.) In 1890 five commodities were important in Anglo-American trade and contributed over 5 per cent of the gross income of at least one state. There were ten great cotton-growing states — Alabama, Arkansas, Florida, Georgia, Louisiana, Mississippi, North and South Carolina, Tennessee, and Texas. Ten other states raised wheat in great quantity — California, Indiana, Kansas, Michigan, Minnesota, Missouri, North Dakota, Oregon, South Dakota, and Washington. Kentucky raised tobacco, Montana produced copper, and the Chicago stockyards made Illinois the world's greatest meat-packing center. (Since virtually all the livestock products went as packed meat rather than as live animals, cattle- and hog-raising states are not included. If they were, they would make the list even longer.)

But by 1954, Britain had found alternative sources of supply for wheat, copper, and meat. Diversification left only four states deriving 5 per cent or more of their income from cotton — Arizona, Arkansas, Mississippi, and Texas. Kentucky and North Carolina earned that much from tobacco-growing. For these two reasons — diversification and the failure of total trade to increase much — the economic bond between the two nations had become, by 1954, much weaker. If we had data on production by constituency in Britain, we should certainly find the same pattern, though perhaps with a less extreme decline.

The same drop is found for the key Senate Foreign Relations Committee. Whereas in 1890 four of the nine members (44 per cent) had ties of some sort to Britain, only two of fifteen members (13 per cent) had them in 1954.

To recapitulate, we had evidence of capabilities among the attentive public in four areas, with two sets of indices (one for each country) for every one of the four. In two cases only, the newspapers in both countries, we found indications that relative Anglo-American attention was at a peak in the 1950's. Even there, it was hardly surprising that this occurred at a time when Britain paid her greatest attention to America. But for the other six indices — student exchange, tourism, and scientific scholarship, each in both countries — we found a decline of capabilities that ranged from moderate to very substantial.

A similar pattern emerges for Anglo-American bonds among members of the political elite: legislators and executive officials. In two instances, personal ties to America among British Cabinet members and Foreign Office assignments, the frequency increased. Personal ties among M.P.'s were about the same in 1954 and 1938, though appreciably higher than before the turn of the century; personal ties in the Senate also remained unchanged. In one instance, economic ties among Cabinet members, there was no significant change. But in seven other cases — ethnic background of members of the American Cabinet, travel by British Cabinet members, United States Foreign Service assignments, economic ties among legislators in both nations, country of birth for members of Congress, ties of Foreign Relations Committee members, and all personal ties in the Senate — there was clear evidence of a decline.

Overall, the evidence of diminishing capabilities (about three to one) is not quite overwhelming, but it is nevertheless impressive. Should it also be strong for mass communication, we would have cause for concern.

7

Mass Communication and Attention

Elite attitudes are highly influential, but in no country, particularly in no democracy, can mass perspectives be entirely ignored. "Elite" and "mass" are merely terms to designate groups at the extremes of a continuum. In the preceding chapter we were concerned with those toward one end of the continuum; in this chapter we study the other end. Nonelite members of the populace may not be important in initiating policy; they may not even, in many circumstances, be important in molding or vetoing it. But mass opinion does set certain bounds beyond which decision-makers may not go. Candidates for public office dare not adopt obviously unpopular positions, and they probably tailor their policy recommendations to what they expect will meet with popular approval. In these negative and passive ways mass opinion does play a role in policy formation. And in the act of voting even many apathetic members of the populace take direct action in influencing decisions by determining who shall occupy the formal policy-making positions.

Migration

Migration is probably the most influential of mass contacts. Immigration brought millions of British subjects to the United States. In addition to making the American cultural heritage overwhelmingly Anglo-Saxon, these migrants provided a continuing source of current contacts between the parent country and her maturing child. It seems as though even now most Britishers have a cousin or other relative somewhere in the United States. They remain bound to those relatives at least by some bond of sympathy with them and with their country, and often by ties of communication — a letter or an occasional visit.

This tie might be less strong if the immigrants failed to be assimilated into their new society. Unhappy immigrants who communicated their bitterness to those at home would become a positive irritant to relations. Natives who regarded a wave of immigrants as threatening to inundate them with alien mores, or endangering their living standards by lowering wage rates, would be unlikely to look with favor on the mother country. Japanese immigration in the nineteenth and twentieth centuries put a severe burden on Japanese-American relations.

But there is little evidence that British migration has ever seriously exacerbated Anglo-American relations. During most of the United States' history most immigrants were from the middle and lower classes. If their wealthy countrymen who temporarily visited North America were distressed by the materialistic or egalitarian values of the new society, the immigrants usually found these traits highly attractive. America was a good place to make one's fortune. Since they shared the language and many of the dominant customs and beliefs of native Americans, British immigrants became assimilated easily and soon thought of themselves as Americans. The second generation of English and Scots was never ill adjusted in the way that the second generations of other nationalities were.[1] The conscious discrimination in favor of British and other Northern European immigrants embodied in the National Origins Act of 1924 and the McCarran-Walter Act testifies to the extent these groups were welcomed.

Migration to the United States has proceeded unevenly, with waves of immigrants coming first from one part of Europe and then from another area. Table 7.1 uses the null-model analysis to indicate the importance of British immigration since 1890.

Migration, as a bond uniting the two English-speaking nations, is clearly far less effective now than it was in 1890. This is true whichever way one cares to look at the matter — as the proportion of Americans with close British relatives and memories of a former life in the British Isles, or the proportion of Britishers with personal ties to residents of the United States. It applies equally whether one looks at the declining number of United Kingdom–United States migrants as a proportion of all migrants, or the declining number of migrants as a proportion of the two countries' total population. The modest absolute increase in British immigrants since 1928 (40

[1] See especially Rowland T. Berthoff, *British Immigrants,* Cambridge, Mass., 1953, pp. 128–210.

TABLE 7.1. Migration from the United Kingdom to the United States as a Percentage of All Immigration to the United States and All Emigration from the United Kingdom, and Indices of Relative Acceptance

	U.K. Migrants to U.S.		
Year	As Percentage of All U.K. Emigrants	As Percentage of All U.S. Immigrants	Indices of Relative Acceptance
1890	56	27	−.32
1913	23	7	−.72
1928	15	7	−.80
1938	6	3	−.91
1954	13	9	−.79
1958	20	11	−.67

SOURCE: Appendix Table 7.1.

per cent) has not even matched the American rate of population increase (44 per cent).

One essential qualification should be made. United Kingdom emigration in 1890 and 1913 included a large number of Irish migrants to the United States. Because of their Anglophobia, their substantial political power in some of the Eastern states, and their constant agitation for Irish independence, the Irish-Americans cannot be termed a link between America and Britain.[2] More probably, Irish immigration constituted a burden on Anglo-American relations. We cannot know what proportion of total United Kingdom emigration was from Ireland, but we do know that even in 1890, when Irish immigration to the United States was the greatest of these six years, Irishmen made up only 11 per cent of all immigrants. The relative number of English-Scots-Welsh was substantially higher (16 per cent) in 1890 than at any time since.

Mail, Telegraph, and Telephone

Since the majority of people, however, are born and die in the same country, the most important means of contact on the individual level are the various systems of communication — postal, telegraphic, and telephonic. In terms of the number of messages sent and received, by far the most significant of these is the mail system. Table 7.2 presents data on the number of letters exchanged. I have used information on the number of letters rather than all pieces of mail, or

[2] H. C. Allen (Great Britain and the United States, New York, 1955, pp. 100–101) and Berthoff (British Immigrants, pp. 202–207) have concluded that Irish immigration was generally detrimental to Anglo-American relations.

even first-class mail. Except for packages, mail other than first-class letters and cards consists largely of advertising material, and we already have direct data on trade. Similarly, a very large portion of all post cards are sent by visiting tourists, and we have direct data on travel.

TABLE 7.2. First-Class Letters Exchanged with Partner Country as a Percentage of All Letters, and Indices of Relative Acceptance

	1890	1913	1928	1938	1954	1958
U.S. to U.K.						
R.A.	−.47	−.32	−.51	−.56	−.67	−.60
Percentage of All First-Class Mail	0.42	n.a.	0.14	0.14	0.10	0.14
U.K. to U.S.						
R.A.	−.46	−.51	−.62	−.65	−.59	−.67
Percentage of All Letters Posted	0.62	n.a.	0.33	0.21	0.49	0.36

SOURCES: Foreign mail from Appendix Table 7.2. U.S. internal mail from Union Postale Universelle, Bureau International, *Statistique générale du service postal, 1890*, Berne, 1892, and *Statistical Abstract, 1960*, p. 510. No adequate data available for 1913. U.K. internal mail from *Statistical Abstract of the United Kingdom, 1889 to 1903*, p. 272; *Statistical Abstract of the United Kingdom, 1924 to 1938*, pp. 324–325; *Annual Abstract of Statistics, 1959*, p. 211.

The trend stands out clearly, and is too pronounced to be the result of any errors in information-gathering. Mail from America to Britain reached its peak in 1913 and has declined steadily since. In the other direction, 1890 represents the closest approach to the expected level, followed by a long and pronounced drop. There was a moderate upturn in 1954 (reversed four years later), but not one great enough even to reach the 1913 mark. The decline is not merely one relative to other foreign nations, as measured by the *R.A.*'s (indices of relative acceptance). In both countries the number of Anglo-American letters declined relative to the number of domestic postings.

The telephone and telegraph constitute newer and faster means of communication. Because of their cost they cannot replace postal communications, but in many situations they become supplements or substitutes.

Unfortunately, no statistics of movement prior to 1938 still survive, but in this case the lack is not serious. For many of the sets of communications data that we have been examining, 1938 represents the nadir of Anglo-American exchange, with the 1950's showing an increase which is modest but still insufficient to reach the high-water mark established in 1928 or earlier. But the *R.A.*'s for telegrams show a very sharp drop even since 1938. The very small improve-

TABLE 7.3. Telegrams Exchanged with Partner Country as a Percentage of All Telegrams Sent, and Indices of Relative Acceptance

	1938	1954	1958
U.S. to U.K.			
R.A.	−.24	−.55	−.51
Percentage of All Domestic and Foreign Telegrams	0.10	0.09	0.12
U.K. to U.S.			
R.A.	−.24	−.52	−.51
Percentage of All Domestic and Foreign Telegrams	3.6	3.2	4.7

SOURCES: Foreign telegrams from Appendix Table 7.3. Domestic telegrams from *Historical Statistics of the United States*, p. 484; *Statistical Abstract of the United States, 1960*, p. 516; *Statistical Abstract of the United Kingdom, 1924–38*, pp. 324–325; and *Annual Abstract of Statistics, 1959*, p. 211.

ment in 1958 comes nowhere near re-establishing the relatively high prewar rate of exchange. And almost alone of all the kinds of data which we consider, the absolute number of telegrams sent back and forth has dropped over the period. This last aspect, however, reflects a trend evident throughout the entire telegraph industry. Air mail makes it possible to get detailed information to Europe in no more than three days. Also, businessmen and private citizens have increasingly preferred the telephone to the telegraph, particularly as the quality of telephone service has improved.

TABLE 7.4. Telephone Calls to Partner Country as a Percentage of All Telephone Calls, and Indices of Relative Acceptance

	1928	1938	1954	1958
U.S. to U.K.				
R.A.	−.98	−.96	−.95	−.90
Percentage of All Calls, Domestic and Foreign	0.00001	0.00003	0.00006	0.00014
U.K. to U.S.				
R.A.	−.98	−.96	−.95	−.89
Percentage of All Calls, Domestic and Foreign	0.0002	0.0004	0.0012	0.0035

SOURCES: Foreign calls from Appendix Table 7.4. Domestic calls from *Historical Statistics of the United States*, p. 480; *Statistical Abstract of the United States, 1960*, p. 512; *Statistical Abstract of the United Kingdom, 1924–38*, pp. 324–325; and *Annual Abstract of Statistics, 1959*, p. 211.

Here the trend runs directly counter to that uncovered so far. Though the number of calls remains small, really minute compared with the total of domestic and foreign calls in both countries, the relative number of calls between Britain and America shows a steady increase. In each year the *R.A.*'s became less negative, though at no point do they remotely approach the indifference level.[3]

This improvement in Anglo-American communications is due at least in part to technical progress. Transatlantic telephone service in 1928 had only been in operation for a year, and the quality of service was not high. As it improved and became more familiar, traffic rose. (On the other hand, the 1928 totals include a large unspecified number of calls which merely passed through the London exchange, originating or terminating on the continent of Europe. Later totals exclude those in transit through Britain.) The jump between 1954 and 1958 is largely accounted for by the opening of the transatlantic telephone cable in September 1956. In the course of a year the number of calls nearly doubled. There was no change in the rates, but the transmission, previously by radio, was much improved, and new circuits were made available by the cable.

Thus, much of the increase in messages between Britain and America represents merely a shift from other means of communication, particularly telegrams. We found that the absolute number of telegrams exchanged fell 15 per cent from 1938 to 1958. Given technical advances and the relatively small cost differential (a telephone call from New Haven to London costs, for three minutes, only twice as much as the cheapest and slowest forty-word telegram), this is not surprising. The relative increase in Anglo-American telephone communication in no way makes up for the decline in telegraph communication. Because of the high degree of substitutability of the two types of messages, a combined index is more satisfactory than two separate ones. As an illustration, we may assume that one telephone call is equal to three telegrams — request, answer, and confirmation. The *R.A.*'s would then be as shown in Table 7.5.

TABLE 7.5. Indices of Relative Acceptance for Telephone and Telegraph Messages Combined

(Each telephone call equals three telegrams.)

	1938	1954	1958
U.S. to U.K.	−.33	−.59	−.57
U.K. to U.S.	−.33	−.58	−.57

No substantial change is evident from the pattern developed for telegrams alone — a sharp decline. The volume of United States—

[3] Nor, of course, would anyone expect them to, considering cost differences. The Sunday rate for a call from New Haven, Connecticut, to London is currently ten times that for a call to Toronto. Surprisingly, the Sunday rate for London is exactly equal to that for a call to Tokyo.

Britain calls is too low to make a significant difference in the combined index. Even if we were to weight telephone calls and telegrams differently — one to one, or one to five, for example — the result would be the same: a substantial fall in the index of relative acceptance for the two combined.

The Mass Media

Communication between two nations is not confined to messages sent directly from one person to another. More general cultural products are inevitably exchanged, particularly between two countries speaking the same language. For most people books, magazines, newspapers, and motion pictures are major sources of both attitudes and information on foreign countries, whether they get opinions and facts directly from the mass media or through "opinion leaders" who act as intermediaries between many people and the media.[4]

The media may do more, even, than provide basic information (or misinformation) and shape attitudes. Frequent exposure to American customs and ways of thought through American motion pictures may contribute heavily to an important aspect of responsiveness — mutual predictability. Simply by familiarizing their audience with American customs and ways of thought, films may help foreigners to know how Americans are likely to react to situations. In addition, they may contribute to predictability from introspection. Insofar as the audience accepts these American mores as its own, nationals of both countries are enabled more easily to foresee the others' actions merely by asking what they themselves would do in similar circumstances. Deutsch et al. found mutual predictability essential to an amalgamated security-community, and very possibly to a pluralistic security-community as well.[5]

To a moderate degree, it is possible that attention to a particular nation in the mass media is an *indicator* of approval; people who go frequently to watch American motion pictures may do so because they like the people, the way of life, the customs presented in the films. Such attention is by no means an infallible indicator, for people may be attracted by the adventure of something strange or want to see something which horrifies them. Yet these last hypotheses by themselves cannot entirely explain the popularity of American films in Britain; some approval, or at least identification with the characters, must unavoidably be present.

[4] On the role of opinion leaders in diffusing the content of the mass media, see Elihu Katz and Paul Lazarsfeld, *Personal Influence*, Glencoe, Illinois, 1955.

[5] K. W. Deutsch et al., *Political Community and the North Atlantic Area*, Princeton, 1957, pp. 56–58, 67.

Despite these reasons for regarding the exchange of cultural products as fostering or indicating greater capabilities, there are grounds for caution. Drew Middleton feels it may have a seriously divisive effect:

> The bridge between the two cultures is slowly being undermined by a flow of popular entertainment that may appeal to the British masses but that sets the teeth of their intellectual leaders on edge.
>
> Understanding of the United States by the upper levels of society — by that strange complex of political, economic, educational, ecclesiastical power known as the Establishment — probably counts for more in Britain than it does in any other country. It is the section of society that is most affronted by the "Americanization" of entertainment in films and television and in cheap books and magazines.[6]

He then quotes C. A. Le Jeune, writing in *The Observer,* who declared that Hollywood films show a country where marriage is "simply a prelude to divorce," where education is "a synonym for necking," and "where drinking is the great national institution shared by male and female." This impression is dangerous, said Le Jeune. "If false, it approaches a national libel, if true it adumbrates a national peril. For who could be strong and durable, loyal in partnership, perseverant and peace-loving in the pursuit of such a kind as this?" The frightening aspect of this comment, says Middleton, is that the critic did not immediately assume the portrait to be a false one.

On the whole, we shall maintain that an increase in the exchange of mass entertainment would contribute to improving responsiveness. Nevertheless a decline in certain areas, particularly films and television, would not be without its blessings. We have some information on the pattern of motion-picture exchange since 1928, though the data are not quite the same on both sides of the Atlantic. (See Table 7.6.)

In America we find that British films have moderately increased their share of the foreign film market. Since foreign films have never accounted for more than a tiny fraction of all movies shown in the United States, this may not seem important. But the share of foreign films has risen in the last few years, especially for the rather elite audiences of the art theaters. Since there are no general worries

---

[6] Drew Middleton, "Cowboys and Indians," *New York Times,* January 19, 1960, 32: 3, 4. For an even harsher reaction see a new book by a former governor of the BBC, Francis Williams, *The American Invasion,* New York, 1962. This dissatisfaction is not confined to the upper levels. A taxi driver in Cornwall, annoyed by the frequency with which American rather than British films are shown on television, remarked to me that it must be because all the television stations (presumably including BBC) are owned by the Americans!

TABLE 7.6. Motion Picture Exchange

	1928	1938	1954	1958
Feature Films in the U.S.				
Number of Foreign Films	193	278	153	266
Number of British Films	37	44	52	63
British Percentage of All Foreign Films	18	16	34	24
Feature Films in the U.K.				
U.S. Percentage of Screen Time	81	79	65	65
Other Foreign Percentage of Screen Time	14	—	—	—
British Percentage of Screen Time	5	21	35	35

SOURCES — 1928: Jack Alicoate, editor, *The 1929 Film Daily Yearbook*, New York, 1929, p. 1045; *The 1930 Film Daily Yearbook*, New York, 1940, p. 479.
    1938: Terry Ransaye, editor, *1939–40 International Motion Picture Almanac*, New York, 1939, p. 886; Alicoate, *The 1940 Film Daily Yearbook*, New York, 1940, p. 39.
    1954: Alicoate, *The 1955 Film Daily Yearbook*, New York, 1955, pp. 248–249; Charles S. Aaronson, editor, *International Motion Picture Almanac*, New York, 1959, p. 26A. Data for showings in U.K. are for 1955. Aaronson gives only the figure of 65 per cent for American films, and it was assumed that virtually all the remainder were British. By law at least 30 per cent of screen time had to be devoted to British pictures.
    1958: Alicoate, *The 1959 Film Daily Yearbook*, New York, 1959, pp. 100, 850.

about the vulgarizing or Anglicizing of American culture, this increase can be considered a modest addition to the Anglo-American alliance's capabilities.

On the British screen, American films have occupied a steadily diminishing proportion of the time. This loss, however, has been entirely to native British films, for the market for other foreign films in England has practically disappeared. Thus while the British show, in their movie viewing, an increasing national self-preoccupation, American films have at least gained at the expense of other foreign pictures. But, as we said, an expansion of the American share would not be an unmixed blessing, nor a diminution an unmitigated disaster.

If we wish to use the decline in American films' proportion of total film time as an indicator of a decline in approval, we must take an additional precaution. According to a law first effective in 1929, 7½ per cent of all screen time had to be devoted to British-made films, with an annual increase of 2½ per cent until it reached 20 per cent. Later legislation reduced the British-made quota to 15 per cent in 1938, but postwar regulations raised it again to 30 per cent in 1954. True, these requirements were slightly less than the proportion of screen time actually devoted to movies produced in Britain (16 per cent in 1938, almost 35 per cent in 1955), but it is difficult to assess the role of the quota in strengthening the competitive position of British producers. Surely the presence of an assured market encouraged them to make more films, and to spend more on production. Yet it seems unlikely that removal of the quota, after it had stimulated production, would have caused a substantial short-run decline in the proportion of screen time allotted to products of the United Kingdom.

Television is of course a postwar phenomenon. While there can be no comparison with 1938, current patterns in this highly influential medium are relevant. Apart from an occasional feature, in the United States no significant portion of broadcasting time is devoted to foreign-made material. The situation is quite different, however, in the British Isles, where products of the American television industry command wide interest, much as Hollywood films did in the early days of motion-picture making. In order to prevent American productions from swamping the British television market, a regulation similar to the moving-picture quota was imposed in 1954 — no more than 14 per cent of air time may be devoted to foreign films.

The British commercial broadcasting system, established in 1955, keeps very close to the limit, and except for an occasional French or Italian film all imported material is American. The BBC shows more British-made programs — in 1954 only about 7½ per cent of broadcasting time went to foreign material, with about two thirds of that from the United States. By 1960 the foreign proportion had risen to 10–12 per cent, of which more than four fifths was American.[7] In fact, the impact of American television is greater than suggested by these quite moderate percentages. The overwhelming majority of American films is concentrated in the peak viewing hours of weekday evenings. If one were to weight American films by the number of viewers watching them (something neither British television authority seems to have done), the proportion of *viewing* time would surely be much more than 14 per cent. As with motion pictures, the effect of American programs, particularly westerns and detective programs, is resented in some circles.

There are some very limited data on the degree to which British readers pick up American periodicals, and vice versa. In the United Kingdom, the most widely read American magazines in 1958 were the *Reader's Digest* (900,000 copies per issue) and *Life* (over 42,000 subscription copies per issue, no data on newsstand sales).[8] Both of these totals were about four and a half times the magazines' United Kingdom sales in 1938. (Both magazines have vastly increased their sales in other countries as well. *Reader's Digest* sold

[7] Personal communications from the British Broadcasting Company and the Independent Television Authority.
[8] Personal communications from *Reader's Digest* and *Life*.

practically no copies in other nations in 1938, but in 1958 sold 7.6 million per issue. *Life International* increased its non-British circulation from 5000 to 290,000 in the same period.) No data are available for sales of other foreign periodicals in Britain, but this figure (1958 sales four and a half times those of 1938) is a substantial improvement over the sales increase of all magazines in the country. (The circulation of 1958 was about double that of 1938.) In number of copies sold, the *Digest*'s achievement is especially impressive.

Figures for the sale of British magazines in America are less satisfactory. The two with the largest American circulation are the air edition of the *Manchester Guardian Weekly* (14,000 copies per issue in 1954) and the *Economist* (6000 copies in 1956).[9] Of all British journals with any significant sale in the United States, only one, the *Guardian Weekly,* kept or would divulge circulation figures for 1938. The *Guardian*'s circulation department estimated that the number of subscriptions from America had at least doubled from 1938 to 1954, almost exactly the same as the growth in sales for all American magazines.[10] Despite the increase, the totals for both the *Economist* and the *Guardian Weekly* are minute compared with the population of the United States or the circulation of domestic magazines there. Yet these two periodicals' circulation is undoubtedly concentrated among elite readers, something that is certainly not true for *Life* or the *Reader's Digest* in England.

In summary, we have found in this chapter clear evidence of expanded Anglo-American capabilities in two areas: British films in America, and American magazines in Britain. In two other cases — American movies in Britain, and British magazines in the United States — the trend was either ambiguous or unchanging. But in five other cases — mail in both countries, telephone and telegraph messages combined in both, and migration to America — the evidence clearly points to diminished capabilities. This evidence is not quite as one-sided as in the preceding chapter on elite links, where the totals of the capabilities for responsiveness showed that four indicators were up, three neutral, and thirteen down; but the bulk of the data points the same way in both cases. When we take the combined totals — six up, five neutral, and eighteen down, plus the four declining indices produced in Chapter 3 — we have grounds for serious concern about the state of the Anglo-American alliance. Furthermore, indicators of American capabilities for responsiveness to Britain are about as likely to have gone down as those for British responsiveness to America; there is no significant difference.

[9] Personal communications from the *Guardian* and the *Economist.*
[10] *Statistical Abstract of the United States, 1960,* p. 521.

The Interchangeability of Indices

The past two chapters also have some methodological significance beyond the study of these particular capabilities. Some of the indices were obtained only after long and painstaking research. A number of them were based on material whose accuracy and comparability were not as high as we might have preferred; others were available for recent years but not for the earlier periods. Some were available for the United States and Britain, two statistically conscious nations, but might not be available for any other two countries, particularly for the early years. Would it be possible to approximate some of the hard-to-find materials with other, more readily fabricated indices? In other words, are at least some of these indices interchangeable?

Our ideal indices should have three properties: (1) The pattern they show should closely approximate the pattern identified by other indices of the same variable. (2) The material should cover a long time-span. (3) The material should be easily obtainable. Four kinds of data in these two chapters meet the last two requirements fairly adequately. They are presented in Table 7.7, along with the set for trade in commodities from Chapter 3, which also meets the requirements.

TABLE 7.7. Years 1890 to 1958 Ranked According to Various Indices of Capability

Index	Rank Order					
	1890	*1913*	*1928*	*1938*	*1954*	*1958*
Mail — U.S. to U.K.	2	1	3	4	6	5
U.K. to U.S.	1	2	4	5	3	6
Migration — U.K. to U.S.	1	3	5	6	4	2
Tourists — U.S. to U.K.	n.a.	3	1	4	5	2
U.K. to U.S.	n.a.	1	4.5	2	3	4.5
Students — U.S. to U.K.	n.a.	n.a.	1	2	3	4
U.K. to U.S.	n.a.	n.a.	1	3	2	4
Trade — U.S. to U.K.	1	2	3	4	5.5	5.5
U.K. to U.S.	1	3	4	5	6	2
Avg. Rank — Last 4 Years Only			1	2	3	4

These indices certainly do not give identical results, but in one essential they show substantial agreement. All show, in the 1950's, a decline from a peak reached in 1928 or earlier. There is, however, little agreement on the ordering of the last three years.[11] This fact indicates that various indices of "capability" are likely to agree only in a very gross manner. Previous theories of international integration which suggested that numerous transaction indices would be closely correlated with each other were oversimple.[12] Major shifts in several indices will probably be repeated in all or most of the others; but in the case of smaller-scale changes, the nuances, there will probably be no such concurrence. When the variation over comparatively short periods is as slight as in this case, an attempt to find extensive agreement on the rankings of six separate years is likely to meet with only indifferent success. But a less fine distinction, such as the statement that capabilities in the 1950's were notably lower than at some other time within the past seventy years, has a great deal more validity.

In any case, we can never expect perfect agreement among the indices. As Paul Lazarsfeld has said,

> Each individual indicator has only a probability relation to what we really want to know. A man might maintain his basic position, but by chance shift on an individual indicator; or he might change his basic position, but by chance remain stable on a specific indicator. But if we have many such indicators in an index, it is highly unlikely that a large number of them will all change in one direction, if the man we are studying has in fact not changed his basic position.[13]

Since we can expect only a probability relation, we must not be concerned if the indices do not agree precisely. Again, in Lazarsfeld's words:

> One pays a serious but unavoidable price for the practical advantages of the interchangeability of indices. Whatever index we use, the items will have some "peculiarities" which result in some cases being misclassified, and therefore the empirical relationships which we find are lower than they would be if we had more precise measures of the variables with which the study is concerned.[14]

But with these cautions, the agreement suggests that the trend we have found for a few mass and elite communications may be generalized. Further investigation into data on other pairs of nations should prove valuable.

[11] The rankings for the last four years correlate with a W of only .17 (using the Kendall Coefficient of Concordance), and almost all of this is due to the general agreement on 1928 as higher than later years. This falls just short of significance even at the .10 level.

[12] See, for instance, K. W. Deutsch, *Political Community at the International Level,* Princeton, 1954.

[13] Paul Lazarsfeld, "Evidence and Inference in Social Research," in Daniel Lerner, editor, *Evidence and Inference,* Glencoe, Illinois, 1959, p. 104.

[14] *Ibid.,* p. 109.

8

Political Socialization

To the extent that Americans come to like Britishers, to approve of Britain, and to value British culture highly, the more readily they may be expected to respond to British requests. We discussed many aspects of this phenomenon in the last two chapters, but there are a number of factors other than those measurable as transactions which operate to increase the favorable content of Americans' attitudes toward Britain, and of Britishers' toward America.

In the United States it is impossible not to be aware of the heritage from Britain. Literary works by English authors are read far more widely than those of any other foreign nation. Many major works by Frenchmen and Germans are neglected — they are unknown, or the language barrier apparently makes them lose too much in translation. Even the very name of our language reminds us continually of its origins and the fact that there are people in another country who use it. Our names, too, remind us of what we hold in common. American Christian names, and to a lesser extent surnames, are like those of the British; we may feel more at ease with a John than with a Jaroslav. And who can repeatedly pronounce the names of places like New Jersey, New York, and New England without recalling occasionally that there is an "old" York, an "old" England?

Our common political heritage is continually impressed upon us. The development of parliamentary democracy, the acquisition of basic rights, lies in a tradition that we know comes from England. The words remind us that the democratic tradition is not entirely indigenous — for example, we have no Parliament of our own to have given us the principles of "parliamentary procedure." It is hard to recall World War II without remembering who fought alone for a year and a half, and who was later our principal ally.

These common elements are not only practically part of the air most adult Americans breathe, but they are heavily stressed in our educational system, from grammar school to graduate school. And additional elements are pointed up in the education of the young and presumably impressionable. In a country which prizes prosperity and material progress, we learn that in the eighteenth century England was the world's most progressive nation, the leader in the Industrial Revolution. Our specialized subjects also emphasize the contributions of Britain and Britons. A study of political philosophy devotes a great amount of time to the outpourings of Hobbes, Locke, Burke, Bentham, Mill, and even John of Salisbury. Furthermore, it is made clear that the ancestry of American thought lies there, not through Rousseau or Hegel. The history of economic thought dwells less on the contributions of Marx and other Continental thinkers than on those of Adam Smith, Malthus, Ricardo, Marshall, and Keynes. A lawyer's training emphasizes the development of the American legal system from English common law. In philosophy we hear of Bishop Berkeley, Locke, Hume, Bertrand Russell, and Alfred North Whitehead. And in the natural sciences what three names are better known than Bacon, Newton, and Darwin? Our cultural closeness to Britain is to some extent reflected in our image of the physical world. In our minds we are likely to exaggerate the detachment of the British Isles from the Continent, and their nearness to us. It would be interesting to know how many Americans are aware that Portugal and Spain are not as far away as England, and that it is a shorter trip from New York to Cherbourg than to Southampton. Many of these same influences also operate, though perhaps with less force, to make Britons feel close to Americans.

We must specify carefully what the effects of this kind of relationship are likely to be. They do not make any significant contribution to our vital ability to *perceive* British needs. (We use the term "perception" to apply not just to the process of seeing that the British government is making a particular demand of our own government, but to seeing the reasons behind that demand.) But a high level of approval does induce us to treat those needs with sympathy and to accord them high priority, particularly in a crisis. Furthermore, it contributes to the phenomenon whereby we see an external threat as common. In principle, the British in 1946 might have visualized Soviet power not as a common danger to Britain and America, but as offering a potential ally for His Majesty against the United States.

The affective element of political socialization is at least partly responsible for the fact that this occurred to hardly anyone.

The Effects of Education

Probably the most potent factor in this respect is the acculturation received during the educational process. One would expect that the great attention American students give to English literature, and to English history with its stress on the development of democracy, would predispose them favorably toward things British. Satisfactory evidence on the degree to which attitudes toward England (rather than just information) would be absorbed during the educational process is scanty. Herbert Hyman refers to a number of studies indicating that the secondary school years form a period when school may be particularly influential, relative to other possible sources, in forming political attitudes.[1] A study by Carl I. Hovland and Walter Weiss testifies to the greater impact of sources of high credibility than those of low credibility on attitudes, even when the attitudes' source is long forgotten.[2] One would expect textbooks to be a very high credibility source for schoolchildren. Most suggestive is a nationwide survey of American adults which asked, "Where do you get most of your ideas about Great Britain and the English people?" Of the sample, 22 per cent mentioned "history" and another 6 per cent "school" as one of their principal sources.[3]

But in a study which has dealt with the dynamics of Anglo-American relations, we can hardly confine this discussion to statics. In both Britain and the United States far more people than ever before are being given secondary education. The increase in America is particularly striking. In 1870 high school graduates represented only 2 per cent of the population seventeen years old; that proportion rose steadily to over 62 per cent in 1956.[4] Should these people be exposed to substantially more information about the United Kingdom, and favorable or at least neutral attitudes, their exposure could work as a potent force to counteract the effects of some of the transactions trends noted earlier.

[1] Herbert Hyman, *Political Socialization,* Glencoe, Illinois, 1959, pp. 99–101.
[2] Carl I. Hovland and Walter Weiss, "The Influence of Source Credibility on Communications Effectiveness," *Public Opinion Quarterly,* XV, 4 (Winter 1952), pp. 635–650.
[3] Office of Public Opinion Research, June 3, 1942, reported in Hadley Cantril, *Public Opinion Research 1935–1946,* Princeton, 1951, p. 975.
[4] *Historical Statistics of the United States, Colonial Times to 1957,* Washington, 1960, p. 207.

In general, the situation is that while more secondary students are exposed to some information on Britain, the amount of attention paid to Britain and the British by those students is less than by high school pupils in the past. The American Historical Association's Committee of Seven urged, in 1899, that all schools offer a course specifically on English history. This committee's report was enormously influential; by 1910, it has been estimated, 43 per cent of all American high schools offered such a course.[5] Since 1910, however, emphasis on English history has declined notably, as Appendix Table 8.1 shows.

In 1922 almost one pupil in eight had a year of English history at some time during his high school career; by 1934 English history, as a separate subject, had vanished from the school curriculum. Medieval and modern history, which, in 1922, gave most of the other students some acquaintance with British history, also has shown a sharp decline in popularity since that time. A new course, world history, has arisen to absorb elements of English, medieval and modern, and ancient history, giving the student a smattering of all. The proportion of pupils in *some* course which touches on English history has remained quite constant: English, world, medieval and modern history combined accounted for about 20 per cent of all high school students in 1922, 21 per cent in 1928, 18 per cent in 1934, and somewhere just under 20 per cent in 1949. But the *amount* of English history to which each student was exposed fell substantially, as the more specific subjects, first English history, then medieval and modern, fell by the wayside and eventually were absorbed into world history. American history, on the other hand, now reaches almost every student during his stay.

To some slight extent this neglect has been made up by the development of another new subject, problems of democracy. This tends to be a very general course, concerned with aspects of sociology, consumer economics, civics, and international relations. One study of the content of problems textbooks gave the average proportion of attention to international relations as 5.5 per cent in 1922–24 and 7.7 per cent in 1935–38. By the end of the 1940's this figure may have risen to nearly 20 per cent. Yet such figures are deceptive, for the amount of attention to international relations varies widely from school to school as well as from time to time. The course is very flexible, and the texts include far more material than a teacher

[5] E. R. Carr, E. B. Wesley, and W. R. Murra, "Social Studies," in Walter S. Monroe, editor, *Encyclopedia of Educational Research,* New York, 1950, pp. 1213–1237.

could cover in a year. Only a few problems are selected for close study. For similar reasons the course syllabuses often put out by state boards of education tend to be even less reliable guides to course content. But on the whole, international affairs can occupy only a definite minority of the time in problems courses; specific attention to Britain is destined to be extremely brief.[6] In addition, certain changes in the geography course may have added somewhat to the study of Britain. While the proportion of students taking geography has remained relatively constant, the emphasis has shifted from the physical and commercial elements to geography as a social studies subject. Unfortunately, there is no way of knowing what proportion of these courses are American geography and what portion world geography.

Not all the attention to Britain need come in social studies, of course. Sympathy for England, a sense of the importance and value of the American cultural heritage from the British, and even some of the like-mindedness that contributes to mutual predictability could equally well come from the study of English literature. Since nearly every pupil is enrolled in a literature course most of the time he is in school, the opportunities for exposure in this area would seem great.

The best means of gauging the content of literature courses is the list of books recommended by the College Entrance Board to those preparing for the College Entrance Examinations. While this list was not binding, the importance of the exams forced schools to follow it quite closely, even for many students not expected to go to college. The first list, compiled for 1901–02, listed 16 books as essential; 13, or 81 per cent of these, were by British authors. In the last compendium, applying to the years 1929–34, 36 books were recommended; 27, or 75 per cent, were British.[7] After that, the board ceased to publish a list, presumably because of schools' objections to the restrictions it imposed. Practice now varies more than it once did, but works by British authors still take up, on the average, about 75 per cent of the time. Shakespeare, *Silas Marner,* and *The Rime of the Ancient Mariner* seem to be read almost everywhere.

But it is not enough to know the amount of attention given to Britain in schools, for that attention might be devoted to promoting hostility toward England and the English. Since at least the turn of the century, educators have been concerned about the possible detri-

---

[6] See Manson Van B. Jennings, *The Development of the Modern Problems Course in the Senior High School,* New York, 1950, esp. pp. 66–68; and J. Burroughs Stokes, "The Changing Content of Modern Problems Texts," *Social Education,* May 1940, pp. 338–341.

[7] Winnifred Quincy Norton, *Entrance English Questions,* New York, 1937, pp. xi–xxvi.

mental effects of nationalistic attitudes inculcated in the schools.[8] During World War I the influence of textbooks on American attitudes toward Britain came in for particular scrutiny from historians Albert Bushnell Hart and H. Morse Stephens and the novelist Owen Wister. Stephens told the 1916 meeting of the American Historical Association, "Americans are taught from childhood to hate Britishers by the study of American history." [9]

Charles Altschul compared the 40 most widely used textbooks in the 1890's with the 53 in widest use in 1916.[10] He found that in the 1890's only 20 per cent of the textbooks made any reference to general political conditions in England prior to the American Revolution and also mentioned some of the prominent Englishmen who devoted themselves to the American cause. Another 45 per cent failed to mention English political conditions, but did refer to Pitt or one or two other pro-American Englishmen. Fully 35 per cent gave the impression that virtually all prominent Britishers opposed the colonists' cause. By 1916 the situation had improved somewhat; the respective figures were 38 per cent, 34 per cent, and 28 per cent, and books in the first category were circulated more widely than before.[11] Efforts to remove bias continued after the war, and despite counterattacks had some success. While no one would suggest that all anti-British implications have been purged, schoolbooks seem likely to produce more favorable attitudes now than half a century ago.[12]

Our conclusions, then, are contradictory. There has been a very great increase in the number and proportion of Americans who are exposed, during their education, to a significant amount of information about Great Britain. To a notable extent that information has lost an earlier anti-British tone. But those students actually in high school in the past were given a deeper and more thorough acquaintance with things British, particularly in their history courses, than are their current counterparts in the more generalized courses.

Overemphasis of trends in high school education, however, obscures changes affecting higher education. Much of the dilution of

[8] See the discussion and bibliography in Merrill F. Hartshorn, "The Improvement of Instructional Materials," *Twenty-Fifth Yearbook of the National Council for the Social Studies,* 1954, pp. 441–473.

[9] Quoted in *ibid.,* p. 443. As early as 1869, Herbert Spencer remarked on "the traditional bitterness against England encouraged . . . even by the lessons in your schoolbooks." (Letter to *New York Tribune* in his *Autobiography,* New York, 1904, II, p. 587)

[10] Charles Altschul, *The American Revolution in Our School Textbooks,* with an introduction by James T. Shotwell, New York, 1917.

[11] *Ibid.,* pp. 21–30.

[12] Hartshorn, "Improvement," pp. 443–447, and I. James Quillen, *Textbook Improvement and International Understanding,* Washington, 1950.

the British content of secondary school courses is now compensated for in college. In the 1950's a far greater proportion of the population had some college education than had even been to secondary school in 1890. The vast majority of American college students are exposed to a substantial amount of information about Britain in literature courses and usually also in a course on international relations, comparative government, or European history. Specialized courses too, as discussed above, tend to contain a high British content.

As with high school students, it is essential to distinguish between the number of people affected and the depth of their acquaintance with things British. There is no evidence that students of today learn more about Britain than did university students three generations ago. What is clear is that because far more Americans go to college far more of them get at least this much acquaintance. Insofar as a much greater proportion of the elites and attentive public is composed of university-educated men and women (in 1954, 83 per cent of United States Senators had completed college, as compared with 40 per cent in 1890), this is especially significant.

In contrast to the notable attention given to England in the American educational system, until recently British secondary education almost entirely ignored the United States. Before the First World War there was almost no separate attention to the United States; it was treated, if at all, as a subordinate part of British or Empire history, or of British literature.[13] For the English schoolboy, American history stopped in 1783. The situation improved only slightly during the next thirty years. History courses were nearly always English, European, or ancient history, almost never world history. One author, studying the contents of 35 of the principal history books used in secondary schools, found that the American Civil War was mentioned in 6, Presidents Lincoln and Wilson in 2, and America's role in World War I in 4.[14] The same author found British texts relatively much more preoccupied with the scientific contributions of their own nationals than were corresponding American books.[15]

Many Britishers woke up to this neglect during the Second World War and took some steps to rectify it. H. C. Allen examined the teaching of American history in Britain in 1954, taking a sample of 25 public schools, 25 leading day or grammar schools, 20 city

[13] Sigmund Skard, *American Studies in Europe,* Philadelphia, 1958, I, pp. 45–57.
[14] R. T. Solis-Cohen, *A Comparative Study of the History Program in English and American Secondary Schools,* Philadelphia, 1939, pp. 83 ff.
[15] *Ibid.,* p. 74.

schools, and 20 county schools. He looked for the proportion of pupils who had "any significant study" of American history, defined as twenty-four periods of forty minutes each during a school life. Of the pupils in these schools, he found that the following proportion met the test: 22 per cent at the public schools, 9 per cent at leading day and grammar schools, 10 per cent at municipal schools, and 15 per cent at the county schools, with an over-all average of 14 per cent.[16] These percentages, however, are too high because his sample was far from random. In addition to grossly overweighting the public and leading grammar schools (only about 2 per cent of British secondary school pupils go to public schools), the best public schools were also overrepresented — the top four, Eton, Harrow, Rugby, and Winchester, were all included. Since public school students do more American history than others, and those in top public schools more than those in the second rank (65 per cent of Eton and Winchester pupils took American history), Allen's results are totally unreliable for the country at large. At best, they suggest only that elite attention to America at this stage is greater than nonelite attention.

A better source is the Ministry of Education's report that perhaps 5 per cent of secondary school students in the 1950's took Certificate Examinations of some sort in American history. In addition, possibly as many as 20 per cent of all students at least had the opportunity to take a course in American history without offering it for examination, though nowhere near this number in fact did so.[17] As to literature, Sigmund Skard declares, "Some American Literature is read, certainly more than before, sometimes even as part of the required syllabus. But it is all dependent on the interest of the teacher, is usually extra-curricular, and hardly contributes much to a rounded picture of the United States." [18] On the university level there has recently emerged, virtually for the first time, a small group of British historians interested in the post-1776 United States. Overall, we conclude that whereas attention to America has increased in the last decade or so, it is still far from substantial. Forces similar to those operating in the United States have been at work, but the American content of British education is much less than that of Britain in the American acculturative system.

[16] H. C. Allen, *American History in Britain,* London, 1956, pp. 4–5.

[17] *Ibid.,* p. 6, and Skard, *American Studies,* p. 77. See O. E. Shropshire, *The Teaching of History in English Schools,* New York, 1936, for data on the number of pupils who take any history course.

[18] Skard, *American Studies,* p. 76.

TABLE 8.1. Percentage of Americans Who Felt Most Friendly toward Britain and toward All Other Countries in Five Surveys

	Percentage			
Question	Britain	All Others	No Opinion	Number =
AIPO — December 1936 "Which of the European countries do you like best?"	46	36	18	2813
AIPO — January 1937 "Which foreign country do you like best?"	43	35	22	2874
AIPO — October 1938* "Which European country do you like best?"	36	35	29	2775
Fortune — November 1938** "Toward which of these foreign governments do you feel most friendly?"	45	32	23	5274
Fortune — November 1938** "Toward which of these foreign peoples do you feel most friendly?"	40	30	30	5274
Benson & Benson — September 1948 "Which foreign people do you feel most friendly toward?"	31	45	24	1015

* For this survey "Britain" includes only those respondents answering "Britain" or "England"; "Scotland" was coded in a residual "All Others" category. On the earlier surveys 1 per cent of the respondents listed Scotland as a favorite country, so properly the figures for Britain would probably be 37 per cent and All Others 34 per cent.

** Unlike all other questions in this table, these were not open-ended. The respondent was given a list of seven European countries and Japan from which to choose.

SOURCE: American Institute of Public Opinion and Fortune Surveys from the Roper Public Opinion Research Center at Williams College, Williamstown, Massachusetts. The Benson & Benson survey appears in William Buchanan and Hadley Cantril, *How Nations See Each Other*, Urbana, Illinois, 1953, p. 216.

The difference between the proportions preferring Britain in 1948 and in October 1938 (which gives the lowest percentage naming Britain of any prewar study) is significant at the .02 level (i.e., the chances are only 2 in 100 that the sample surveys would produce such a finding if there was not really such a difference in the population at large). The difference between the 1948 proportion and that in January 1937 (the most nearly identical question) is significant well above the .01 mark.

Mass and Elite Opinion

But these trends are merely in forces which tend to promote mutual approval; they are not in themselves measures of that approval. They give no evidence that the acculturation has been effective and not offset by other influences, such as the general decline in communication and attention. By far the most direct, and probably the most accurate, method of ascertaining the degree of popular approval on both sides of the Atlantic is through the analysis of survey data.

Many nationwide surveys conducted over the past twenty-five years have asked for Americans' opinions of England, or Britons' attitudes toward their American cousins, but few questions have been repeated over the years in the same or similar form. The most important difference in phraseology is the substitution of the word "government" for "people" in a question like "Toward which of these foreign peoples do you feel most friendly?" Another difficulty may stem from comparing open-ended with closed questions — that is, one that asks a respondent toward what country he is most friendly, and one which asks toward which country on a particular list he feels most friendly. This may be important in the United States if, as was the case in one survey, Canada is omitted. But fortunately the basic question was asked often enough to give us several cross checks and show that variations in phraseology did not, in this case, make a critical difference. (See Table 8.1.) This sort of question has been asked only twice in the United Kingdom, so a different set of queries is needed as a supplement. (See Tables 8.2 and 8.3.)

TABLE 8.2. Percentage of Britishers Who Felt Most Friendly toward America and toward All Other Countries in Two Surveys

	Percentage			
Question	America	All Others	No Opinion	Number =
BIPO — July 1939 "Which foreign country do you prefer?"	33	49	19	1000
BIPO — July 1948 "Which foreign people do you feel most friendly toward?"	29	56	15	1195

SOURCE: Data on the 1939 survey were provided by Social Surveys, Ltd., in London; the 1948 survey is reported in Buchanan and Cantril, p. 140. The difference is significant at the .05 level.

TABLE 8.3. Percentage of Britishers Who Felt Friendly, Un-friendly, and Neutral toward the United States in Six Surveys

	Percentage			
Question	Favorable	Unfavorable	Neutral, No Opinion	Number =
BIPO — March 1941 "How do you feel toward the United States?"	88	2	10	1000
BIPO — October 1956 "How do you feel toward the American government?"	52	11	37	2000
BIPO — October 1956 "How do you feel toward the American people?"	64	9	27	2000
USIA — October 1958 "What is your opinion of the United States?"	61	9	30	611
USIA — November 1959 "What is your opinion of the United States?"	63	8	29	1000
USIA — February 1960 "What is your opinion of the United States?"	66	6	28	1221
USIA — May 1960 "What is your opinion of the United States?"	51	13	36	1150

SOURCE: British Institute of Public Opinion data provided by Social Surveys, Ltd. Findings by the United States Information Agency appeared in the *New York Times*, October 27, 1960, 28: 4–5. The difference between the result of the 1941 study and each of the later ones is significant at the .001 level.

One might expect that because of temporary conditions or the current policies of a foreign power, the power's popularity might fluctuate widely without any change in basic underlying variables. But in the cases shown in the tables we are able to examine a number of surveys conducted at different periods, with the basic result always the same — a sharp decline, since the beginning of World War II, in the mutual popularity of Britain and America in each other's eyes. In Table 8.1, five different questions on four different surveys all show significantly wider approval of Great Britain than does the survey of 1948.

Different surveys produce equivalent results in the British Isles. With both sets of questions there is a significant drop in American popularity between the prewar and postwar periods. The latest decline, in May 1960, probably represented a temporary response to the U-2 incident and the collapse of the summit conference, particularly since the division was so stable on the earlier post-1945 surveys. But overall, the question was asked in so many different forms, and at so many different times, that it surely seems a valid indicator of opinion change. On the level of popular approval, the two countries have drifted apart during the last generation. This occurred despite the trends in their educational systems which should have brought them closer together, all else being equal.

The finding discredits two hypotheses put forth by Buchanan and Cantril. They suggested that two of the principal reasons for the great popularity of countries like Britain and America in each other's eyes were their shared experiences in fighting World War II together, and a feeling of solidarity in the current "Bi-Polar World." [19] Yet some factor or factors far more powerful than their common causes operated to pull them apart over the period. Perhaps, as is suggested elsewhere in this study, the experience of alliance is not necessarily one which ties nations together. The resentments, distractions, and strains on each other's capabilities may just as well become disrupting forces.

Other kinds of trends are discernible over a longer period. A number of writers have interpreted the American Revolution as one which was initiated by the colonial gentry but which got out of hand and became a lower- and middle-class revolt against vested interests and governing cliques.[20] As a result the lower classes in America had substantial political power from the birth of the Republic, and especially after the age of Jackson. But this revolt never occurred in Britain, and the working class there achieved power very slowly, reaching its peak only in the last two decades. There is little evidence that this group currently is more favorably disposed toward the United States than upper-status groups, but it was once. Despite unemployment caused by the Northern blockade of Confederate cotton

[19] William Buchanan and Hadley Cantril, *How Nations See Each Other,* Urbana, Ill., 1953, pp. 39–44.

[20] See C. L. Becker, *History of Political Parties in the Province of New York,* Madison, Wis., 1909; J. F. Jameson, *The American Revolution Considered as a Social Movement,* Princeton, 1906; and A. M. Schlesinger, *Colonial Merchants and the American Revolution,* New York, 1918. Not all historians agree with this interpretation, but most critics argue, not that the lower classes failed to achieve substantial power, but rather that they had it anyway, long before the Revolution. See Robert E. Brown, *Middle-Class Democracy and the Revolution in Massachusetts,* Ithaca, 1955.

exports, English textile workers maintained a sympathy for the Union during the Civil War that was not shared by the aristocracy.[21] Part of this attitude was undoubtedly a sympathy for the country where the democratic revolution had succeeded. The rise in power of British labor since 1890 may have helped to strengthen the bond between the two countries. In the United States, just because the democratic revolution succeeded, there has been a certain antipathy to the class-bound British that probably persists even now.[22] But because the lower classes had much power even from the beginning, it has not been a factor important in the *trend* of Anglo-American relations. Possibly their antipathy has been weakened somewhat by their greater exposure to pro-British influences in American education in recent years. Intensive research on these matters might prove extremely profitable.

TABLE 8.4.   Favorable Judgments as Percentage of All Judgments by Britain and America of Each Other and of All Outside World

	London Times		*New York Times*	
Years	*(1)* *Of U.S.*	*(2)* *Of All Outside World*	*(3)* *Of U.K.*	*(4)* *Of All Outside World*
1890–1913	59	52	49	44
World War I	83	24	93	27
World War II	85	57	69	63
1946–1949	66	43	64	36

SOURCE: Columns (2) and (4) from Ithiel de Sola Pool, *Symbols of Internationalism*, Stanford, 1951, p. 23; column (3) from *ibid.*, p. 33; column (1) adapted from figures on p. 25 with aid of column (3). Insufficient data provided on interwar years.

There are indications of a distinct rise in approval among the elites. Pool's study of prestige-paper editorials, referred to in Chapter 6, examined the degree to which they expressed approval of each other's countries. Table 8.4 shows the results of this study.

[21] In the survey material cited earlier, there is no significant correlation between status or income and friendliness toward the United States. On earlier attitudes, note Herbert Spencer's comments: "Their social position, their class-interests, their traditional opinions, have always predisposed our 'upper ten thousand' to look coolly on a society like yours. And irritated as they were by having the success of American institutions held up to them as a reproach, it is not surprising that they were ready to say and do unfriendly things whenever the opportunity offered." (Letter in *Autobiography*, p. 589)

[22] Buchanan and Cantril, *How Nations See Each Other*, p. 140, show a highly significant (.001 level) correlation between high income and pro-British attitudes.

If we exclude the wartime periods, in the elite papers of both Britain and America we find a growing proportion of favorable judgments over the years. And in each case they approve more of each other than of the rest of the world, giving grounds for optimism about the bonds between the two nations. It may be significant, nevertheless, that mutual approval dropped sharply after the wars. Pool declares simply that great one-sidedness of judgments is typical of an overly self-conscious alliance. As proof he cites the degree of British and American approval of Russia during the Second World War.[23] (It should be mentioned that Russian-American and Russian-British approval during World War II, while high, was not quite as high as that between the United States and England.) Of the decline since, he says that the British-American alliance is extremely close, close enough "not to be threatened by honest discussion." He may be correct, but the data could equally well illustrate a weakened alliance if one were to start with the assumption that it had become enfeebled.

Cultural Differences and Uniformities

Great Britain and the United States are culturally very similar: Britons and Americans tend to value the same things, to share similar attitudes. They tend to have very similar attitudes toward authority and to react in like and mutually predictable ways.[24] Under most circumstances we can better predict how a Britisher would act than how an Indian or even a Spaniard would.

To be specific, similarity of culture means a high degree of predictability from introspection. This is likely to be especially helpful in avoiding frictions. The Russians, for instance, have what we consider an almost pathological fear of penetration, of the presence of foreign agents for espionage or sabotage.[25] Americans, perhaps, are devoted to the proposition that policy must be based on near-perfect information. Neither party seems fully aware of the strength of these attitudes in the other. To the extent that these hypotheses are correct, they explain much of the divergence between the American and Soviet approaches to nuclear test inspection. In Anglo-American relations it seems plausible to suggest that the two nations, partly because of cultural differences, react differently to a threat to their supplies from overseas. Americans may react with stockpiling, or

[23] Ithiel de Sola Pool, *Symbols of Internationalism*, Stanford, 1951, p. 33.
[24] Gabriel A. Almond, *Citizenship in Modern Democracies*, Princeton, forthcoming, explores these matters.
[25] Nathan Leites, *A Study of Bolshevism*, Glencoe, Illinois, 1953, pp. 288–303.

building up alternative sources of supply. Englishmen, on the other hand, may respond with positive measures to keep the particular supply line open. (Obviously, cultural differences are not the entire explanation. On this matter wealth and the degree of dependence on overseas supply are highly relevant also.) Neither can understand just why the other's reaction takes the form it does. These are quite speculative hypotheses, but they serve to illustrate the way in which cultural factors can cause frictions through misunderstanding. One of the strengths of Anglo-American relations is that this friction is very slight compared with that between nations of more dissimilar cultures.

Similarity of cultures is important, in a negative way, in reducing frictions, but its role as a positive force in promoting responsiveness is more tenuous. If we and the British shared the same attitudes toward supply lines, it would be easier for us to understand why they were willing to fight for the Suez Canal; in this sense, we could more readily perceive the psychological basis of their demands. But it would not help us to see the basis of the need in the particular case, i.e., the degree of their dependence on this lifeline. Only an appropriate level of transactions can carry this kind of information. And a willingness to meet the demand depends on the degree to which we consider it in our interest to do so (conditions in the entire world are relevant here) and on the degree of sympathy and approval we feel toward the British. Similarity of culture makes a modest positive contribution to responsiveness, especially as we tend to approve of those who are like us, but in general it is far more influential as a means of eliminating friction.

As with approval, trends are extremely important. We referred earlier to the decreasing predominance of citizens of British origin in the American ethnic make-up. Not only are descendants of the later immigrants a greater proportion of all Americans, but they are also beginning to form an appreciable proportion of the attentive public and even of the elites. John Fitzgerald Kennedy's election to the Presidency merely emphasizes a process that has occurred in business, the media, and local, state, and national government throughout the country. Of itself this would tend to diminish the elements of similarity between British and American culture, but it has been counteracted by the substantial assimilation of these immigrants into Anglo-Saxon norms and culture. President Kennedy, at Choate and Harvard, experienced the full upper-class education of British-Americans. This assimilation is reflected throughout American life; the foreign-language press, for example, has only a fraction of its onetime readership. Yet the process is not entirely one-way. The contents of the melting pot, though they remain dominated by the original flavor, are not that alone — the immigrant nationalities have modified Anglo-Saxon strains as well. The widespread adoption of Italian food illustrates in a trivial and obvious way a process that has not been confined entirely to the trivial and obvious.

There cannot, of course, be any process comparable with this in Britain, but the emergence of the British lower class as a political force has in an important way tended to increase the similarity of the British and American political cultures. The process of leveling and equalization are far from complete, but they have progressed a long way since 1890. In the words of one perceptive commentator:

> There is reason to think, however, that fundamental changes are occurring in the relations between government and citizen. Ordinary people in Britain are entering more into politics, and public opinion is becoming more ebullient, restive, and assertive. The lower class no longer feels exaggerated respect for its betters. . . . British democracy is still deferential, but it is less so than a generation ago, and before long it may be very little so.[26]

To sum up, there is evidence that at the elite level American and British attitudes toward each other have improved substantially during the past seventy years. Over a shorter period, the last twenty-five years, it seems clear that mass sympathies for the other country have weakened. On balance, the British and American political cultures probably have become more alike with the assimilation of non-Anglo-Saxon immigrants in the United States and the wider acceptance of egalitarian values in Britain. The strength of a contrary trend, the dilution of Anglo-Saxon culture in the United States, is difficult to evaluate, but it seems unlikely to outweigh the effects of the other two forces. In a later chapter we shall speculate on the possible results of these trends under various conceivable circumstances.

[26] Edward C. Banfield, "The Political Implications of Metropolitan Growth," *Daedalus,* Winter 1961, p. 67.

9

Testing Capabilities:
The House of Commons and the Senate

One serious gap remains to be filled — we must show that the decline in capabilities is relevant to the making of political decisions. In earlier chapters we assumed, sometimes on the basis of ambiguous evidence from other studies, that the various links under consideration did tend to make individuals responsive to the other nation's needs. There was no evidence, however, that in the specific case of Britain and America these ties made an important difference. Particularly in this case, where so many channels of mass communication exist, the presence or absence of a direct personal tie might not, to any significant degree, affect the likelihood that a particular decision-maker will be responsive. If not, it would be hard to prove that a decline in many gross links, such as the proportion of the two economies engaged in Anglo-American trade, would seriously affect actual responsiveness. We shall fill this gap by examining the personal backgrounds of individual members of the House of Commons and the Senate, and by comparing their votes or public statements on policy matters.

Ties and Responsiveness: Commons

For the House of Commons, I chose to analyze public statements on policy rather than voting patterns. A Member of Parliament virtually *never* votes against his party; and almost all votes, certainly all votes on issues even remotely associated with foreign affairs, are ones on which the party takes a stand. If he does defy the whips, he risks expulsion from the Parliamentary party, abandonment by his constituency organization, and defeat in the next general election. A single lapse may be overlooked, but repeated violations of discipline will almost certainly end his political career. Even "crossing the floor" to the other party offers little hope — no member has done so, and been returned at the next election, since 1945. This is not to imply that British parties are dictatorial and can march M.P.'s into their lobbies at will. There may be much pushing and hauling before a policy is settled, and the leadership must always beware of antagonizing the rank-and-file too seriously. But once policy is set and made a matter of public record, the M.P. who attacks it does so at his great peril. Thus, an examination of voting records would tell us little about a Member's true feelings.

Although an M.P. seldom votes against his leaders, he may abstain from voting somewhat more freely. Abstention is a recognized way of showing disagreement and is less likely to be punished by the leadership unless done repeatedly. Unfortunately, the recording of abstentions (or better, absences) at divisions shows no significant pattern. Abstention can show those who are really interested how one feels on a matter — constituents, interest groups, or fellow Members can note one's abstention, and the leaders against whom one wants to protest will surely notice it. But even on an important measure there usually are many involuntary absences due to illness and business or personal demands for Members' presence elsewhere. One who merely reads the report of a division several years after the event, without knowing the reasons for a particular M.P.'s failure to be recorded, can rarely discern a significant pattern.

But it is not unusual for a Member, even though he may vote as directed in the end, to criticize a policy during debate, to ask a hostile question during question time, or to oppose the policy in a speech to his constituents or another group. He feels particularly free to do so during the period before an official party position has been adopted. For example, the Labour party directed its members to abstain on ratification of the 1954 London and Paris agreements to rearm a sovereign West Germany. Yet by the time the vote was taken, almost half the Labour M.P.'s had expressed an opinion either in Parliament, in letters to newspapers, or in outside speeches reported by a London or major provincial paper. In addition to providing information on Members' real feelings about matters which come up for division in the House, this kind of analysis also gives their views on a great number of issues that are never made a matter of record vote.

Much of this material, and practically all of it for the earlier years analyzed, came from the Parliamentary debates themselves. For 1938 and 1954 this could be supplemented by reports of debates at the annual party conferences, and by party publications which cull from newspapers and private speeches relevant statements — particularly those which might embarrass the opposition. These include the Tory *Hints for Speakers* and the *Liberal Magazine*. For 1954 there was also a superb collection of clippings at the Conservative and Unionist Central Office in London, containing a complete file of all reports of statements by M.P.'s in the London press, the most important country papers, and periodicals like the *New Statesman*. Though the files for a few deceased M.P.'s had been disposed of, there were still, in 1960, clippings on over 90 per cent of the 1954 members of the Commons. Because these supplementary sources were not available for 1890, and only in part for 1938, the following tables record far more expressions of opinion in 1954 than in the two earlier years combined.

The following types of issues or statements were considered as involved in Anglo-American relations. A detailed list of particular issues is in Appendix C.

1. Explicit criticism or approval of the other government or nation. (Criticism of individuals was not included unless it appeared that the speaker meant it to apply to the government itself or to all or most members of the other nationality. Thus, criticism of President Eisenhower would probably be recorded as an attack on the United States, but remarks about Senator McCarthy might not be.)
2. A call for weaker or stronger ties with the other country.
3. Policies intended to increase mutual capabilities for responsiveness (whether by the creation of common institutions or by such means as eliminating restrictions on travel).
4. Ratification of a treaty signed by both governments.
5. A direct economic interest of the other country (tariffs or foreign aid).
6. Restrictions on the freedom of the government to conclude international agreements (the Bricker Amendment).
7. An expressed desire by the other government.

The various kinds of ties an M.P. might have with America were identified and classified in the same way as in Table 6.7. There were economic ties of several sorts: "strong" personal ties of birth, education, marriage, or residence; and "weak" personal ties of travel, war service, and honors. In addition, I obtained data on membership in the Pilgrims of Great Britain in 1938 and 1954 and in the English-Speaking Union in 1954.[1] These associations have the specific aim of

---

[1] From correspondence with the secretary of the Pilgrims and conversation with the secretary of the English-Speaking Union. In the latter case, the records of membership in 1954 had been destroyed, and the secretary gave

promoting closer Anglo-American relations. I also had some supplementary sources on travel to America by Members of Parliament in 1954. Publicity material provided by the party headquarters frequently mentioned Members' travel experiences. In addition, I learned from several individuals about particular M.P.'s who had visited in the United States before 1954. Thus, quite a few more M.P.'s will be listed in the following tables as having personal ties to America than were so listed in Chapter 6, where the emphasis was on comparability from one year to the next. Even so, there must have been a number with ties that could not be identified. The class of M.P.'s without ties means, in the following tables, merely those with no known links. Nevertheless, we shall see that there is a significant difference between the responsiveness of M.P.'s who we know have ties and those for whom there is no such evidence.

The information on attitudes is analyzed in two ways. First, every M.P. is classified either as responsive, unresponsive, or neutral — "neutral" meaning here that no policy statement on any of these issues was recorded. Second, it was useful to record the number of statements on separate issues made by each M.P. Thus, if a Member is recorded as responsive on one issue and unresponsive on two others, he is treated as, on balance, unresponsive, and a one is entered in the appropriate cell on the *left*-hand side of Table 9.1. But on the *right*-hand side of the table we list individual statements on issues, so a one is recorded under "responsive" and a two under "unresponsive." The totals will not always add up to 100 per cent because figures have been rounded.

In every subsection of Table 9.1 the same pattern holds. M.P.'s with ties of any sort to the United States are more likely to speak up on matters affecting Anglo-American relations than are M.P.'s without ties. And when they speak, they are more likely to be responsive. This is true whether each particular M.P. is characterized as responsive or unresponsive, or whether the statements are examined individually. In many of the subsections of Table 9.1 there are not enough cases for the results to be statistically significant even at the .10 level, but they are so in the three with the greatest number of cases. For M.P.'s, the relationship between ties and responsiveness is significant at the .02 level in the table for all years combined. And for statements, the relationship is significant at well above the .01 level both for 1954 and for all years combined.

For 1954, there are enough cases to control for party affiliation. (See Table 9.2.) The results are the same. For individual M.P.'s,

---

me the names only of those he was certain were members then. That list is therefore accurate as far as it goes, but is not all-inclusive.

TABLE 9.1.   Percentage of M.P.'s with and without American Ties
Who Were Responsive, Unresponsive, and Neutral, and of Responsive and Unresponsive Statements

1890

M.P.'s	Res.	Neut.	Unres.	Statements by M.P.'s	Res.	Unres.
U.S. Ties (N = 24)	8	88	4	U.S. Ties (N = 4)	50	50
No U.S. Ties (N = 118)	0	96	4	No U.S. Ties (N = 5)	0	100

1938

M.P.'s	Res.	Neut.	Unres.	Statements by M.P.'s	Res.	Unres.
U.S. Ties (N = 31)	16	81	3	U.S. Ties (N = 8)	88	12
No U.S. Ties (N = 101)	8	88	4	No U.S. Ties (N = 19)	79	21

1954

M.P.'s	Res.	Neut.	Unres.	Statements by M.P.'s	Res.	Unres.
U.S. Ties (N = 40)	20	60	20	U.S. Ties (N = 56)	48	52
No U.S. Ties (N = 89)	16	52	33	No U.S. Ties (N = 125)	26	74

All Years Combined

M.P.'s	Res.	Neut.	Unres.	Statements by M.P.'s	Res.	Unres.
U.S. Ties (N = 95)	16	74	10	U.S. Ties (N = 68)	53	47
No U.S. Ties (N = 308)	7	81	12	No U.S. Ties (N = 149)	32	68

the association of ties and responsiveness is as hypothesized, but not
to a statistically significant degree. For the analysis by statements,
however, the association is significant at the .01 level. The uniformity
of direction identified in the two sections of the table and the high

TABLE 9.2.   Percentage of M.P.'s with and without American Ties
Who Were Responsive, Unresponsive, and Neutral, and of Responsive and Unresponsive Statements, with Party Affiliation Controlled,
1954*

M.P.'s	Res.	Neut.	Un-res.	Statements by M.P.'s	Res.	Un-res.
Conservative (N = 64)	(16)	(67)	(17)	*Conservative* (N = 44)	(50)	(50)
U.S. Ties (N = 26)	19	65	16	U.S. Ties (N = 20)	70	30
No U.S. Ties (N = 38)	13	68	19	No U.S. Ties (N = 24)	33	67
Labour (N = 62)	(18)	(40)	(42)	*Labour* (N = 132)	(26)	(74)
U.S. Ties (N = 14)	21	50	29	U.S. Ties (N = 36)	36	64
No U.S. Ties (N = 48)	17	37	46	No U.S. Ties (N = 96)	22	78

* Three M.P.'s — two Liberals and one Irish Nationalist — are not included.

significance often found form as persuasive a proof as could be expected with these data.

Note that the association between party and responsiveness is also quite strong, since Conservatives are much more likely to be responsive than are Labourites. In the "M.P.'s" section of the table the relationship is significant at the .02 level; in the "Statements" part it is significant at .001, an extremely high level. The relationship between party and responsiveness, in fact, is stronger on both sides of the table than is that between ties to the United States and responsiveness.[2] A Labour M.P. *with* a tie to America is less likely to indicate responsiveness than is a Conservative M.P. *without* an identifiable tie. We can only speculate on the reasons. *Part* of the explanation undoubtedly is that Conservatives tend to get most of their ideas from other Conservatives, and the same is true of Labourites. Since almost twice as many Conservatives as Labourites have known ties with America, their views probably carry a heavier "weight" in the informal opinion-forming processes of their party. Similarly, the greater "weight" of men with ties in the Conservative party must give them a better chance of invoking party discipline in their favor. Although discipline is not enforced nearly so stringently in speeches as in voting, it is nevertheless a factor. But possibly the most important element lies in bonds with America of which we have no knowledge. It seems very probable that Conservatives, having on the whole more money, are more likely to have traveled to the United States than Labourites; and having more business connections, they are more likely to have an economic link with the United States that was not caught in the rather wide-meshed net used to find M.P.'s with commercial ties.

Ties and Responsiveness: The Senate

One of the principal flaws in this kind of analysis is its implicit assumption that all topics on which an opinion might be expressed are of equal importance, both to the speaker and to the other government in question. Thus an M.P. might criticize the United States for its shipping subsidies, aid to Franco Spain, and lack of civil liberties, but support the American-backed program of German rearmament. Quite possibly, the United States government would value the support on German rearmament highly enough to offset the other criticisms, and in an important sense the M.P. would be more "pro-

---

[2] For "M.P.'s" the contingency coefficient for party and responsiveness is .29 and that for ties and responsiveness just .04. For "Statements" the comparable figures are .25 and .18.

American" than another Member whose attitudes on all four issues were the opposite. Thus there might be a serious fallacy in simply counting the number of issues on which the Member supported or criticized American policy. Yet in practice there is no thoroughly satisfactory way of weighting the issues. No two observers could agree whether a statement on German rearmament was worth two statements on other policies, or worth four pronouncements, and so on, down a list of twenty additional issues.

In the particular case, this handicap was not too serious. For the three years under study, nearly three quarters of the M.P.'s expressing opinions did so uniformly — they were either always responsive to the United States, or always unresponsive, thus substantially eliminating the weighting difficulty. Still, a more systematic method of solving this problem would be desirable, and it is offered by Guttman scale analysis. The essential principle of scale analysis is this:

> The items can be arranged in an order so that an individual who agrees with, or responds to any particular item also responds positively to all items of lower rank order. The rank order of items is the scale of items; the scale of persons is very similar, people being arranged in order according to the highest rank order of items checked, which is equivalent to the number of positive responses in a perfect scale.[3]

The classic illustration is a group of questions regarding height. If you ask a man if he is over six feet tall and he responds affirmatively, you know that he will also answer yes to questions asking if he is over five feet ten inches in height, or over five feet eight.

By finding that the issues in Anglo-American relations could be scaled, we would sidestep the "weight problem." That is, we might find that with regard to responsiveness to the United States, the four issues — Spain, civil liberties, subsidies, and German rearmament — ranked in that order. A man who opposed American aid to Spain would be unresponsive on all other issues. Similarly, if he defended the state of American civil liberties but criticized American shipping subsidies, he would also support assistance to Spain but oppose arming the Germans. We have not solved the weight problem in the sense of saying which issue is more "important," but we have avoided the necessity of worrying about it. We do not have to decide whether support on German rearmament is "worth" opposition on the other three matters, for such a situation will never occur. The procedure

[3] Bert F. Green, "Attitude Measurement," in Gardner Lindzey, editor, *Handbook of Social Psychology*, Cambridge, Mass., 1954, II, p. 353. Scale analysis was developed by Louis Guttman, in Samuel Stouffer *et al., Measurement and Prediction*, Vol. 4 of *Studies in Social Psychology in World War II*, Princeton, 1950, pp. 60–90.

gives us a method of ordering M.P.'s from most responsive to least responsive in a meaningful and consistent way.

The result is that we can describe the pattern of responses as "unidimensional" in scale-analysis terms. The items in the scale measure related attitudes on a particular topic. We cannot be sure what basic feelings are responsible for the statements made by the various M.P.'s, but we can be reasonably sure that all the particular measures were regarded as aspects of one general policy by the Members. A man who is normally highly responsive will not have been unresponsive on one issue because of extraneous factors.

The discussion in the last two paragraphs is of course an oversimplification. Hardly ever is unidimensionality so perfect that there are no variations within the scale, no "errors" where a man is responsive when we should expect him to be unresponsive. Other factors do operate to some extent, but the amount of variation must be very limited if we still are to treat the list of issues as forming a scale. By convention, the response of no more than one man in ten may be in "error" on any item, and the total number of "errors" for all items may not exceed 10 per cent of the number of items times the number of men. Thus the effect of extraneous variables is kept to a minimum.

It must be emphasized that the creation of a scale does not eliminate the need for sound judgment by the researcher. One might indeed be measuring a single dimension, but it need not be the dimension which one is really trying to measure. In deciding what issues to try to put into the scale, and in interpreting the meaning of that scale when completed, one must know what the issues signified and have a set of independent criteria for picking them out. In this case I used the criteria specified earlier for issues involved in Anglo-American relations. No issues which did not meet the original criteria were proposed, and it was essential that at least most of those items which did meet the criteria be capable of incorporation into the scale.[4]

This procedure makes it possible to rank legislators from most responsive to least responsive. The data are too incomplete to apply this method to the study of M.P.'s attitudes — most Members do not express themselves on any given issue — but I have been able to apply it to voting in the United States Senate. In most of the analysis below, it will be necessary to simplify the results, merely classifying lawmakers into three groups — responsive, moderate, and unresponsive — of as nearly equal size as possible. But the reader should remember that the information was made available through a complete ordering.

[4] For further information and list of votes, see Appendix C.

Like any other quantitative tool which imposes a certain amount of simplification on a complex reality, this procedure has its faults. It cannot tell us whether a legislator holds a particular opinion firmly or with little intensity. His action may stem from deep conviction or strong interest-group pressure, or he may simply be "logrolling" for support on issues of more importance to him. Perhaps an influential legislator determines the votes of a number of "satellites" on an issue.

These refinements can be made only with such other approaches as interviewing and analysis of debates and public statements. But if these two methods are used in tandem, it is possible to get the benefits of both while avoiding most of the pitfalls which either alone sets. The analysis of public statements is peculiarly suited to the House of Commons, where roll-call votes are relatively rare and a Member seldom votes against his party. On the other hand, the examination of voting patterns is peculiarly suited to the Senate, where the opposite conditions prevail. If, using the two techniques, one in each body, we find that similar variables have similar effects on lawmakers' attitudes, we shall have very strong evidence of the validity of the relationships so identified.

TABLE 9.3. Percentage of Senators with and without British Ties Who Were Responsive, Moderate, and Unresponsive

1890

Senators	Responsive	Moderate	Unresponsive
U.K. Ties (N = 49)	37	33	31
No U.K. Ties (N = 35)	9	46	46

1954

Senators	Responsive	Moderate	Unresponsive
U.K. Ties (N = 23)	48	22	30
No U.K. Ties (N = 73)	27	33	40

Both Years Combined

Senators	Responsive	Moderate	Unresponsive
U.K. Ties (N = 72)	40	29	31
No U.K. Ties (N = 108)	21	37	42

Just as with M.P.'s, we find a consistent relationship between the possession of personal or economic ties and responsiveness. For 1890 the relationship is significant at the .01 level; for 1954 and for the two years combined it is significant at the .10 level. A similar pattern emerges when we control for party affiliation. Since the conditions of partisanship were quite different in the two years, we shall give no totals for both combined.

TABLE 9.4.   Percentage of Senators with and without British Ties Who Were Responsive, Moderate, and Unresponsive, with Party Affiliation Controlled*

1890

Senators	Responsive	Moderate	Unresponsive
Democratic (N = 37)	(57)	(43)	(0)
U.K. Ties (N = 27)	67	33	0
No U.K. Ties (N = 10)	30	70	0
Republican (N = 47)	(0)	(34)	(66)
U.K. Ties (N = 22)	0	32	68
No U.K. Ties (N = 25)	0	36	64

1954

Senators	Responsive	Moderate	Unresponsive
Democratic (N = 48)	(40)	(25)	(35)
U.K. Ties (N = 15)	40	20	40
No U.K. Ties (N = 33)	39	27	33
Republican (N = 47)	(23)	(36)	(40)
U.K. Ties (N = 8)	63	25	13
No U.K. Ties (N = 39)	15	38	46

* The year 1954 excludes one Independent.

In two of the cases in Table 9.4 the control for party affiliation emphasizes the importance of personal and economic bonds. For Democrats in 1890 and Republicans in 1954, the relationship is marked and highly significant (.01 level). For Republicans in 1890 and Democrats in 1954, however, there is no such relationship. But as we shall show, the latter finding is due to the fact that in 1954 constituency ties were entirely without effect in promoting responsiveness. If only direct ties, economic and personal, are considered, those 1954 Democrats who have them prove highly responsive.

As is evident from the most cursory examination of these tables, party affiliation was an important variable. Particularly in 1890 party discipline (or perhaps like-mindedness, we cannot tell which) was extremely powerful in foreign affairs. We cannot be sure why, but an explanation would undoubtedly include many of the same factors as were offered regarding the difference in responsiveness between the Conservative and Labour parties. This sheds light on the political situation of the late nineteenth century when the Democratic party was often accused of being pro-British, despite its dependence on the votes of Irish-Americans. Here is evidence that the Democrats were, in an important sense, much more "pro-British" than their opponents. On every issue affecting Anglo-American relations a majority of Democrats was ranged on the responsive side against a majority of Republicans. Exactly 62 per cent of the Senators never voted against the party on these issues — 21 Democrats and 31 Republicans. The "moderate" section includes *all* who ever voted against their party.

We can use this information to illustrate the influence of ties in another way. In 24 instances a Democrat voted against his party in an unresponsive manner; in 31 cases a Republican went against his party in order to be responsive. If we distinguish between those Senators with and without ties and make a ratio of the number of votes against party over the number of Senators in each class, we have the figures given in Table 9.5. Note that the existence of a tie with Britain has a

TABLE 9.5. Votes Cast against Party per Senator, Senators with and without Ties to Britain, 1890

Senators	Ratio of Responsive Votes	Ratio of Unresponsive Votes
Ties to U.K.	0.73	0.33
No Ties to U.K.	0.60	1.50

greater effect in moderating opposition to British wishes (column 2) than as a positive force in promoting responsiveness (column 1).

Kinds of Ties

I also wished to know whether two or more links per lawmaker would be more effective than a single tie. Table 9.6 gives data for the House of Commons. In the left-hand side of the table we see that Members with two ties were actually *less* likely to be responsive than those with only a single tie. On the other hand, Members with two or

TABLE 9.6. Percentage of M.P.'s with and without American Ties Who Were Responsive, Unresponsive, and Neutral, and of Responsive and Unresponsive Statements, with Number of Ties Controlled, All Years Combined

M.P.'s	Res.	Neut.	Unres.	Statements by M.P.'s	Res.	Unres.
Two or More Ties				Two or More Ties		
(N = 28)	21	61	18	(N = 28)	64	36
One U.S. Tie (N = 67)	13	79	7	One U.S. Tie (N = 40)	45	55
No U.S. Ties (N = 308)	7	81	12	No U.S. Ties (N = 149)	32	68

more links tended to speak out somewhat more often, whatever the content of their remarks. In the right-hand half of the table there is a slight tendency, significant at the .10 level, for responsiveness to be more frequent where there is more than one tie.

Examination of the Senate was also inconclusive on this point. Although in 1954 only two Senators had more than one discernible bond with the British, and both of them were highly responsive, the cases were obviously too few to give any satisfactory indication. For 1890, however, the results were just the opposite of what one would expect. Though not to a statistically significant degree, Senators with two or more ties tended to be *less* responsive than those with only one. On this evidence, then, we must conclude that the existence of any link at all is far more important than the reinforcement of that link by one or two additional ones.

In addition, it seemed necessary to see whether the kind of tie made any difference, whether either economic or personal ties were more significant than the other. Table 9.7 lists separately all M.P.'s with economic ties, all with no economic but "strong" personal ties, those with only "weak" personal ties, those whose only connection with the United States is through the English-Speaking Union or the Pilgrims, and finally those with no known link at all.

TABLE 9.7. Percentage of M.P.'s with and without American Ties Who Were Responsive, Unresponsive, and Neutral, and of Responsive and Unresponsive Statements, with Type of Tie Controlled, All Years Combined

M.P.'s	Res.	Neut.	Unres.	Statements by M.P.'s	Res.	Unres.
Economic Ties				Economic Ties		
(N = 53)	11	83	6	(N = 22)	73	27
"Strong" Ties (N = 15)	20	60	20	"Strong" Ties (N = 27)	48	52
"Weak" Ties (N = 19)	21	63	16	"Weak" Ties (N = 19)	63	37
ESU-Pilgrim (N = 8)	25	63	13	ESU-Pilgrim (N = 10)	50	50
No U.S. Ties (N = 308)	7	81	12	No U.S. Ties (N = 149)	32	68

The association of responsiveness with economic ties is evident on both sides of the table, and is significant at the .01 level in each case. Among those with various kinds of personal ties to the United States, it makes little difference whether the bonds are "weak," "strong," or merely those of membership in an organization like the Pilgrims. Possibly some differences would show up in a larger sample, though they are not evident here. But there is a *slight* difference, significant (at the .10 level) only in the right-hand half of the table, between all those with just personal ties and those with commercial bonds. Possibly economic self-interest plays a part. More likely, however, the difference is due to the fact that the ties of commerce are current ones: the legislator has a continuing channel of information and opinion from the United States. Most personal ties, on the other hand, lie in the individual's past, and it may have been many years since he talked to many Americans. Since most of the American policies in question, such as German rearmament and China policy, were of relatively recent vintage, it is not surprising that men with past but not current contacts with the United States should fail to perceive American wishes or their justification.

Notice that men with personal ties to America of any kind are more likely to speak up on matters affecting Anglo-American relations. Only 62 per cent of those with personal ties said nothing, whereas 81 per cent of those with no ties are unrecorded. They are even somewhat more likely to record unresponsiveness than are those without ties (17 per cent to 12 per cent). Perhaps this is because men who have been abroad or have personal contacts with foreigners naturally have more interest in foreign affairs (whether contacts cause interest, or vice versa, or whether it is a mutually reinforcing process is not relevant here). But it may also be that the experiences of these men have in some instances made them "anti-American." Clearly, it is a danger to be considered. If a wider experience of foreign contact in a population is likely, in general, to increase responsiveness, it may also result in a certain concomitant increase in the level of hostility as well.

We cannot reproduce the analysis of Table 9.7 for the Senate, because in the two years under study a total of only five Senators had personal ties of any nature without also having economic ties to the United Kingdom, and this is too few to produce interesting results. But it is possible to compare the effect of all kinds of direct ties, personal or economic, with that of constituency ties. Table 9.8 lists all Senators with constituency economic ties, those with only direct bonds, and those with none at all.

Although the number of Senators who have only direct ties to Britain is too small for us to talk of statistical significance, the figures are interesting nevertheless. They suggest that whereas constituency ties were once powerful forces in producing responsiveness, they are no longer very important. In fact, in 1954 Senators with no links at all were more likely to be responsive than were those whose links passed through their constituencies. This apparent shift is not surprising when one examines the changes in America's economic structure since the turn of the century. In 1954 no state derived more than 12 per cent of its income from a commodity important in Anglo-

TABLE 9.8. Percentage of Senators with Constituency Economic
Ties, Direct Ties Only, and No British Ties Who Were Responsive,
Moderate, and Unresponsive

1890

Senators	Responsive	Moderate	Unresponsive
Constituency Ties (N = 46)	39	30	30
Direct Ties Only (N = 3)	0	67	33
No U.K. Ties (N = 35)	9	46	46

1954

Senators	Responsive	Moderate	Unresponsive
Constituency Ties (N = 12)	25	25	50
Direct Ties Only (N = 11)	73	18	9
No U.K. Ties (N = 73)	27	33	40

American trade. But in 1890, seven states gained more than 12 per
cent of their income from cotton: Texas (55 per cent), Mississippi
(46 per cent), South Carolina (41 per cent), Arkansas (33 per cent),
Alabama (32 per cent), Georgia (31 per cent), and Louisiana (19
per cent). Wheat contributed at least that much to three other states:
North Dakota (55 per cent), South Dakota (29 per cent), and Minnesota (17 per cent). No wonder, then, that the economic nature of
his constituency made so much less difference in the way a Senator
voted in 1954 than it did in 1890. Anglo-American commerce has
diminished greatly both as a power base and as a means of communicating to legislators who are not themselves directly tied in with it.
Possibly also the British government's deliberate discrimination, for
balance-of-payments reasons, against imports from the Dollar Area
alienated some Senators from states producing goods whose export
to Britain continued, but in limited quantities. In any case, the above
figures provide dramatic evidence of the South's diminished "internationalism," which many writers have noted.

The conclusion that the effectiveness of constituency ties in promoting responsiveness is directly proportional to the weight of the economic interest in the constituency rests on scanty evidence, but it
can be buttressed with another set of data. For 1954 and 1890, I
ranked the states involved in Anglo-American trade according to the
amount of income derived from goods important in that trade, and
then ranked their Senators by degree of responsiveness. For 1954
(when no state derived more than 12 per cent of its income from such
products), the correlation between the two rank orders[5] was only

[5] I have used the Kendall Rank Correlation Coefficient.

.14, and not statistically significant. But for 1890, the same procedure produced a correlation of .34 (significant at the .05 level) for Democratic Senators and the astonishingly high correlation of .86 (significant at the .001 level) for Republican Senators. With this evidence, it is hard to imagine how the precipitous decline in Anglo-American commerce over the past seventy years could fail to work to the detriment of continued responsiveness from American policy-makers.

In the previous chapter we suggested that higher education in the United States, and particularly legal training, was probably important in instilling a favorable attitude toward Britain and a readiness to meet her needs. The lawyer's training might be particularly important in this respect, since such a high proportion of the American political elite was originally prepared for the bar. Table 9.9 divides Senators according to the amount and kind of education they obtained.

TABLE 9.9. Percentage of Senators with Legal Training, Other Higher Education, and No Higher Education Who Were Responsive, Moderate, and Unresponsive, 1890 and 1954 Combined

Senators	Responsive	Moderate	Unresponsive
Legal Education (N = 133)	32	37	32
Other Higher Education (N = 24)	29	25	46
No Higher Education (N = 23)	13	26	61

Whether or not the legislator has had legal training does seem to make a difference, for lawyers were significantly (.01 level) more responsive than were Senators who had no higher education at all. But we cannot be certain whether it is the law training or merely university education in general that makes the difference. The latter group of Senators fell between the other two classes, less responsive than one but more so than the other. In neither direction was the difference statistically significant. An additional caution must be noted. Quite possibly it is not education that is relevant at all, but simply a third variable which tends to be associated with substantial schooling. We should expect an individual with a higher education to be exposed to more kinds of international communications than a man who never went beyond secondary school. There is no way we can, with these data, control for these other, less visible kinds of communication; the possibility is merely offered as an extra reason for treating this finding with restraint.

At this point let us consider two possible criticisms of the above findings. One is that we have the chain of causality wrong — people who already look favorably on another country are then willing to develop ties with it, not the reverse, though the association shows up equally in the analysis. With regard to bonds of education, travel, business, and particularly membership in Anglo-American organizations, this objection obviously carries some weight, but with many other ties self-selection is not a factor. A man has no influence over where he is born and is unlikely to have much more regarding where he does military service in wartime. Many of the business firms in question — Lloyds, Macmillan, Simmons — have international ties that long antedated the Members' or Senators' association with them. Nor are they companies whose bond with the other country would be a major factor in attracting the legislator.

Another potential objection concerns the degree to which these findings can be generalized. Although these influences may be important for ordinary legislators, they may not be effective on such others as members of the executive, who must take a wider view and who are subject to immensely more varied pressures. Especially in Britain fifty or more years ago, Cabinet members were likely to be rather wealthy landowners, and perhaps were less affected by narrow economic concerns. Joseph Chamberlain in the 1890's, for example, heartily championed an Anglo-American *rapprochement,* but he may well have had no strong economic interests in the United States. He wanted friendship with America to counterbalance the new threat of German power. The point, however, is that other men also feared Germany's might, but were not necessarily led to embrace the republic across the seas. But Chamberlain did, and it is perhaps no coincidence that he had an American-born wife. There is no attempt to argue cause in this particular case — he may have married an American because he already liked Americans generically; his marriage may have only reinforced an initial liking for Americans; or it may in fact have been no more than a coincidence. Yet since the association of links with responsiveness is so notable for M.P.'s and Senators, it may affect Cabinet members similarly. This seems particularly plausible because we are *not* arguing that one becomes responsive in any simple, direct way to one's economic stake in another country's welfare, but rather that the existence of an economic or personal link opens a man to messages he would otherwise never hear.

Sources of Friction

Finally, we shall reiterate our earlier conclusions about the extent and severity of Anglo-American economic rivalry. I identified all those M.P.'s who were attached to firms with subsidiaries or investments in countries where British holdings were less than 75 per cent of the Anglo-American total — that is, countries where in the termi-

nology of Chapter 4 America and Britain were in competition, or
where the United States was dominant. Of the 132 members of the
1938 House sampled, 15, or 11.4 per cent, were attached to such
companies. In 1954 the proportion had fallen to 12 of 129, or 9.3
per cent. Though not statistically significant, this change is in the
hypothesized direction, suggesting that fewer legislators were subject
to this kind of Anglo-American friction in the 1950's than before the
war. In addition, there is evidence that the irritation was never very
serious anyway, as was also suggested in Chapter 4: M.P.'s attached
to such firms were no more likely to be unresponsive than were Members with no ties to America at all. (Of 27 M.P.'s whose companies
had holdings where America was dominant or the two countries
competed, only two were unresponsive.)

We cannot repeat this analysis for Congress, since in 1954 there
were only three Senators with links to firms that might be engaged in
investment rivalry, and each of these also had direct economic bonds
with Great Britain. But in its place we can examine the effect of
British postwar quantitative restrictions on imports. Of the 96 Senators, 31 were tied to firms which produced goods that could be imported from the Dollar Area only by the procurement of specific,
individual licenses. The British government generally tried to limit
the importation of these goods, and where possible discriminated in
favor of soft-currency suppliers. Here again the mode of identification
is a crude one, for most imports from America, excluding agricultural
and mineral raw materials (but including food, cotton, and copper),
were subject to quantitative restrictions.[6] With some products the
limitations were applied rigorously, and in other cases licenses were
granted freely to all applicants; there is no way of knowing in any
detail what the pattern was. Yet even this measure produces the
interesting results shown in Table 9.10.

TABLE 9.10. Percentage of Senators with and without Ties to
Firms Producing Goods Whose Importation into Britain Was
Restricted — Responsive, Moderate, and Unresponsive, 1954

	Responsive	Moderate	Unresponsive
Restricted (N = 31)	23	19	58
No Restrictions (N = 65)	37	35	28

Senators associated with firms whose exports to Britain are limited
are much less likely (significant at the .01 level) to be responsive

[6] For the complete listing, see Board of Trade, Import-licensing Branch,
Notice to Importers No. 635, London, 1954. All goods not listed there were
imported on government account only.

than are legislators without such ties. The substantial removal of these restrictions since 1958 should reduce what really was an important irritant.

To summarize, we have found that:

1. Legislators with economic or personal ties to the other country are more likely to be responsive to the needs of that country than are legislators lacking those ties.
2. This holds true when party affiliation is controlled, though party is itself an important variable.
3. It makes little difference whether a legislator has a number of ties to the other country, or only one.
4. There is some evidence, though not enough to be conclusive, that economic ties are more likely to be effective than personal ones.
5. The importance of a constituency tie is directly proportional to the weight of the economic interest in the constituency.
6. Senators with education in the law are more likely to be responsive than Senators without higher education.
7. Anglo-American investment rivalry does not seem to diminish responsiveness among M.P.'s.
8. British trade discrimination did seem to reduce responsiveness among Senators.

10

The Military Link

Superficially, it would seem that one vital aspect of Anglo-American relations has had a history quite different from the general trend we have found so far. That aspect is the growth in the depth and extent of military interdependence. Whatever may be said about a decline in the strength of economic or cultural links, have not the defense establishments of the two nations, in response to mutual dangers from outside, become ever more closely intermeshed since 1914? We shall spend the rest of the chapter examining this question, and in the following chapter we shall assess its significance as a force affecting integration.

The capabilities of military integration may take the shape of formal international or supranational institutions, informal practices, or the exchange of persons. Supranational institutions may often be the most effective of these capabilities, but a poorly operating, understaffed, or underpowered organization may well be inferior to one or all of the other possible forms a capability may take. Our earlier arguments about the relative merits of pluralism and amalgamation are relevant here.

There is also responsiveness itself, made possible by the capabilities. In fact, the growth of capabilities may be due to the previous existence of responsiveness, in a deliberate effort to increase that responsiveness. We shall deal with a number of capabilities created specifically for such a purpose. This is in contrast to the capabilities which have so far concerned us — those which have been substantially, though seldom entirely, autonomous of government control which seeks to develop them as capabilities per se. Finally, remember that the amount of capability needed in a situation depends upon the loads it must bear. In certain noncritical situations a low level of capability would not be of major concern, but when loads are high, even a greater amount of capability might be insufficient.

In this chapter we shall depart from the particular years we have analyzed so closely until now. To look at 1890, 1913, 1928, 1938, and 1954 in isolation would grossly distort the military picture, for such growth in military collaboration as has occurred has not been steady, but highly intermittent. Co-operation between the armed forces of the two countries was practically *nil* before World War I; the facilities built up between 1917 and 1919 were dismantled immediately thereafter. They had to be reconstructed from scratch during the second cataclysm. The arrangements of World War I were precedents, memories and lessons to those who participated, but the arrangements themselves had been inactive for twenty years. Even before V-E Day in 1945 the dismantling began again. While the destruction was not as complete as it had been in 1918, much rebuilding was required for NATO.

Thus we shall use four separate periods for comparison: those years in each of the great wars when the United States was a participant, the years immediately preceding American entry into World War II, and the NATO co-operation of the early 1950's. It will be instructive to compare the NATO period both with the wartime alliances and with the peacetime arrangements of 1939–41. The discussion will be topical, considering several types of capability and responsiveness separately, with the arrangements examined chronologically within each section. A postscript on recent developments in NATO will follow, for in at least one respect any trend toward closer integration has been halted during the past few years.

Strategic Planning and Co-operation

Before the First World War there was no joint strategic planning of any kind. Many American officials, in fact, had not abandoned the idea that war with Britain was a possibility, and had planned accordingly.[1] But when war came to the United States, it became necessary for that country to mesh its program with the Allies'. Strategic planning was then nominally the responsibility of the Supreme War Council, a committee of heads of governments. President Wilson was basically suspicious of the Entente's political aims, and though he decided to co-operate fully on military matters, he carefully avoided

[1] See Chapter 1.

political entanglements; he insisted that the United States was an Associated, not an Allied, Power. Nevertheless, he appointed Colonel House as his political representative, named General Tasker Bliss his military representative, and permitted American officers to join the Permanent Military Representatives.

The Supreme War Council was a political body and did not attempt to direct military operations in the field. It only discussed questions of policy affecting the military situation, the character of military operations, and the distribution of manpower and supplies. All decisions had to be unanimous. The Permanent Military Representatives had no executive authority. The members' decisions required approval by their superiors, who frequently withheld approval or bound their representatives' negotiating positions in advance. Permanent organs equipped to advise on the various fields of Allied activity were lacking. Even in advising, the Americans had only limited influence. According to the Army's plans, American forces were not expected to play a major part in the war until 1919. As long as this illusion persisted, the American chiefs' leverage over their allies was limited. And the principal strategic decisions, especially great land concentration on the Western Front, were made before America became active anyway. Strategic co-operation between Britain and America was thus never very close.[2]

When war loomed again in the late 1930's, a new beginning had to be made on strategic co-operation. As early as 1937 the Navy Department sent Captain Royal Ingersoll to London for "purely exploratory" conversations with the Admiralty. By 1940 each power had a joint planning staff in the other's capital. Though conversations remained on an *ad hoc* basis, the British were very free about telling the Americans of their war plans. The American and British service chiefs met at the Atlantic Conference, but produced little more than agreement on co-operation for the escort of convoys. The "true opening of formal permanent relations" between the American and British staffs occurred in early 1941, though they were neither binding nor at the highest military level.[3] The agencies for this consultation were the British Joint Staff Mission and the United States War Plans Divi-

[2] See Tasker Bliss, "The Evolution of the Unified Command," *Foreign Affairs*, I, 2 (December 1922), pp. 1–30; Sir Frederick Maurice, *Lessons of Allied Co-operation: Naval, Military, and Air, 1914–1918*, New York, 1942; Ernest R. May, "Wilson," in May, editor, *The Ultimate Decision: The President as Commander-in-Chief*, New York, 1960, pp. 111–131; and David Trask, *The United States in the Supreme War Council*, Middletown, Conn., 1961.

[3] Mark S. Watson, *Chief of Staff: Prewar Plans and Preparations*, Washington, 1950, p. 384.

sion. President Roosevelt preferred to let the military take the lead in these matters, and kept aloof while America remained neutral.[4]

Once the war began, collaboration was far closer between the two English-speaking powers than between any other two nations. The British Chiefs of Staff Committee (Chief of the Imperial General Staff, First Sea Lord, and Chief of the Air Staff) served as a corporate authority for issuing unified strategic directions in wartime. On the American side, the Army and Navy chiefs had long met as the Joint Army-Navy Board. In February 1942 they added General Arnold of the Air Force to become the Joint Chiefs of Staff. Arnold was added to make a negotiating team comparable with the British unit.

Together the six men constituted the Combined Chiefs of Staff (CCS), but an important distinction must be made. This name was applied both to the body of the six chiefs which met periodically, as at Casablanca, and to the permanent group at Washington. The latter consisted of the American Joint Chiefs and three high-ranking British officers who were nevertheless subordinate to their chiefs in London. The CCS had full powers (in the case of the British representation in Washington subject to approval by London) to act throughout the military sphere. It had direct strategic control over the European-Atlantic Area. The United States assumed "principal responsibility" for military operations in the Pacific and China while Britain did the same for the Middle East and Southeast Asia, but the CCS retained general jurisdiction.

Far more than the Supreme War Council of World War I, the CCS set up specialized committees to deal with logistics, intelligence, transportation, communications, munitions allocation, meteorology, shipbuilding, and military government. The Combined Staff Planners assisted and drew up papers, but like the Supreme War Council the CCS never had any notable staff of its own. Throughout the period it was largely dependent on the separate national staffs for papers and recommendations — integration never approached the creation of an international secretariat.

Although there was no joint political body of superior authority, like the Supreme War Council, to hamstring the CSS, it was not free of political control. In Britain, the Chiefs of Staff were members of the Defense Committee, which included senior Cabinet members and the Prime Minister as chairman. Churchill kept immediate as well as

[4] Ray S. Cline, *Washington Command Post: The Operations Division*, Washington, 1951, pp. 1–49; Maurice Matloff and Edwin M. Snell, *Strategic Planning for Coalition Warfare, 1941–1942*, Washington, 1953; Roland G. Ruppenthal, *Logistical Support of the Armies*, Washington, 1953, I, pp. 1–14; and Watson, *Chief of Staff*, pp. 369–405.

ultimate authority over his military commanders. On the American side, Roosevelt's control of the armed forces was usually indirect; he avoided "meddling," and there were few occasions, particularly toward the end of the war, when he overruled them. Nevertheless, the control was there and was exercised. Most important was the case in 1942 when the Joint Chiefs, disgusted by British foot-dragging on the plan for a cross-Channel attack, threatened to de-emphasize Europe and concentrate on the Pacific war. Roosevelt immediately intervened to forestall them.[5] Samuel Eliot Morison, discussing this point generally, declared:

> But there were also occasions when the only way that the British Chiefs of Staff could get out of something that the Prime Minister insisted on was to signal Field Marshal Sir John Dill, their representative in Washington, to see General Marshall and beg him to induce the President to persuade Churchill that what he insisted on simply could not be done. Conversely, when the Combined Chiefs of Staff made a decision that Mr. Churchill did not like, he sometimes tried to work on Mr. Roosevelt to have it overthrown.[6]

Roosevelt and Churchill, whether acting individually or together, kept ultimate responsibility for decisions on strategy. The exceptionally good relations between them reduced many frictions that would have been serious in other circumstances.

The American Joint Chiefs came into existence, as a body, to deal with the British Chiefs of Staff. In other ways, too, the American organization came more and more to reflect the British pattern. Particularly in planning techniques the requirements of coalition warfare encouraged similarity.[7] But perhaps the most significant measure of integration at this point has been suggested by Ernst Haas.[8] In his study of the European Coal and Steel Community he examined the degree to which interests and interest groups developed on crossnational lines, thus counteracting the divisive effect of purely national cleavages. In the present case, for instance, did the two naval chiefs ever find that they had common interests which opposed those of the other chiefs, or did the Americans and British always present a united front to each other in their conferences?

At the Casablanca Conference in 1942 the British Chiefs of Staff had carefully worked out their plans and presented the conferees with

[5] William R. Emerson, "F.D.R.," in May, *The Ultimate Decision*, p. 156.

[6] Samuel Eliot Morison, *Strategy and Compromise*, Boston, 1958, pp. 14–15.

[7] Maurice Matloff, *Strategic Planning for Coalition Warfare, 1943–1944*, Washington, 1959, p. 111; and Franklyn A. Johnson, "The British Committee of Imperial Defence: Prototype of U.S. Security Organization," *Journal of Politics*, XXIII, 2 (May 1961), pp. 231–261.

[8] Ernst Haas, *The Uniting of Europe*, Stanford, 1958.

numerous detailed papers. The Americans had not prepared such a united front, and as a result the British were able to commit the group to a Mediterranean Campaign in 1943 rather than the cross-Channel attack, which most of the Americans desired. Both General Marshall and General Wedemeyer were disheartened by the outcome and determined not to repeat it. Henceforth the American position hardened, and the discussions more closely resembled negotiations between two parties. The results of later conferences were considered more satisfactory from the American side.

> The Army planners . . . who helped in preparations for *Trident* concluded that the American staff had done much better than at Casablanca. They agreed that the United States should plan to send a large delegation to the next conference, due to be called within the next few months, and that 11 members of it should work together beforehand. They advised settling well in advance what would be the agenda, anticipating British arguments and preparing the American case for the JCS [Joint Chiefs of Staff] thoroughly and in time for everyone to know exactly what it was. Above all, they wanted to be sure that the President and the JCS were willing to support the case as worked out in detail by the joint staff.[9]

In the last two years of the war the Americans tended more and more to make their own decisions, either overriding the British chiefs or simply not consulting them. This was a reflection of the increasing margin of American military strength over that of the United Kingdom, and later of the shift in attention from Europe to the Pacific, an area long recognized as a primarily American responsibility. But the British, as their relative military strength declined, attempted to use the CCS as a means of maintaining something like equality of influence.[10]

There were differences of national character, history, and political philosophy, but differences of perceived national interest were probably most important. The British felt that a Mediterranean attack was essential; the American military men, with different strategic concepts and, more important, an overriding concentration on military rather

---

[9] Cline, *Washington Command Post*, pp. 221–222. See also pp. 218–248; Matloff, *Strategic Planning, 1943–44,* pp. 106–107; and Matloff, "The Anvil Decision: Crossroads of Strategy," in K. R. Greenfield, editor, *Command Decisions,* New York, 1959, p. 294. Forrest C. Pogue, in "SHAEF — A Retrospect of Coalition Command," *Journal of Modern History,* XXIII (December 1951), pp. 329–335, expresses a dissenting opinion, however, saying that never on such matters as the Mediterranean-European strategy did the debate ever become a purely British versus American affair, and he mentions several instances where one of the chiefs sided against his compatriots.

[10] John Ehrmann, *Grand Strategy, VI, October 1944–August 1945,* London, 1956, pp. 47–49.

than political tasks, could not agree. Consensus on strategy at sea was prevented by the United States Navy's concentration on the Pacific while the British were vitally concerned with the Atlantic lifeline.

The degree of co-operation in strategic planning was limited; but by common agreement, whatever the measure, it was very much greater than twenty-five years earlier. The alliance produced an agreed strategy for most theaters and, in the words of one author, "formed the closest and most far-reaching combination of sovereign states, on the basis of equality, that has yet been seen." [11]

On the state of this type of co-operation in the early 1950's we have far less information, particularly about the interests expressed in high-level military deliberations. Most negotiation occurred through NATO. The North Atlantic Council of ministers or heads of government met three times a year. Decisions in this body had to be unanimous. Under the Council was the Military Committee, which met once or twice annually and included a chief of staff from each member nation. The Standing Group was in permanent session in Washington and provided strategic direction and co-ordinated defense plans. It was composed of senior military officers of the United States, the United Kingdom, and France — not, as in the corresponding arrangement of World War II, the JCS or their immediate subordinates. [12] This group's decisions were, of course, subject to approval by the members' political and military superiors. An international Staff-Secretariat, composed of nationals of all members, represented a slight improvement over previous arrangements, but in 1954 it numbered less than 600, including messengers and guards. (The comparable figure for the Pentagon is 31,000.)

In one sense there was, through 1954, less disagreement about strategy than ten years before, largely because of the force of circumstances. NATO's primary concern was the defense of Europe; that could only be achieved by land forces in Europe, backed up by the United States nuclear deterrent. No such fundamental option as the Mediterranean versus the Western European attack plan of World War II offered itself. Yet there was room for much disagreement on the relative weights of the Shield and the Sword, and to some extent about the relative priorities of Europe and the Far East. In the words of one author,

[11] *Ibid.*, p. 130. See also Forrest C. Pogue, *The Supreme Command*, Washington, 1954, p. 50.
[12] Until 1953 the Chairman of the United States JCS was the day-to-day American representative on the Standing Group. After that, his functions were delegated to another senior officer, and the prestige of the Standing Group was allowed to decline.

It is inevitably difficult for a large group of countries to develop a common and efficient strategy and balanced military forces. The main difficulty is, of course, that the military interests of the coalition partners are not sufficiently convergent and that, in the absence of federation, mutual trust in the dependability of allies is incomplete and subject to doubt and corrosion. It is a weakness of the alliance that this difficulty has not been mitigated by closer co-operation.[13]

The capabilities for responsiveness in this area of military affairs were, in 1954, appreciably greater than in 1917–18, and without question were stronger than ever before in peacetime. Nevertheless they probably fell short of what was achieved in World War II.

Unity of Command

Tactical planning and command in the field is every bit as important as strategic planning to the building of an integrated military force. In World War I, the British suggested the most extreme form of linkage by proposing that American troops serve in the British Army under British officers. The situation on the Western Front in late 1917 and early 1918 was critical, and the Allies were anxious to get American troops into the front lines as soon as possible. The United States Army then expected that it would be unable to make a significant contribution before 1919. Therefore the British, particularly General Haig, pressed for the amalgamation of British and American forces: one United States company to be included in each of as many British battalions as possible or, alternatively, one American battalion in every British brigade. Haig's attitude toward the American troops was not without a condescension which severely irked Pershing. The American General felt that this British pressure reflected not only a desire for speed but also a wish to prevent the establishment of an independent American army. He refused to permit amalgamation, and Washington supported him entirely. Considerations of national sentiment, fear of political opposition in the United States, and concern over the Anglo-American frictions that might consequently arise influenced the decision.

Finally, according to the Milner-Pershing and Abbeville agreements of 1918, it was decided that the combat elements of six divisions would be *trained* for ten weeks, battalion by battalion, with British units. Higher commanders and staff officers would be assigned for

---

[13] Klaus Knorr, "The Strained Alliance," in Knorr, editor, *NATO and American Security*, Princeton, 1959, p. 5. See also Ben T. Moore, *NATO and the Future of Europe*, New York, 1958, pp. 76–89.

training and experience with the British. As soon as possible all troops were to be re-formed under American command. The Americans persevered with the creation of their independent army, and the British have never repeated the attempt to amalgamate the forces of the United States with their own.[14]

Unity of command in the field was approached by steps, though never too closely. At first, after much urging by Bliss and some of the other military chiefs, a general reserve was created, but in name only. It was controlled by the Permanent Military Representatives, in consultation with the national Commanders in Chief, who were to determine its development, strength, and use. It was found to be a clumsy and impractical scheme for command by committee. On April 3, 1918, Marshal Foch was charged with co-ordinating the action of Allied armies on the Western Front. He held strategic direction of the troops, but the national commanders kept tactical control. Each could, in principle, appeal to his government if he considered that Foch's orders endangered his army. Every nation retained a separate section of the front, and the Allied forces were composed of self-sufficient national units under a supreme commander. In practice, integration was perhaps somewhat more complete than it appeared. Wilson was particularly careful to respect Foch's decisions. Though he had previously given Pershing a free hand, when it appeared that his general was not co-operating sufficiently with the Marshal, Wilson was quick to assert his ultimate authority. When asked by Pershing or Bliss to approve a decision, the President always first inquired whether Foch had been consulted, and whether he agreed. In Bliss's terms, Foch's "good sense, kindly tact, personal magnetism and supreme professional qualifications . . . secured the degree of co-operation necessary for success and made him in fact if not in name the inter-Allied Commander-in-Chief on the Western Front." [15]

Thus a very limited plan for unified command was worked out. It operated only on the very highest level, however, and was largely dependent on the personality of Foch and the self-restraint of leaders like Wilson.

Unity of command came to mean a little more on the naval side. An Allied Naval Council, composed of the Ministers of Marine and the chiefs of the naval staffs, had powers to recommend to commanders and report to their governments, but the individual responsi-

[14] On this attempt, see Robert Blake, editor, *The Private Papers of Douglas Haig, 1914–1919,* London, 1952, p. 525; Rufus Isaacs, *Rufus Isaacs, First Marquess of Reading,* London, 1945, II, pp. 88–91; and John J. Pershing, *My Experiences in the World War,* New York, 1931, I, especially pp. 307–309.

[15] Bliss, "The Evolution of the Unified Command," p. 30.

bility of the Chiefs of Staff and the Commanders in Chief at sea was untouched. For the United States and Britain, it was the relationship of Admiral Sims with the British chiefs in London that mattered. Policy decisions were reached jointly, as Sims struggled with the British over the convoy question and insisted on being shown all the material available to the Admiralty before making up his mind on a matter. Command was unified. Sims effectively placed the direction of American naval units in Europe in the hands of the British; American destroyers in Ireland came under the operational orders of Admiral Sir Lewis Bayly. Sims's Chief of Staff became the United States Chief of Staff for Admiral Bayly; he was the first foreign officer to have his name entered on the British Navy List. As a deliberate gesture to demonstrate Anglo-American co-operation, for five days in June 1917 Sims commanded a portion of the British fleet while Bayly was away. But despite all this, Sims was never supreme in his own service. His actions remained subject to approval in Washington, and the interaction that occurred in London and at sea was not matched at the governmental level.[16]

This whole structure was naturally disbanded between the wars. Before United States entry into the second conflict in 1941 there could, of course, be no joining of commands, but American military planners had considered possible arrangements. The Navy war plan in force at the time of Pearl Harbor contemplated sending most of the Asiatic fleet into the Southwest Pacific, where it would co-operate with the British. Air Force plans included the dispatch of United States bombers to Britain, but while the British would assign the strategic tasks, the bombers would be kept in large groups to retain American command.[17]

When the United States did become involved, integration was more nearly complete in Europe than elsewhere. The Allied chiefs were able to build upon their experiences in World War I, and then in the Mediterranean in 1942–43, to produce the most nearly integrated multinational command system of modern warfare.

As plans for the European Command were being worked out in 1943, General Dever, commander of the European Theater of Operations for the United States (ETOUSA), insisted that the Supreme Commander of the Allied Expeditionary Force, when appointed, should report directly to the Combined Chiefs of Staff, not through his

[16] Elting E. Morison, *Admiral Sims and the Modern American Navy,* Boston, 1942, pp. 338–391.

[17] William Hardy McNeill, *America, Britain, and Russia: Their Co-operation and Conflict, 1941–1946,* London, 1953, p. 12, and Watson, *Chief of Staff,* p. 381.

national Joint Chiefs.[18] He expected that the Supreme Commander would be British, and wanted this as an assurance of protection for American interests. Actually, General Eisenhower became Supreme Commander. The British were compensated by having SHAEF in London, where the American JCS feared the Commander would be unduly subject to Churchill's influence. (The JCS sometimes hastened negotiations by allowing Eisenhower to represent them in London on matters of broader Allied interests, but did this rather seldom for fear he would be too heavily swayed by the British chief.)[19] Thus an integrated command was set up, with certain precautions for each party's interest.

A joint staff was organized at SHAEF, with British and American officers very carefully selected for their ability to work with officers of the other nationality.[20] This staff tended to assume more important tasks with the passage of time. It co-ordinated policy on administration, health, purchasing, hiring of labor, intelligence, and similar matters. Note, however, that the term is "co-ordinated" — detailed implementation of the staff's decisions was left to its subordinate commands and national agencies. In most cases its decisions were recommendations, not orders. On all matters of administration, the British and American forces continued to report directly to the appropriate national authorities. But *informally,* the degree of integration became substantial. Important decisions affecting American forces were unavoidably made by Eisenhower at SHAEF, and for convenience he came to rely for advice on the SHAEF binational staff rather than on the staff at the United States Army's separate European headquarters (ETOUSA). Consequently the United States representatives at SHAEF began to act as the senior American staff, and in mid-April the theater commander in Paris was forced by circumstances actually to designate the American staff members at SHAEF as the acting general staff for ETOUSA. A similar conflict between SHAEF and another American agency, Communications Zone, was similarly resolved largely in SHAEF's favor.

[18] When General Eisenhower was Supreme Allied Commander in the Mediterranean, Prime Minister Churchill frequently communicated directly (through the British Joint Chiefs) with Eisenhower's subordinate British commanders (Matloff, *Strategic Planning,* p. 273). This was quite definitely outside the formal command pattern of either the Mediterranean Command or that eventually set up in Europe. He did so much less frequently after Eisenhower was made chief of the AEF.

[19] Pogue, *The Supreme Command,* pp. 40–41.

[20] Eisenhower's insistence on this requirement is illustrated by a tale which is now familiar. An American officer might safely call a British co-worker a bastard, but to refer to him as a *British* bastard was a sure way of being returned to the United States on the next ship.

The command of forces actually in the field was integrated only near the top. General Montgomery was appointed to command both British and American forces for the assault on Normandy, with General Bradley as his second-in-command. But the reorganization of September 1, 1944, raised Bradley to commander of the Twelfth Army Group, all American troops, on the central front and left Montgomery in charge of the Twenty-first Army Group, composed of British and Canadian forces, in the north. Thus, as in 1917–18, each nation had its own section of the front, subject, however, to firmer formal and informal control from the Supreme Allied Commander than was true in the first war. Integration was also high at Air Force headquarters in Europe and at Fifteenth Army Group headquarters in the Mediterranean.

This was the peak of intermeshing; in no other theater was the level nearly as high. In the early war months General Wavell was made Supreme Commander in Asia and the Pacific, but on American insistence he had no power to relieve national commanders, to interfere in the disposition of forces, or to commandeer their supplies — Eisenhower in Europe was to have all these powers. Higher direction came from the CCS.

By mid-1943, three separate regional commands had been set up in the Far East: the Pacific Ocean, Southwest Pacific, and Southeast Asia commands. Lord Mountbatten headed the latter, with General Stilwell as his second-in-command. British officers had authority for the three separate forces: air, ground, and naval. While the CCS made decisions on strategy and allocation of forces for the Southeast Asia Command, the British Chiefs of Staff retained operational jurisdiction. China remained exclusively under American direction.

Integration was much less complete in the Pacific Ocean and Southwest Pacific Area commands, largely because the United States provided almost all the forces. Admiral Nimitz and General MacArthur reported directly to the American JCS, not to the CCS, on all matters. The CCS had only indirect control of them, and co-operation was poor. With the Japanese attack on Midway imminent, the Americans requested that a British aircraft carrier be transferred to them from the Indian Ocean, and were refused. Just previously Churchill had remarked to Harry Hopkins that the two fleets were acting as though they were two totally independent forces.[21] By 1944, when it became possible for the Royal Navy to take a more active part in the Pacific, the United States planners decided against asking for their participation. Though they could have used any British task forces, they feared that problems of command, planning, and particularly logistics

[21] Robert E. Sherwood, *Roosevelt and Hopkins,* New York, 1948, p. 525.

would complicate matters and slow down the quickening pace of the war.

Thus in Europe the Anglo-American command was substantially more unified than it was in World War I, but in Asia collaboration was not even as close as that of the AEF of 1917–18. The national staffs united within themselves to resist outside pressures, and the employment of national forces remained largely a matter for diplomatic negotiation.

In 1954, the only significant instance of a unified command of British and American forces existed through NATO, where the organization bore a strong resemblance to that of SHAEF. There was a Supreme Allied Commander (SACEUR), and below him various regional ground, sea, and air commanders, each leading forces contributed by more than one nation. Three types of military units were distinguished: those over which SACEUR had operational control of training and development, those merely earmarked for his control in time of war, and those which remained entirely under national command. NATO control was most effective in the Central Europe Command, which included both British and American ground forces. Significantly, it included only part of the British and American tactical air forces in the area, and none of their strategic bombers — owing primarily to American unwillingness to share information or control of nuclear weapons. Even in Central Europe the NATO commander's control was likely to be firm only in time of maneuvers, as indicated by Lord Ismay's statement that SACEUR might "deal direct with national authorities . . . to settle with them how the forces could be employed in peacetime." [22] Naval forces under Supreme Allied Command Atlantic were merely earmarked. British- and French-earmarked units were prepared and used for the assault on Suez without the knowledge of SACEUR. And, of course, forces could always be withdrawn entirely from NATO control, as the French withdrew their naval units subsequently.

On the other hand, a permanent, integrated military staff had, by 1954, grown up at NATO headquarters. It had assumed important tasks, though in all probability not to the extent that SHAEF headquarters once took over the functions of ETOUSA's staff.

On these counts, then, we may safely say that the capabilities for unified command of American and British forces in 1954 fell somewhere between that of World War I and SHAEF in World War II. They were clearly greater, however, than ever before in peacetime

---

[22] General Hastings Lionel Ismay, *NATO: The First Five Years*, Bosch-Utrecht, 1955, p. 72.

and, if war had developed, might have become as great as a decade earlier.

Standardization of Equipment and Logistical Integration

Another dimension of co-operation between two armies is the degree to which they come to use the same equipment and the same supply lines. This may reach the point where neither party can fight a war without the active co-operation of the other, or it may stop far short. Anglo-American military integration has never reached the extreme of intermeshing, but it has been important on several occasions.

In 1917 the United States found itself with nowhere near the amount of equipment necessary for the millions of men it wished to put into the fighting, and without sufficient time to retool its industry to produce those goods. Thus it turned to its allies, who possessed a certain amount of surplus productive capacity. Since most of this capacity was to be found in France, that is where the bulk of American equipment came from — artillery, Hotchkiss machine guns, Chauchat automatics, and ammunition. Of 43 American air squadrons, 30 were equipped with French planes, 10 with aircraft of American manufacture, and only 3 with British planes. Some tanks were assembled in France according to an agreement whereby the British built the hulls, the United States the motors and chassis, and both shipped the parts to France for assembly; but most American tanks were of purely French manufacture. Therefore the American Army was much more similar, in equipment, to the French forces than to the British. In the other direction, the United Kingdom bought many war supplies in the United States, but these tended overwhelmingly to consist of raw materials rather than military ordnance. The most important exception was the DH-4, a British-designed bomber.[23]

Little was done on the matter of combining supply lines. Foch, Pershing, and the Italian Military Representative at various times made suggestions for pooling food, oil, munitions, tanks, and aircraft, but the British were opposed. No quartermaster general, they said, could be responsible for his armies if a higher authority could transfer his stocks. Pershing declared that no commander would forgo control of his supplies any more than he would lose direct command of his army. A Military Board of Allied Supply was organized in May 1918,

[23] H. Duncan Hall and C. C. Wrigley, *Studies of Overseas Supply*, London, 1956, p. 100; Pershing, *My Experiences*, I, pp. 131, 161, 232; and Marcel Vigneras, *Rearming the French*, Washington, 1957, pp. 2–6.

but its wings were clipped by the following limitations: (1) its powers
applied only to supplies in France; (2) it could not interfere with the
ration or with the armies' distributive machinery; (3) decisions had
to be unanimous; (4) its decisions were to be communicated to the
chiefs of the appropriate departments of the various armies and given
effect by them. Other than this halting step, arrangements were made
for an Allied motor transport reserve and a Franco-American ammunition pool. There were a few other agreements "for pooling resources without interference with the internal affairs of armies," but
there was not time for them to become effective.

By the middle of 1940, Britain was placing large orders for equipment in the United States. The nature of these orders was influenced
by the demise of France in June 1940. French orders from the United
States had been far larger than those of the British, and were for
equipment that could not be used by American troops. Should Britain
also fall, American officials believed, the United States would be left
with millions of dollars of nonstandard and therefore useless arms.
For this reason, and to avoid the delay of retooling American facto-
ries, the British had to agree to order only equipment which was also
produced for the American Army. In effect, they had to adopt American equipment. Except for United States use of the Bofors antiaircraft
gun, standardization, though substantial, was all in one direction. An
Anglo-American Standardization of Arms Committee met, but its
powers were limited to discussion and recommendation. There was at
this time, however, a substantial mutual exchange of secret scientific
information, especially about radar, antisubmarine devices, and aircraft equipment.

After the beginning of 1942 still more American-type equipment
was produced for Britain. All aircraft built for the British in the
United States were American models, though the Liberator and
Mustang designs were heavily influenced by British suggestions.
Nearly half of Britain's tanks came from America; the basic design
was American with notable British improvements. The United Kingdom's dependence was particularly striking in the case of heavy trucks
and tank transporters, self-propelled artillery, and transport aircraft,
nearly all of which were American-designed and built. The same was
true of over two thirds of its escort vessels, auxiliary aircraft carriers,
and landing craft, though in the first two cases again the influence of
British design was heavy. The most extreme possible case of weapons
standardization was represented by the reluctant British agreement,
in 1941, to equip ten divisions solely with American arms and
material. Neither this plan nor anything like it was ever carried out.

Only a few pieces of British equipment were adopted by the American army — the 6-pounder antitank gun, the 4.5-inch medium gun, and the Oerlikon antiaircraft gun. Strong efforts to persuade the United States to produce the Spitfire, Beaufighter, and Sterling aircraft all failed. A number of weapons that the United Kingdom authorities refused to forgo were eventually built for them in Canada.

Where standardization failed, co-ordination of production helped reduce the loss. The Americans relaxed their ban on building British-type equipment to make .303-inch rifles and ammunition; 12 per cent of all rifles produced in the United States during 1942–43 were of this nonstandard type. The only other important instance was in the manufacture of the Universal Carrier, which accounted for more than a third of American armored-vehicle production, excluding tanks, in 1944. While limited, this co-ordination effectively reduced the waste that would have occurred had Britain been forced either to do without this equipment or to make it herself. On the highest level it was represented by a basic adjustment imposed by lack of ships for transport; the original war plan of the United Kingdom was modified to put a higher proportion of its manpower into the armed forces, while the United States formed a smaller army and produced more munitions than had been expected. Collaboration on scientific research, especially on radar and the atomic bomb, was of course very close and highly successful.[24]

Co-ordination of production, however, fell far short of what might be expected in a single country. While taking American equipment, the British often continued to build for themselves corresponding arms of British design. For example, it would have been most efficient for Britain, whose tank production was dependent on United States machine tools and components, to stop production and take all its tanks from America, where there was a surplus.

> But over and beyond those arguments [fears of assignment difficulties and the conviction that British tanks were superior] was a consideration of high national policy; to put it bluntly, a country whose army was wholly dependent on a foreign source of supply for so important a piece of equipment *could not easily maintain the status of a fully independent Great Power*.[25]

No statement could better illustrate the limits to the very real and substantial degree of standardization and supply integration achieved.

---

[24] On these matters see H. Duncan Hall, *North American Supply*, London, 1955; Hall and Wrigley, *Studies of Overseas Supply;* F. W. Mulley, *The Politics of Western Defense*, New York, 1962; and Watson, *Chief of Staff*, p. 316. J. P. Baxter, 3rd, *Scientists Against Time*, Boston, 1948, is useful on scientific co-operation.

[25] Hall and Wrigley, *Studies of Overseas Supply*, p. 19 (emphasis mine).

Logistical unification was no further advanced in World War II than in World War I. United States forces in Britain purchased many goods locally, but from the moment that they became American property they were sent through American supply lines. For SHAEF, logistical responsibility remained with the British Service Ministries and the United States War and Navy departments. General Eisenhower could only co-ordinate, and apart from the occasional and unsystematic supply of material from one army to the other, nothing was done. Had the British fleet moved into the Pacific in 1945, it would have provided its own logistical support.

In the middle 1950's there was almost certainly less standardization of equipment than there had been ten years earlier. For NATO as a whole, it had not gone much beyond small pieces of equipment like spark plugs, rims and tires, and lamp sockets. Many larger items were supplied by United States military aid, either from American manufacturers or by offshore purchases, but few arms were used universally. Between Britain and America alone the situation was better, for the United Kingdom had adopted a number of major items: the American 105-millimeter tank gun, the F-86 fighter, and the Corporal and Thor missiles. The United States accepted and produced the British Canberra bomber. Agreement was also reached and implemented on a standard antiaircraft gun, naval ammunition, and quite a number of small components. An Anglo-American Technical Property Committee existed for the exchange of patents, and joint-development projects resulted in American adoption of the steam catapult and the angled deck for aircraft carriers, and RAF methods of servicing aircraft. Co-operative research is currently under way on vertical take-off and landing aircraft. But in the most important area, nuclear weapons, the close wartime co-operation ceased with the passage of the McMahon Act in 1946. Only in 1958, *after* the British had developed an H-bomb independently, did Congress amend the act to permit exchange of information on atomic weapons.[26]

Standardization went no further than this. On the debit side, the 1953 agreement on a standard 30-caliber rifle cartridge has yet to be fully implemented by the United States. The British spent many years developing and producing three classes of V-bombers at enormous expense. Each of these bombers, says one author, was only a marginal improvement on the American B-47 and came into service only long after improved versions of the B-47 could have been made available. The Blue Streak missile, whose development as a military weapon

[26] Ismay, *NATO: The First Five Years*, p. 129; United Kingdom Central Office of Information, *Anglo-American Co-operation*, London, 1958, pp. 11–13; and Ministry of Defence, annual *Statement on Defence*, London, 1950–60.

was abandoned only in 1960, was to have been better than the Thor, but not the second generation of American missiles. The same author points out the expense involved in America's policy of building a mammoth navy in American shipyards when the United States is the world's highest-cost producer of ships.[27] Neither country was willing to become dependent on the other for production of such crucial items.

NATO's "common infrastructure" marked a marginal improvement over the arrangements of World War II. It included air fields, pipelines, and communications systems, which were paid for by member governments and used by NATO forces in Europe. Yet infrastructure meant only the provision of certain common physical facilities, not a system of unified supply lines. Each member continued to supply its own troops.

The indications of responsiveness may be summed up as follows: In standardization and co-ordination of production, NATO's performance fell between that of World War I and World War II, though clearly nearer the latter. Logistical integration as developed in infrastructure was somewhat further advanced than ever before, but its extent still was not great.

Joint Agencies — Powers and Effectiveness

Apart from the conduct of war by the military forces themselves, the most important aspect of any multinational war effort is the degree to which the economies of the participants can be linked to supply each other and to avoid waste from competitive purchasing and duplication. We shall examine the many agencies which have at various times been set up by Britain and America to handle these problems, and analyze the working of these institutions.

World War I undoubtedly represents the period of least attempt and least success in this respect. A number of bodies, including the Inter-Allied Munitions Council, the Inter-Allied Food Council, the Wheat Executive, and the Allied Maritime Transport Council, were set up. Of these, the Maritime Transport Council was the most important, and it typifies the organizational principles of all. An original proposal for an international board with executive authority over a common pool of Allied tonnage was quickly rejected. Instead, the Council existed to exchange information among the member governments, and to co-ordinate their policies and efforts. The point of executive action on ship movement was always at the national level; the Council was only to influence those actions by providing informa-

[27] Malcolm N. Hoag, "What Interdependence for NATO?" *World Politics*, XII, 3 (April 1960), pp. 370–371.

tion and recommendations. Its permanent staff was composed entirely of staff members from the various national agencies, though the chief representatives were members with real authority in their governments so that decisions, once reached, might be implemented effectively. Only one small "pool" of 500,000 tons of chartered neutral shipping was under the Council's direct control.

There were further limitations on the Council's activities. It had no influence over the use of passenger ships for troop transports; this was always a matter for direct negotiation between the British and American governments. America's association with the Council was always somewhat tentative; in the words of the chairman of its Executive, the United States representatives "had a less direct and decisive influence in their national administration than their colleagues" on the Council.[28] Most important, the only country with any number of ships to offer was Britain. France and Italy had relatively small merchant marines which were fully occupied. The United States, though it had a large fleet, was busy transporting troops to France and supplying them. While the British hardly had a surplus of ships, they were the only ones to assign very many to the needs of other Allies. In this situation there was little opportunity for international control. Finally, even had the desire for very close integration been present, which it was not, the comparative novelty of economic-planning techniques would have made its implementation difficult.

World War II, when a number of combined boards flourished, represents a far more interesting period. The most ambitious was the Combined Production and Resources Board, nominally assigned to integrate the countries' war production programs, and particularly to determine what part of American production would go to Britain. But at the time it was organized (January 1942), neither country had yet resolved the administrative procedures for its own economy, and the Board never fitted into those procedures when they became fixed. The United States armed services particularly failed to co-operate with the Board: one author charges that this was deliberate and stemmed from the highest military authorities.[29] On balance, the Combined Production and Resources Board was ineffectual. It compiled data and made recommendations regarding production, but the real power of allocation remained with the purely American agencies. Probably its most important function lay in providing the British with a formal, permanent channel for their demands on the American economy.

Another agency set up at the same time was the Combined Raw

[28] J. A. Salter, *Allied Shipping Control,* Oxford, 1921, p. 176.
[29] S. McKee Rosen, *The Combined Boards of the Second World War,* New York, 1951, p. 148.

Material Board, but its precise powers and jurisdiction were never defined. Efforts to clarify its mandate were resisted in "high quarters." [30] Its members acted on instructions from their government departments. Its staff was very small and was provided entirely by the various national agencies. The Board was dependent on those agencies for information, which it could not always obtain from them, and of course dependent on them for carrying out its recommendations. It was never properly integrated even with the other combined boards, let alone the national departments. In general, the members had to avoid over-all planning and limit their activities to problems which had already arisen. They had some success in dealing with raw materials to be obtained from outside British or American territory, avoiding the waste of competitive bidding, but "the notion of a common United States–United Kingdom pool as such had not been fully accepted by either country, and their national agencies as a rule looked after their own raw materials very closely." [31]

Even more ineffective was the Joint Food Board, which also was restricted to recommending allocations, and perhaps still more than the other boards waited for problems to be referred to it. Its relations with American agencies were particularly difficult, and it was always plagued with jurisdictional difficulties. Many of the most important discussions on food, as in the meat crisis of 1945, took place over its head, directly between London and Washington. One other material-allocating body, the Munitions Assignments Board under Harry Hopkins, merits attention. It had real powers of allocation, primarily because of Hopkins's personal authority and because it did *not* suffer the handicaps of a true combined body, but was an American committee to which British, Russian, and other representatives came with their pleas.

Transportation along the North Atlantic lifeline to England had also to be co-ordinated; this task fell to the Combined Shipping and Adjustment Board. From the start the idea of a common pool and joint planning was rejected, and the Board had no powers of final allocation. The terms of the executive order establishing it were that executive power would be "exercised solely by the appropriate shipping agency in Washington and by the Minister of War Transport in London." Co-operation between these authorities was poor, and when, in June 1943, the British desperately needed ships, President Roosevelt himself had to make the assignment *by transferring the ships to British control.* W. H. McNeill declares:

[30] *Ibid.,* p. 38.
[31] *Ibid.,* p. 27.

In effect then, the British Ministry of War Transport and the War Shipping Administration managed two separate fleets of ships. Anglo-American pooling of resources was limited to the occasional lending of a ship from one to the other for some particular voyage or series of voyages.[32]

Thus the performance of these boards in synchronizing the two economies was not nearly so impressive as their titles might imply. Some of the difficulties were largely the result of the way the boards were organized. They had the power to appoint their own staffs, but no funds of their own. Staff members' salaries were paid by their respective ministries or agencies, and they largely continued to think of themselves as employees of those agencies or ministries. Matters would have been much improved if each agency had had its own staff drawn from a full-time binational secretariat. Some national bias in data-gathering and analysis would have been eliminated, and much information that was never provided, or came only after long delay, would have been available when needed. S. McKee Rosen suggests that if the boards had been given clearer mandates and possibly had been composed of less senior officials (who might have had more time and energy to devote), they would have been more successful.[33] But neither government wanted the boards to have clear mandates which would give them powers of control and allocation. In the words of one of the chief production planners in the British war economy, "No government could possibly delegate or assign to outside agencies the power required to distribute and pool the war effort." [34]

Yet it would be a mistake to disparage the importance of these bodies simply because their powers were advisory rather than executive. Had they been able to reach decisions within themselves and then to obtain, by whatever means of persuasion, the co-operation of their individual governments, they would have been highly significant. But neither was possible. They had little prestige with their national agencies and were frequently ignored. Most often they were unable to reach important agreements internally, and instead opinion divided along national lines. The British members of three or four different boards could all be found advocating the same point; though the American representatives were often unable to agree among themselves, they seldom made common cause with the British. Only rarely was there a united effort by a board against one or both governments.

[32] McNeill, *America, Britain, and Russia*, p. 134.
[33] Rosen, *Combined Boards*, pp. 262–265.
[34] Sir Arthur Salter, "From Combined War Agencies to International Administration," *Public Administration Review*, IV, 1 (Winter 1944), p. 3.

NATO exhibits no organizations as significant even as those of 1942–45. There were, in the middle fifties, various groups to study possible commodity shortages in wartime, such as the planning committees for petroleum, coal and steel, food and agriculture, and industrial raw materials. They had, however, no power beyond that of drawing up recommendations to be submitted in time of war, and were merely embryos of combined boards. In addition there was the Planning Board for Ocean Shipping, which, like its predecessors in two wars, was "to plan the most efficient use of resources," and to make other preliminary arrangements for wartime. But unlike its predecessors, it was expected in case of war to have a pool containing the great majority of all members' ships at the disposal of a body called the Defense Shipping Authority. This Authority, if it came into being, would represent a very substantial advance over previous Allied co-operation. Whether it would in the event be given real powers is dubious, but during the semi-peace of the 1950's it had neither authority nor active function. None of these boards and committees had any significant staff.

By general agreement, NATO's capabilities in this respect fell short of the achievements, however modest, of the early forties, and were hardly an improvement over those of 1917–18. The machinery of day-to-day co-operation was absent.[35]

Exchange of Personnel

In a study which has paid so much attention to the element of personal contact, it would be inappropriate to close this discussion without some analysis of the exchange of military personnel. One type of capability is the degree to which officers of one nationality come into contact with those of the other. Such contacts are likely to give them an appreciation of the methods of the other army and of the attitudes of its officers. Insofar as the contacts are found rewarding, they tend to strengthen the bonds of sympathy between the armies as well.

Information on *all* contacts of this sort is neither available nor essential. One of the most important contacts is the interchange of

[35] See Ismay, *NATO: The First Five Years,* especially pp. 145–149, and "Staff for the Cold War," *Round Table,* June 1951, pp. 207–211. The latter clearly exaggerates the extent and intensity of Anglo-American co-operation in the last war, but its discussion of the differences between that and the NATO period is enlightening. But in any case, there is no doubt that NATO's integration in this respect, however ephemeral, is greater than that between Britain and America in 1941, when the few agencies that existed, such as the Anglo-American Food Committee, were even more lacking in authority and importance.

officers between the various service colleges. The most common level for this exchange is of career officers of the approximate rank of colonel. It was attempted, therefore, to find information on the number of American and other foreign military officers studying at British staff colleges, and the same for foreign officers in American service schools. The results were disappointing, since data of this sort often are either not collected at all or, more likely, are for some reason kept secret.

A few figures, however, are available from British sources on the number of foreign officers at four institutions in the United Kingdom: the Imperial Defence College, the Joint Services Staff College, the Army Staff College, and the Royal Navy College. Because the Imperial Defence College was closed during World War II and the Joint Services Staff College only opened in 1947, we shall, for 1953–55, give totals both for the four and for the Army and Navy colleges alone in Table 10.1.

TABLE 10.1.   Commonwealth, American, and Other Foreign Army and Navy Officers at British Staff Colleges

| | 1943–45 | | 1953–55 | | | |
| | (1) Army and Navy Colleges Only | | (2) Army and Navy Colleges Only | | (3) Four Colleges | |
	Number =	Per-centage	Number =	Per-centage	Number =	Per-centage
Commonwealth	176	65	45	47	84	60
United States	25	9	11	12	17	12
Other Foreign	72	26	39	41	39	28
All Non-British	273	100	95	100	140	100

SOURCE: War Office, *Army Orders*, London, 1943, 1944, 1945, 1953, 1954, 1955; and communication from the Admiralty. Number of Commonwealth officers at Royal Navy College was unavailable.

Since there were practically no exchanges of this sort in 1917–18, the amount of interchange in all three columns of the table clearly represents an improvement over the situation then, but the difference between the two later periods is not substantial. Comparing columns 1 and 3, we see a slight rise in the proportion of American and other foreign officers; the comparison of columns 1 and 2 shows an equally small increase in the American percentage, though an appreciable decline of Commonwealth and increase of foreign officers. Contacts with American officers as a proportion of contacts with all non-British officers thus increased very slightly for British officers studying there. Of the principal American military colleges — National, Army, Naval, and Air War colleges — only the Naval War College operated during World War II, and only the Air War College accepts foreign officers. During 1953–55 it had eleven British and three Canadian officers enrolled.[36] This gives slight indication of increased capabilities, but firmer conclusions would require data on the many lower-level service schools, and that information is not available. A few American and British officers also attended the NATO Defense College in the latter period.

These findings are the only ones which suggest that an aspect of Anglo-American military capabilities for responsiveness was stronger in the 1950's than in the Second World War. It must be emphasized, however, that the data are only a fraction of what we would like to know about officer exchange. They say nothing about Air Force personnel, or about British and American officers in other countries, and not enough about the proportion of British officers among all foreign personnel in the United States.

The other major source of military contact is at bases — namely, the great number of American military establishments in the United Kingdom. These contacts were much less numerous in the 1950's than during World War II. Army, Navy, and Air Force personnel, *with* their dependents, totaled only 75,000 in 1960 as compared with twenty times that number — over one and a half million — at the World War II peak.[37] This decline must have been a heavy counterweight to the increased exchange among service schools.

Conclusions on the Trend

First, the degree of military collaboration during World War II was not as great as might be imagined from the impressive-sounding titles which accompanied it in this "closest and most far-reaching combination of sovereign states." The Combined Chiefs of Staff were dependent on their national staffs. They usually divided along national lines, and their chief function was to bridge the gap between two different national outlooks. The British members never exerted any appreciable influence over operations in the Pacific. SHAEF did repre-

[36] Personal communications from the war colleges.

[37] Ruppenthal, *Logistical Support*, p. 233, and *New York Times*, November 18, 1960, 9: 3–4. While many of the troops in Britain at the May 1944 peak were combat troops practically "in transit" to France, the proportion was not as great as might be supposed. Only 40 per cent were ground forces. The other 60 per cent were air force, supply, and headquarters personnel.

sent a well-integrated international command, but unity of command never went below the level of Generals Montgomery and Bradley. Nothing approaching this unity existed outside the European Theater. Standardization of equipment, though impressive, left much to be desired, and logistical integration was *nil*. The combined boards were without authority and often nearly without influence.

No one pretends that the degree of integration among the Army, Navy, and Air Force of the United States is as great as it might be, but on all counts (probably least so in the case of logistics) it was and is much greater than that between Britain and America in the Second World War.[38] Although it would be a mistake to ignore what was achieved, an easier mistake would be to exaggerate it.

The NATO arrangements of the early and middle 1950's and the closer Anglo-American ties supplementing NATO were undoubtedly the closest ever between the two nations in time of peace. But given our conclusions on the all-time peak of military co-operation of the forties, it certainly was at a lower level in 1954. The capabilities for strategic planning and co-operation were only slightly less close, but unity of command in Europe fell a little further short. Agencies for co-ordinating Anglo-American productive and transport capacity were hardly of more importance than in 1918. Integration on the level of logistics and equipment was low. Our limited data do, however, suggest that the exchange of military personnel was at least equal in the two most recent periods. On balance, we would rank the four periods in this order, from the lowest level of capabilities to the highest: $1939-41 < 1917-18 < 1953-55 < 1942-45$. The degree of co-operation in the latest period is probably closer to that of World War II than World War I.

It is more difficult to compare the amount of resulting responsiveness, since the loads are heavier in wartime than when both partners are at peace. Yet as manifested in such areas as strategic planning, and in the general field of logistics, standardization, and co-ordination of production, it seems clear that responsiveness was at least not higher, in the early NATO period, than ten years before.

Postscript: The Anglo-American Alliance since 1954

During the First World War the British recognized that it was essential for America to be kept at least neutral. Their program of

---

[38] This might well be the most appropriate standard against which to measure the degree of military integration between Britain and America — to my knowledge, no one has attempted the task. But valuable as the comparison might be, it is peripheral to the purpose of this study, which is to compare Anglo-American integration at one point with that which existed in earlier or later years.

restricting neutral trade with the Continent was designed to limit the United States' commerce as much as possible without provoking its leaders to embargo supplies and equipment vital to the Allies. While in the end many British leaders regarded it as essential that America take up arms, and all welcomed the event when she did so, the sense of need of active military assistance was not nearly so great as it was to be in 1940 and 1941. Churchill expressed that desperate sense of dependence upon the United States when he heard the news of Pearl Harbor:

> No American will think it wrong of me if I proclaim that to have the United States at our side was to me the greatest joy. . . . at this very moment I knew the United States was in the war, up to the neck and in to the death. So we had won after all. . . . England would live; Britain would live; the Commonwealth of Nations and the Empire would live. . . . Once again in our long Island history we should emerge, however mauled or mutilated, safe and victorious.[39]

From the vantage point of North America that dependence was never so strong. Few leaders, and certainly not President Wilson, thought that the security of the United States depended on a British victory in World War I.[40] Even if we now believe that to have been the case, few saw it then. By 1941, however, the situation was different. While many isolationists could see no danger, both the Democratic Administration and the Willkie wing of the G.O.P. recognized that Britain must not fall. Yet to most of them even then, a German victory meant, not certain doom for the United States, but only a highly dangerous situation, one which would strain the Western Hemisphere's resources to their limit.

But by 1950, leaders on both sides of the Atlantic had come to realize that the defeat of one partner meant certain defeat for the other. Like the statements of the two previous paragraphs, this is a generalization; it held true more for Britain than for America, but it was generally accurate.

In the past few years, nevertheless, two currents, one more disquieting than the other, have appeared in British thought. They have manifested themselves in the field of co-ordination in weapons development and employment, but indicate a sharp and serious decline in responsiveness and mutual predictability.

For the first decade after World War II, Britain had no significant

[39] Winston S. Churchill, *The Second World War*, New York, 1951, II, pp. 606–607.

[40] Charles Seymour, *The Intimate Papers of Colonel House*, Boston, 1926, I, pp. 293, 298–299; and Robert E. Osgood, *Ideals and Self-Interest in America's Foreign Relations*, Chicago, 1953, pp. 155–194.

strategic bombing force of her own and was dependent on American nuclear power for protection. This, however, was a division of labor that was forced upon her by her economic weakness, not one that she voluntarily accepted. American passage of the Atomic Energy Act and the abrupt cessation of Lend-Lease disillusioned Prime Minister Attlee about the possibilities of close Anglo-American co-operation in the postwar world. Thus as early as 1947 he gave the order for British research and development on nuclear weapons to proceed. By the middle of the 1950's that program was well advanced, and Britain had recovered much of her economic strength.

The first indication of a change in British policy appeared in the *Statement on Defence* of 1954, which proposed a gradual change "in the direction and balance" of effort.[41] More emphasis was to be placed on the RAF strategic bombing force, and less on the Army. This shift became greater with each succeeding year. Britain must have "its own stock" of nuclear weapons; the deterrent was to get "highest priority." The 1956 *Statement on Defence* declared that the United Kingdom "must make a contribution to the Allied deterrent commensurate with [its] standing as a world Power." [42] In official pronouncements this view reached its peak with the 1957 *Statement:* "While Britain cannot by comparison [with America] make more than a modest contribution, there is a wide measure of agreement that she must possess an appropriate element of deterrent power of her own." [43] The building of the British H-bomb, the production of three classes of V-bombers to deliver it, and the development of the Blue Streak missile all reflected this policy.

This duplication of the American deterrent was a serious failure to observe a division of labor within NATO. Malcolm N. Hoag has presented a cogent, well-reasoned argument, on *strategic and economic grounds,* for concentrating the NATO deterrent base on North America, planning to avoid if possible the use of tactical nuclear weapons in Europe, and concentration by European nations on the provision of sufficient conventional forces to withstand even a massive nonnuclear attack in Europe. Any European attempt, he says, to provide a strategic deterrent must be inadequate for economic reasons and in any case will immeasurably increase the damage to Europe by drawing heavy fire in war.[44]

On these grounds the argument is very compelling, but it presupposes a European willingness to depend on the United States to

---

[41] House of Commons, *Accounts and Papers,* Cmd. 9075, London, 1954, p. 6.
[42] House of Commons, *Accounts and Papers,* Cmd. 9695, London, 1956, p. 4.
[43] House of Commons, *Accounts and Papers,* Cmnd. 124, London, 1957, p. 3.
[44] "Interdependence for NATO?" pp. 369–390.

deter the Soviets from using or threatening to use nuclear weapons on
Europe. A government's willingness to implement Hoag's reasoning
depends on two factors. One is the degree to which it is confident of
American readiness to retaliate in case of: (*a*) Soviet nuclear attack
on the European country alone, not including North America, or
(*b*) a Soviet threat to some interest which the European country
feels is vital to itself, but which stops short of a direct nuclear attack.
(The danger of *b* may be mitigated by the presence of Western forces
prepared to fight a limited war.) More important even than the
European government's confidence in American willingness to risk
massive destruction in its defense is its confidence that the Soviet
Union finds the threat credible — American intentions must not only
be "correct," but they must also be expressed in sufficiently convincing form. A high degree of responsiveness is required on both
sides of the partnership; Americans must perceive European vital
interests and respond appropriately, and Europeans must perceive
correctly American intent. For the United States it may also require
a high degree of "we-feeling," of wide self-identification which could
not conceive of allowing the European state to be submerged.

Britain's deliberate turn away from a division of labor within
NATO was a powerful indication of the lack of mutual responsiveness
in the Anglo-American alliance. It would be a mistake to assume
that this was the only factor at work, as it would be foolish to insist
that mutual responsiveness was lower between Britain and the United
States than between other European nations and the United States.
Though her confidence in America was undoubtedly higher than
other countries', a less dependent policy was more nearly within her
reach. Britain had more technical skill and experience and could bear
the economic burden more easily. Perhaps she was more prone to
underestimate the cost of an independent deterrent. And there were
other arguments, aside from a fear of American desertion, which
could support such a policy. It seemed that an independent nuclear
force might be cheaper than large conventional forces; if the first
could be substituted for the second, it would be an economy measure.
Inertia also helped — once British scientists had designed the weapons and their delivery systems, it would have required a sharp reversal to forgo their production when it was seemingly within grasp.
Finally, the desire to have more influence within the Anglo-American
alliance was certainly a factor. Only with her own nuclear striking
force (and consequently the threat, however vague, to "go it alone")
could Britain, it was felt, hope to affect American policy on matters
that were of interest to Britain. Prime Minister Macmillan expressed
this belief:

It puts us where we ought to be, in the position of a Great Power. The fact that we have it makes the United States pay a greater regard to our point of view, and that is of great importance.[45]

This attitude, though questioning American responsiveness to subordinate British needs (and British confidence in that responsiveness), does not necessarily imply any decline in the fundamental matter of responsiveness — America's readiness to defend Britain from nuclear attack. But of all the reasons suggested for the attempt to provide a British deterrent, there is little doubt that the most powerful argument, to the well-informed, was a declining confidence in American willingness to risk massive destruction on Britain's behalf.[46]

Duplicating the American deterrent, even on a very small and inadequate scale, meant weakening the *collective* strength of Anglo-America by departing from the division of labor. But for Britain, it was seen from a national point of view as a step toward greater influ-

[45] *The Times* (London), February 24, 1958. Quoted in Harold Sprout, "Britain's Defense Program," in Princeton University Conference, *Britain Today: Economics, Defense, and Foreign Policy,* Princeton, 1959, p. 60.

[46] In addition to Sprout, see Knorr, editor, *NATO and American Security,* and Robert E. Osgood, "NATO: Problems of Security and Collaboration," *American Political Science Review,* LIV, 1 (March 1960), pp. 106–129. A particularly fine analysis of the influences persuading various types of Britishers of the usefulness of an independent deterrent is provided by Leon D. Epstein, "Britain and the H-Bomb, 1955–1958," *Review of Politics,* XXI, 3 (July 1959), pp. 511–529.

In identifying this decline in confidence, it is not necessary to imply any growing American conception that Britain was "dispensable," or any new failure of communication which prevented the United Kingdom from perceiving American determination to stand by it. The appalling explosion of anger at the United States after Suez represented a feeling that Britain had been betrayed and could never again trust her ally. A change in the Anglo-American link resulting from such a decline in capabilities is quite possible, but the more important change was certainly in the realm of loads. New developments in military technology exposed the United States to heavy destruction and made an American strategy of massive retaliation far less credible than before.

Note also Robert E. Osgood's observation (*NATO: The Entangling Alliance,* Chicago, 1962, p. 170) that allies' willingness to engage in a division of labor depends "on their assessment of the compatibility of their vital interests with the military strategy and foreign policy that interdependence promises to serve. In other words, before accepting the limitations of specialization and integration, each ally must ask, 'Interdependence for what?' and assess the answer to that question in terms of the contribution of NATO's strategy to his military security and the compatibility of that strategy with his foreign policy inside and outside the NATO area. Therefore, the determination of allied strategy and the proper strategic function of each ally within the overall plan must be prior to the achievement of interdependence, and interdependence must be subordinate to the requirements of allied military collaboration and political consensus." He indicates (p. 218) that Soviet threats to bomb London during the Suez crisis strengthened British determination to have their own deterrent.

ence and security. Since then, the British government has come to wonder whether it was worth the price. The V-bombers have proved an insufficient, even pitifully insufficient, force to create the threat intended. To build and maintain them required a dangerous reduction in the nonnuclear forces of all three services. Most important of all, it became prohibitively expensive to develop new weapons — that is, missiles — to replace the bombers when they became obsolete. The government's change of heart first became evident in the *Statement on Defence* for 1959, but there could be no doubt when, in April 1960, it decided to abandon the Blue Streak. The cost of perfecting and manufacturing it was simply too much. Britain could not match the superpowers' efforts at a price she was willing to pay.

At present British deterrent forces consist of the V-bombers and sixty Thor missiles under joint British and American command. Each has a veto on their use through the double-key system. The V-bombers are closely integrated into SAC — so much so that while he always retains a veto on their employment, a British Prime Minister might find it difficult to use them if the United States opposed their use. After the V-bombers become obsolete, the United Kingdom, while continuing to make its own nuclear warheads, will be dependent on rockets of American manufacture for their delivery. The government has admitted it will no longer have a truly independent deterrent — if indeed it ever had one. We thus see a partial return to the original division of labor, though the decision to continue producing nuclear warheads keeps the return partial.

The precise reasons for the reversal are not hard to imagine. First, the economic cost of a British deterrent was driven home to those who thought it a measure for saving on defense. Second, the United States had undoubtedly been somewhat more successful in convincing the British government of the value of the American pledge to stand by its ally. Insofar as responsiveness improved in this way, the price of an independent deterrent seemed less worth paying. After all, if American intentions had been sufficiently in doubt, Britain could somehow have managed to shoulder the cost.

Even in 1957 we must emphasize that there was, in Conservative circles or in the right wing of the Labour party, little hope for a totally independent policy. Britain's military dependence on the United States has two facets. First, there is an *immediate* dependence which means, in effect, that Britain cannot survive unless the United States is actively committed to her defense. This immediate dependence is what the Conservative government tried unsuccessfully to break. It wanted Britain's security to depend on her own capabilities if the United States should insist on being neutral in the face of a Russian nuclear threat to Britain. But there was no thought of challenging a *secondary* kind of dependence stemming from the recognition that Britain could not stand alone if the United States were to fall. Britain was willing to pledge herself to fight for the United States' existence and to make a contribution to joint defense. Russia's submergence of America would mean the end of Britain's sovereignty.

A far more disquieting threat to the Anglo-American alliance appeared more recently, for it is directed to secondary dependence. Left-wing members of the Labour party, long dissatisfied with the alliance, demanded "the unilateral renunciation of the testing, manufacture, stockpiling, and basing of all nuclear weapons in Great Britain." [47] There was some ambiguity about their attitude toward NATO, but it appeared that they would insist on Britain's withdrawal from the alliance if NATO refused to abandon nuclear weapons.

Despite the violent opposition of Hugh Gaitskell and the parliamentary party's leadership, the 1960 Annual Conference of the Labour party passed two resolutions endorsing unilateral nuclear disarmament. The Conference rejected a Gaitskell-supported resolution affirming Britain's intention to remain in NATO. Although the resolutions, by their passage, officially became party policy, Gaitskell promised to ignore them. About 70 per cent of the Labour Members of Parliament stood with him. He fought unceasingly throughout the ensuing year and succeeded in reversing the decision at the 1961 Conference. Because of his efforts the Labour party is again officially committed to NATO and the acceptance of American nuclear protection; but a deep split in the Labour movement remains, and nearly half of all party activists are of the unilateralist persuasion.

While Communist influence in the nuclear disarmament movement is more than negligible, the position is supported by non-Communist leftists of many persuasions. Should their demands be implemented, the consequences would be to reduce drastically Britain's military cooperation with the United States in all respects. Clearly the unilateralists strike against what we called immediate dependence — they are not willing to have Britain defended by nuclear weapons, whether British or American. Except for the extreme pacifists, they presumably would accept American conventional military assistance.

More seriously, these attitudes require a break with secondary dependence as well in their demand for the withdrawal of missile bases. In addition to not wanting to be defended by the United States, the unilateralists may not be willing to join in that country's defense if it became involved in a war. Some justify their position by means of the following logic: Arms races cause war; if Britain abandons

[47] *The Times* (London), October 6, 1960, 18:5.

nuclear arms, the other powers will be forced to follow suit; therefore there will be no arms race and no nuclear war. A few would delete the adjective "nuclear" from the conclusion, feeling that any kind of war would be unlikely. There are many men like these who seriously believe their policy would prevent world war, but for others it indicates a desire to be able to stand aside should America and Russia come into conflict. A few see the result of such a collision as the exhaustion of the participants and a new era of security and influence for Britain; more recognize that Russia might win but find the prospect of Soviet domination less objectionable than death in atomic war. In either case, these men are prepared, if necessary, to keep from the United States the aid that might mean the margin between victory and defeat or stalemate. This notion of security, or even of a tolerable existence in a world with a devastated America, is for most Britons a new one.

The sources of the unilateralist position are as diverse as the kinds of reasoning used to support it. In part they are technological. The development of missiles and the H-bomb makes it virtually certain that Britain could not survive an atomic war in recognizable form.[48] Rising fears of the genetic consequences of nuclear war have played a role. In part the attitude stems from twelve years of domestic political frustration for Labour; the resounding 1959 defeat makes *some* major policy revision seem essential if the party is ever again to achieve a majority. Stalin's death, the moderate reforms in Kremlin rule, and the Soviet coexistence campaign have played an important part. Khrushchev has made deliberate large-scale Soviet aggression appear unlikely, and even the consequences of Russian domination less disastrous. One commentator has declared, "I can only report an increasing tendency on the Left to argue that the differences in human freedom are by now matters of degree rather than principle. . . ."[49]

Past American foreign policy was also an influence. "Brinkmanship" and alleged American impetuosity and irresponsibility contributed to a distrust of American intentions and/or good judgment. But the death of Secretary Dulles and the subsequent moderation of United States policy went almost unnoticed, perhaps because the

[48] Note Secretary Forrestal's remarks on the decision to dispatch B-29's to British bases in 1948: "We have the opportunity *now* of sending these planes, and once sent they would become somewhat of an accepted fixture, whereas a deterioration of the situation in Europe might lead to a condition of mind under which the British would be compelled to reverse their present attitude." (Quoted in Walter Millis, Harvey Mansfield, and Harold Stein, *Arms and the State,* New York, 1958, pp. 226–227)

[49] John Cole, "The Struggle for the Labour Party," *The Guardian,* January 4, 1961, 6:4.

policy was less a cause of distrust than an excuse for it. Thus the roots are also intellectual. The British left has long regarded America with ambivalence. The United States has been a positive symbol as the great center of democracy and egalitarianism, but a negative one as the capitalist power par excellence. By the very nature of its economic system it must be imperialist. Admiration and deep suspicion are combined. Present conditions provide a catalyst for anti-American manifestations, but do not by themselves produce such sentiments.[50]

Probably the pacifist tradition of the British left is an equally important factor. In opposition between the wars the party stood for disarmament and lamented the government's failures to make any progress in this area. In 1935 the party leader, George Lansbury, refused on pacifist principles to support the rearmament necessary to make collective security measures effective against Germany and Italy. Lansbury was deposed, but for years thereafter many Labour M.P.'s refused to vote for even the meager rearmament programs offered by the National government. This attitude has persisted. In the postwar years leftist groups have continued to work for total disarmament, or failing that, at least the renunciation of nuclear weapons by all nations. Many who are not totally pacifist join the latter cry from a moral outrage against nuclear weapons. They see British unilateral abandonment of them as "giving a lead to the world."

Thus the sources of the current antinuclear weapons campaign are many. Its proponents converge, for different reasons, on a program which gives agreement only through a certain ambiguity. For many, the moral element is so strong that they have not yet thought through the logical political consequences. Nevertheless these views are strongly held, and widely enough that they once were carried against the most vigorous opposition of the party leadership. These sentiments are firmly rooted in past habits of thought and are fed by current international conditions.

However secure labor support for the western alliance may now seem, the unilateralists have many sources of strength. Gaitskell's victory was achieved by converting a few people heading some of the major trade unions. Some of his supporters were motivated less by anti-unilateralism than by a simple desire to maintain a moderate leader with a wide electoral appeal.[51] If certain trends — Labour's frustra-

---

[50] David Marquand, "England, the Bomb, the Marchers," *Commentary,* XXIX (May 1960), pp. 380–386, stresses the role of anti-Americanism in the unilateralist movement.

[51] Though it defeated unilateralist motions, the 1961 conference passed, by three quarters of a million votes, a resolution against the establishment of American Polaris bases in Britain. See Leon Epstein, "Who Makes Party

tion, Russia's coexistence policy, the development of still more fearsome weapons and delivery systems, the failure of disarmament negotiations — continue, the demand for a break with the American alliance may grow. The danger is probably not immediate. Acceptance of the unilateralist position would condemn the Labour party to continued minority status for the next few years. Even the most ardent unilateralists recognize that their policy does not now command majority support in the country.[52] But they are content to wait and argue, confident that someday a Labour party committed to nuclear disarmament will regain power. Meanwhile their pressure can make it difficult for the government to commit itself any more deeply to its nuclear alliance with the United States. No one can be complacent about the state of Anglo-American relations.

Policy: British Labour, 1960–61," *Midwest Journal of Political Science,* VI, 2 (May 1962), pp. 165–182.

[52] Surveys indicate that a substantial majority of the population wants Britain to retain her own nuclear capability — though a majority opposes the placement of American missiles on British territory. See Alastair Buchan, "Britain Debates the 'Balance of Terror,'" *Reporter,* April 3, 1958, p. 10.

11

Toward Greater Integration

Much of the analysis in this study has been concentrated upon trends in patterns of communication and attention. Clearly, these trends are not all that is relevant to the relations between Britain and America or between any other two nations. One particularly significant variable is the pattern of events in the international arena. A common external threat can push together two nations whose attention and communication capabilities are not high, and it may keep their policies in alignment over a substantial period of time. It does this principally by forcing each of the partners to give special weight, special priority, to the demands of the other. Thus, even though transaction rates may be unchanged, each partner finds the other readier to respond to his needs. This external threat was a most important element in Anglo-American relations during the period before World War I and has been very influential, though to an uneven degree, during the last twenty-five years. In addition, the fact of an alliance may cause each government to make special efforts to increase the attention it gives to the other. Both may more readily perceive, as well as be more willing to respond.

But trends in the international system are not, by themselves, enough to maintain this relationship — they are not sufficient for the continuance of an integrated community. This is not always recognized. The notion that military and strategic considerations will always bind Britain and the United States together is a tenacious one. A recent study of the American-British-Canadian relationship pointed to

> . . . operative forces that are more urgent than the mere belief in an underlying identity of interests — forces that are the effective agents

for translating that sense of identity into the instruments for positive and unified action . . . the most potent and immediate of these forces is a sense of real and present danger to the Free World as a whole.[1]

We should know better. Even the narrowest military alliance requires more than objective military necessity to keep it together — Iraq and Cuba should have suggested that. McNeill, recalling World War II, wrote,

> Yet a consideration of the course of Anglo-American relations in the autumn of 1944 and the spring of 1945, when Germany's defeat was already certain and before the Americans recognized any definite threat from Russia, suggests how easily Anglo-American friendship and co-operation could be interrupted by lack of common danger.[2]

An alliance may be a precarious thing. Americans have tended not to worry too much about the state of their relations with Britain in particular, but a recurrent fear has been that the Soviets, by turning on a peaceful-coexistence campaign, could cause NATO in general to relax and disintegrate as the apparent threat diminished. This is a narrow view, which perceives only one of the factors that could cause an alliance to weaken. Yet in the light of the previous chapter, it recognizes what was, and is, a real danger.[3]

To maintain an alliance over a long period requires more than immediate peril. If the threat recedes, the alliance, unsustained by other factors, may collapse and defy rebuilding should the danger reappear. More seriously, one or both partners may imagine mistakenly that the threat has receded; if then the alliance is enfeebled, the cost will be heavy. Yet more dangerous is the possibility that other interests will come to take priority over the threat which once brought the partners together. The avoidance of widespread radioactive poisoning may seem more important than avoiding military defeat. Lesser interests may encourage chance-taking — the desire to influence the other partner's policy may cause one to duplicate part of his defense establishment. This may be seen as weakening the *joint* strength somewhat, but the loss may appear small compared with the national gains. Should there have been a misjudgment — if the weakening in joint strength should prove the margin of defeat in an unexpected war — it would then be too late to avoid the consequences.

[1] Edgar McInnis, *The Atlantic Triangle and the Cold War*, Toronto, 1959, p. 20.

[2] William Hardy McNeill, *America, Britain, and Russia: Their Co-operation and Conflict, 1941–1946*, London, 1953, p. 748.

[3] By contrast, a relaxation of international tension would not seem likely to cause the disintegration of the United States–Canada tie.

Furthermore, an alliance by itself may impose burdens which make its continuance difficult. In terms of our model, the additional loads may exceed the capabilities which it adds:[4]

1. The economic burdens of defense may divert resources away from essential uses at home; key groups in the population may find their interests neglected and blame the expense of the alliance.
2. Attention may be diverted from other interests, foreign or domestic, whose neglect will thrust great difficulties onto one or both partners.
3. The military concentration may draw the attention of one member away from his partner's other vital concerns; a member's limited capacity for responsiveness can be too heavily concentrated on the military situation, while the other partner's sense of frustration continues to grow.

Doubtless an alliance brings with it increased capabilities for its own maintenance: Military personnel meet and travel between the countries, and they come both to like their opposite members and to appreciate and understand their problems. Political and military institutions are set up, increasing and channeling the capacity for responsiveness. Yet it is unlikely that military dependence will, by itself, create new capabilities to match the loads it places on existing capabilities. In Godechot and Palmer's terms, *"il faut que plus qu'une telle interdépendance pour constituer une civilisation."* [5] More precisely, it requires more than a military interdependence just to maintain that interdependence in working order.

The Anglo-American alliance is probably stronger on the surface than underneath. If the governments permit the links to weaken further, they must be prepared to face the consequences of diminished responsiveness someday.

It is not easy to predict just what these consequences may be, but a brief résumé of the principal trends will help give perspective:

[4] Deutsch *et al.*'s findings are relevant. They found that alliances to meet a foreign military threat were sometimes helpful but by no means essential to the growth of integration. The effect of a military threat was likely to be transitory, and permanent unions derived their support from other factors. Often the military threat caused some parts of the community to feel that they had been excessively burdened, and in other cases preoccupied the governing elites so that they became unresponsive to the needs of their own or their partner's populace. An alliance, far from being necessary to integration, often contributed to disintegration. (See pp. 44–46, 60–61, 156–157, 190–191 of *Political Community and the North Atlantic Area*, Princeton, 1957.)

[5] Jacques Godechot and Robert R. Palmer, "Le Problème de l'Atlantique du XVIIIème au XXème siècle," *Relazioni del X Congresso Internazionale di Scienze Storiche*, Florence, 1955, V, p. 234.

1. The relative frequency of Anglo-American links in the executive and legislature in both countries has declined.
2. Mutual attention and communication among members of the attentive public has diminished.[6]
3. Mutual attention and current communication at the mass level has generally declined, though there are a number of exceptions.[7]
4. Educational attention, which should promote favorable deep memories even though it cannot easily communicate current needs, has increased.
5. Elite approval, as reflected in the prestige newspapers, is up.
6. Mass approval, as measured by survey research, has declined.
7. Although they were never as divisive as has sometimes been held, certain previous irritants — trade restriction and discrimination and investment rivalry — have receded, and an increasing similarity of the two cultures promises to reduce other possible sources of friction.

Factors 4, 5, and 7 are elements which may make it increasingly likely that Britain and America will not desert each other in a crisis. They may be abetted in this by those ties under 3 which have grown stronger. One would feel more certain of this, however, if 6 also showed improvement. Though they had substantial opposition from other parts of the government, the American President and Cabinet were not unresponsive to Britain's needs in 1939–41 and 1946–49. It was mass support of an activist policy that was felt most keenly to be lacking. The fact that elite approval of Britain has risen during the last generation is not sufficient comfort. Emergency aid for Britain may draw upon a wider elite base of support than ever but still face substantial opposition from below.

In the United States this decline in mass support is probably not a serious concern. Whatever the trends in approval, the American government did, on numerous occasions after World War II, make substantial contributions to British and Atlantic defense — the British Loan, the Marshall Plan, NATO, and the Mutual Security Act. The pressures of a clear and present danger from abroad were largely responsible. Yet in a way this is just the point. It was not difficult to convince many that if Britain fell to the Soviets, American security would be grievously endangered. But current trends in technology

[6] Though newspaper attention has risen in both nations, all other elements — trade in merchandise, trade in services, tourist exchange, student exchange, and scholarly attention — have weakened.

[7] Mail, telephone and telegraph communications, and migration are down, but the exchange of magazines and films has either increased or remains about the same in both countries.

make military attempts to defend Britain increasingly hazardous. Massive retaliation has lost its sting. Though American security would still be intensely threatened by the fall of Britain, it would be equally endangered by some kinds of military action to prevent that fall. One answer to the dilemma is of course to create a relationship, of implicit and explicit threats and promises, which will obviate any choice between the loss of our ally and nuclear catastrophe. This was the purpose of the massive-retaliation doctrine. But the decline in mass approval may make the threats and promises increasingly less credible.

A more serious danger to the maintenance of joint defense, however, comes from the British side. As the smallest and weakest of the three major nuclear powers, the British are becoming more and more aware of the dangers. It is there that the decline in mass approval is particularly disquieting. Despite the presence of a few "name" figures like Lord Russell, the leaders of the British unilateralist movement are not drawn from the traditional elites. By the unilateralists' own admission, every daily, weekly, or Sunday paper with a circulation over 100,000 is on the other side.[8] The leaders are primarily trade-unionists and left-wing intellectuals without current university attachments. Yet this movement was temporarily strong enough to set official Labour policy in defiance of the party chief.

Furthermore, mass approval of America, not just mass opinion on other issues, is crucial here. The unilateralists do not prefer the Soviet Union to the United States; the contrary is still true. But the Khrushchev "thaw" in Russia, coupled perhaps with an increasing disillusionment with American capitalism, has narrowed the gap between their attitudes toward the two countries. Their relative preference for the United States has diminished to where they are not unwilling to contemplate a world from which the United States has vanished and the Soviet Union is battered but victorious. While this is not an agreeable vision, it is better than one of nuclear destruction for themselves. Thus we must be concerned, for the long run, over the decline in mass approval of the United States. It threatens to prevent mutual responsiveness even in crises.

But this danger is a long-term one and depends for its seriousness upon future developments in East-West relations and in military technology. Either a satisfactory arms-control agreement or a renewed Western capacity to fight limited war would substantially remove it. In the sense of abjuring violent conflict between themselves, and an

[8] Francis Flavius, "*The Guardian* Puts Us in the Picture," *Tribune*, January 13, 1961, 4:5.

ultimate willingness of each partner to preserve the other from extinction, the marriage may be stable for a long time to come.

This does not say that the marriage need be a happy one. Stability and happiness do not necessarily go together. External pressures and their own basic "affection" are not enough to ensure that differences of interest or opinion will be settled easily or amicably. A couple may become increasingly dependent upon each other for support, but their arguments may become increasingly bitter.

Elite approval and cultural similarity make modest contributions to mutual responsiveness on normal, noncrisis matters — we discussed the means by which they do so in Chapter 8. The improvements noticed [9] are heartening in this respect, but they are by no means sufficient. Responsiveness depends particularly on the level of communication and attention, and it is in this area that we find a serious downturn.[10] Without the facilities to identify each other's needs a will to meet them is impotent. (The one important instance of increasing attention — education on both sides — is much more influential as a means of increasing approval than in providing current, up-to-date information on the other party's needs.) Meeting those needs at the governmental level often requires the existence of interest groups which can be mobilized to support a responsive policy. The decline of trade, listed under elite communication, is worrisome in this respect also.

Let us review three sets of less-than-crisis issues which are certain to arise between the United States and the United Kingdom during the next few years, and the degree of responsiveness that might be expected on each. First is the matter of peacetime military interdependence. The two nations might, in a showdown, stand together as before, but the changes in the world arena and the decline in attention and mass approval militate against any closer linking of their armed forces or defense policies. Only with the renewal of an openly aggressive Soviet foreign policy, pursued in a way that lent itself to perception as a mutual threat, can one visualize much additional support for further military interdependence. The proposal for a NATO independent deterrent is, after all, a proposal for greater mutual dependence among European states but less dependence on America.

Second, there is the whole class of issues that can broadly be labeled "colonialism." The Kennedy Administration has been making a major effort to strengthen its ties with the emerging nations of the

---

[9] Numbers 4, 5, and 7 in the outline on p. 199.
[10] Numbers 1, 2, and 3.

world. On matters where these nations can make "colonialism" seem
to apply, the Administration may give less, not more, weight to the
views of the "colonial" powers, among whom Britain must still be
numbered. The relative decline in attention to Britain will encourage
this tendency, and American cultural memories of 1776 make it unlikely that there will ever be much mass support for "colonialist"
policy. In the long run, relief may come as Britain liquidates the remains of her empire; but for many years there will undoubtedly be
instances where "colonialism" will come up in an economic rather
than a political sense — foreign investors' property will be nationalized, for example. Possibly this will happen often enough to the
United States, as well as to Britain, to produce a common front of
sorts. The necessity to get along with the underdeveloped countries,
however, may produce a situation where Britain and the United
States, despite outcries about their losses, will not protect each other
from expropriation.

A third type of issue is the economic. As a connecting link, commerce has been of diminishing significance, and current trends indicate that it may continue that way. Some trends in mass and elite
opinion suggest that it will also decline as an irritant. Elite and attentive public acceptance of the principles of free trade is stronger in
the American Northeast than ever before. On the other hand, it is
probably weaker than ever before in the newly industrializing Southeast, and powerful labor unions increasingly clamor, with their em-
ployers, for tariff protection. The effects of hard-core unemployment
and the gold outflow have also been detrimental. But as long as the
world economy remains on a relatively even keel, this is unlikely to
become too serious. After all, the decline in economics as a bond has
the beneficial effects of simultaneously reducing a source of irritation.

In this study we have expressed great concern over the weakening
of certain bonds between Britain and America, and some might insist
that so much concern is misplaced. Although the two nations may
not be quite as near as they once were, they still are very close.
Except for Canada, Great Britain is surely America's closest ally,
and of all countries outside the Commonwealth none has closer bonds
with Britain than does the United States. If these bonds are now not
quite as strong as they once were, that is not surprising, since both
countries now have more far-flung interests than ever before. Many
more world-wide problems compete for their attention, and a slight
loosening of the Anglo-American bond is of little concern. After all,
its strength ensures that it is the last that will be broken. So why
not attend to the feebler ones first?

The answer is twofold. First, though the Anglo-American tie is one of the strongest, it is surely one of the most essential. Again with the possible exception of Canada, no country is as vital to the United States in the cold war as is the United Kingdom. For Britain, *no* other alliance could match in security that presented by America. If anything should break that tie, both countries would find it nearly impossible to find compensation. Thus we should be sure to build our foreign policies on the most stable foundations, and only then turn to strengthening the superstructure.

Second, there is no assurance, whatever its strength, that the Anglo-American bond will be the last to break. The odds perhaps suggest that it will be last, but the probabilities are not high enough to satisfy us. An additional load may appear with little warning, and whereas a weak bond may survive light loads indefinitely, a heavy weight may break a strong bond after only a short pull.

A rather elaborate metaphor may help to elucidate the argument. Imagine the security of the United States as a treasure chest suspended by a net, the net being tied to fifty posts by a rope to each post. Each post represents another nation, and each rope an alliance or mutual-defense pact. Some of these ropes are tied to key portions of the net; others are of marginal importance. Each rope is of a different strength from the others. These are the capabilities. In the present case the rope to Britain is both strong and anchored to a vital spot. Imagine further that fifty men of various strengths come to pull on these ropes every day, and that the men change ropes at random, pulling on one rope one day, another the next. These are the loads. Some men can break the weaker but not the stronger ropes; possibly some can break no rope at all. Probably the most powerful man can break even the toughest rope, though this is not certain. In this situation the Anglo-American rope, as one of the strongest, is one of the most likely to survive; but despite the probabilities, should it meet a very powerful man early, it *could* be one of the first to break.

Let us add another dimension to the metaphor: a contest between rot which weakens the ropes over time and a harassed rope-mender who is trying to keep them all strong and secure. Thus some ropes gradually become vulnerable, and others, through reinforcement, become stronger than ever. If the rope-mender is both lucky and wise in the apportionment of his time and resources, he may be able to preserve the net's treasure indefinitely. If he is unlucky or foolish, it will be lost. In these circumstances, for how long dare he neglect the Anglo-American rope? He may wait for a very long time, and even then the rope will probably be one of the toughest remaining, but it will be weaker than before and within the strength of more of the men pulling. The chances will thus become greater that it will break.

And since it is such a key rope, the cost of losing it would be heavy. Would he not be wise to tend it carefully and keep it strong?

Finally, let us add one more dimension. Assume, not that the men are guided daily to their ropes at random, but that they are directed deliberately so that the most powerful men are often sent to pull on the strongest ropes. Here is not a neutral nature, but a malevolent, rational enemy seeking to destroy American security. Would the rope-mender not be still more foolhardy, under these circumstances, to neglect his key ropes just because they were strong at the beginning?

By emphasizing the danger of the broken rope this metaphor, however useful, obscures another point which must be made. In addition to breaking the rope, analogous to the end of the Anglo-American alliance or perhaps of the security-community, the decline of capabilities relative to loads presents a more immediate threat. Inadequate capabilities, by preventing a high level of responsiveness, result in mutual frustration — important interests are left unsatisfied. Britain and America are highly important to each other; each has the economic, military, and diplomatic strength to meet or deny major needs of the other or to help the other gain benefits from a third party. Obviously, the United States can indulge or deprive Britain more than vice versa, but Britain's power is not to be ignored. To the extent that responsiveness fails, they must conduct their other international relations with less than optimum strength, and in prevailing international conditions the loss may be critical. (Without Marshall Plan aid, Britain's resistance to the Soviet Union would have been severely weakened.) George Kennan admirably sums up the argument:

> The day that Englishmen and Americans come to regard their mutual differences as more important than the need for a common front in the face of Communist power in Russia, there will no longer be any future for any nation in the Western world. Conversely, so long as the minimum of Anglo-American solidarity is preserved — so long as the English-speaking nations continue to manifest in their own mutual relations the genius for tolerance and accommodation that lies at the heart of their domestic life the Communist victory will never be complete. . . .[11]

How might we mend the rope? For suggestions, let us consider some of the ways in which the United States could try to prevent the nuclear disarmers in Britain from gaining further support:

1. It could see that the American view is presented logically to the British, with an attempt to convince them of its soundness, their own illogic, and the disastrous consequences of their program.

[11] George Kennan, *Russia, the Atom, and the West*, New York, 1957, p. 101.

2. It could work to strengthen the sense of mutual identification, of "we-feeling," that Britons have for the United States. Since the English could not respect themselves if they allowed their Scottish compatriots to be obliterated, the Americans might try to get the same attitude attached to them. America could try to become a friend they could not morally desert.

3. The government might try, on a wide variety of issues, to persuade the British of its good intentions and the logic of its policies, thus restoring confidence in its good judgment.

4. It might try to show them the extent to which their own interests depend upon American well-being, such as that the health of the British economy could not continue if the American economy faltered. Not only might it try to show that this kind of dependence existed, but it might attempt to increase it objectively, as by enlarging the proportion of Britain's trade that goes to America.

5. It might take steps to help its own decision-making system to become more responsive to British needs and wishes, thus decreasing the feeling of frustration across the Atlantic.

Each of these suggestions necessitates strengthening the ties of communication and exchange of persons between the two nations. The first four require that an increasing proportion of Britain's attention be directed to the United States. Point five is the obverse: it requires that an increasing proportion of American attention be directed to the United Kingdom. All five points demand that the current declining trend in Anglo-American communications and attention be sharply reversed, on both mass and elite levels.

The means of beginning to reverse this trend are innumerable, and the attack would have to be pushed on many fronts. Probably the most important would be a conscious decision to accord the other's requests a heavier weight in decision-making than they have been given in the past. This might take the form, for instance, of an over-all higher priority to British needs, which would, especially on colonial matters, widen the gap between the United States and the emerging nations. For obvious reasons such a policy is not lightly to be recommended, but there is a more agreeable alternative. One of the chief reasons for present irritation over American policy toward colonialism is its instability. In an attempt to please both the emergent and the colonial nations, we often anger both alternately. Instead, we might deliberately adopt a stronger and more consistent anti-colonial policy. The British would certainly be angered by this, but we might compensate them by important concessions in some other area, such as economics or the sharing of military secrets. Such an arrangement, whether reached implicitly or by official negotiation, might enhance Anglo-American relations over the years. The shift to greater consistency in actual and symbolic responsiveness might well pay off in closer co-operation in many areas of foreign policy.

Other possible steps would be:

1. The expansion, relative to other sections, of those sections of policy-making organs which are concerned with the other partner — i.e., the British Commonwealth Office of the Department of State.
2. The maintenance and, if possible, expansion of official intelligence-gathering agencies in the other country.[12]
3. The provision of more funds for the exchange of persons — students, academics, opinion-leaders, military men, and political figures.
4. The elimination of restrictions on travel between the two nations, particularly the United States requirement that British subjects obtain visas before entry. This would merely reciprocate a British policy in effect since the end of World War II.
5. A reduction in trade restrictions — i.e., the American tariff and, on the other side, what remains of quantitative restrictions and preferences which favor Commonwealth over American goods. On these grounds, at least, British participation in the European Common Market would not be desirable if it diverted trade from the United States. The Trade Expansion Act, however, is a step in the right direction.
6. A reduction in the rates for postal, telegraph, and telephone communication between the two nations, preferably the application of domestic rates to such traffic.[13] This might profitably be extended to books and periodicals.
7. Exemption of each other's products from national quotas in the mass media, such as British limitations on the percentage of foreign films and television programs which can be shown. Alternatively, existing quotas might simply be enlarged.
8. The elimination of restrictions and duties on the importation of books and periodicals printed in English.
9. An expansion of the amount of attention given to each other in

[12] Recent reductions in the budgets and staffs of United States embassies in Europe to provide funds and personnel for the new embassies in Africa illustrate precisely what should not be done, especially in the long run.

[13] The cost of this step would be moderate. The United States already applies the domestic postage rate to mail destined for Canada and Mexico, and the General Post Office has estimated (in a personal communication) that it would cost the United Kingdom about £1.65 million annually to apply the domestic rate to first-class mail sent to the United States.

the educational process (especially in Britain), with an attempt to eliminate unfavorable biases from educational materials.

Some of these recommendations would meet with determined opposition from domestic pressure groups, and some might be undesirable for reasons other than the one here advanced. Some, though not all, would mean greater attention to Britain at the expense of other nations or of domestic events, and in many instances this would not be desirable. Because of other short-term dangers some contrary steps, such as reducing the London embassy, may be unavoidable. Where possible, it would seem best to make the shift to mutual Anglo-American attention at the expense of domestic attention, on the grounds that under twentieth-century conditions errors in the international arena are likely to be more costly than errors at home.

Even if implemented, these recommendations would not immediately produce a drastic improvement in Anglo-American relations — they are not panaceas, nor are they dramatic. But they serve as examples of the kind of steps which would, over a number of years, substantially improve each nation's capacity for attention and responsiveness to the other. If these and similar measures are carried out, the Anglo-American alliance will be better able to withstand the stresses which will inevitably afflict it. They will not, by themselves, lead to the *de jure* unification of Great Britain and America, a goal which is in any case not necessarily to be desired. But they can lead to a lasting, stable, and mutually rewarding relationship between the two great English-speaking peoples.

12

Notes on a Theory of Integration

In this study we have specified in theory and examined empirically a number of variables which have often been neglected in the analysis of international politics. We have developed a theory that responsiveness is largely a function of the ratio of loads to capabilities at any time, and have looked at many transactions which make up capabilities for attention, communication, and mutual identification. We have also specified and examined some of the internal factors which affect responsiveness but which are not measurable as transactions. In the preceding chapter we considered some of the ways in which changes in the world political arena may affect relations. Finally, in a test case on legislators we showed that these transactions and internal factors do make a difference in the way men behave.

We have also expressed some tentative conclusions about trends in responsiveness, offering substantial evidence that in many important respects Britain and America have become less responsive to each other's needs than they were several decades ago. At the very least we have shown the weakness of such optimism as H. C. Allen's:

> With the election of Eisenhower and the prospect of possibly four years or more of power and influence wielded by these two men [Eisenhower and Churchill], who above all others were responsible for and symbolized the supreme achievement of Anglo-American unity in World War II, it is hard to believe that all will not be well.[1]

These words were written less than three years before Suez. Yet the attempts of this study represent only the beginning of what must be a serious and determined effort to measure responsiveness with

[1] H. C. Allen, *Great Britain and the United States,* New York, 1955, p. 983.

precision. Part of the solution may come from considering responsiveness in over-all terms. The discussion may have to be limited to one or more particular areas of policy at a time so as to avoid the "index problem" which results from trying to combine such disparate elements as an increase of military responsiveness with a decline in the field of economics.

Also, this discussion has not considered a number of other elements which influence responsiveness. There is a whole class of variables which may be described as internal factors; that is, they are not measurable as international transactions. One of these is the size and influence of interest groups. In Chapter 3 we put forth the working hypothesis that changes in size are correlated with changes in influence. The changes are not necessarily proportional, but at least they occur, and in the same direction. We recognized the limitations, and in some circumstances absolute error, of this assumption; nevertheless we found it a useful and seldom seriously damaging one to work with. Yet because it is so central to much that was done, it needs to be explored and tested rigorously in a number of circumstances. Interest-group analysis, with all the attention and resources devoted to it in recent years, has hardly begun to solve this problem. Is the assumption valid? With what time lags? Under what conditions?

In the particular case of Anglo-American relations, attention must be given to interest groups other than those directly involved. In the opening theoretical statement we insisted that the weight of a load at any given time depended in part upon the number, weight, and direction of other loads, both domestic and international. If powerful domestic interest groups are pressing the same demands as those coming from one's ally, it may be easy to meet his demands even if little attention is given him or little priority is assigned to his needs. In both countries groups which have an interest in the Western alliance and the cold war may, at present, help to keep responsiveness at a high level. But should nuclear disarmament become official policy in Britain, armament and alliance-oriented groups in the United States might widen the resultant breach. Domestic interests pressing in a direction opposite from the partner — business demands for a higher tariff, for instance — may make it practically impossible to indulge the partner's needs even when attention and priorities are high.

It is not only the particular formal or informal associations often meant by the term "interest group" which change in size and influence. In much of the world whole strata of populations, lower-class and middle-class, are gaining political power for the first time. The following example illustrates a situation whereby the relations between two states might change radically without any variation in attention, communication, or attitudes. Suppose that for decades power in a Latin American country had been essentially in the hands of wealthy landowners and businessmen with important commercial ties to the United States. For these men the ties were sources of reward, and so they contributed to maintaining responsive relations. The middle and lower classes, however, may have regarded those commercial ties as means of exploitation, and so they were associated with deprivations. With the economic development of the country, this nonelite portion of the population slowly acquired political interest and some bases of power. Following a revolution in which their representatives gained power, there might be a long series of hostile acts directed against the United States. Yet this transfer of power postulates no change either in transactions flows or in the number of people holding pro-American views. It means only internal changes in political power.[2]

On the face of it, this kind of change does not appear to have affected Anglo-American relations much. Britain undoubtedly has seen a great increase in the political efficacy of the working classes over the past century, but there is little evidence that they are more anti-American than the upper class. In the United States there is a striking correlation between high income and pro-British attitudes, but lower-class political power, starting as it did from a higher level, has probably not increased nearly as much as in England over the same period. This whole problem, however, deserves thorough investigation.

We have shown that members of the Cabinet and legislature of both countries are, in general, less likely to have bonds with the other country than were their counterparts in the past. Yet the Cabinet and legislature hardly exhaust the list of bodies important in the formation of foreign policy, and in many ways they are not even typical. For example, entry into the House of Commons, possibly via trade-union ranks, may be somewhat easier for a member of the working class than admission to the highest levels of Her Majesty's civil service. If working-class men are particularly unlikely to have contacts with the United States, the decline in links among M.P.'s may be sharper than in the civil service. Similar data must be found for the leaders of major interest groups, editors, publishers and journalists, and other key members of unofficial policy-making groups.

The finding that legislators with ties are more likely to be responsive than those without ties does not necessarily apply to men like officers of the Bank of England. High civil servants' backgrounds and

---

[2] This hypothetical description actually fits rather closely the events in Argentina during recent decades. See Ysabel Rennie, *The Argentine Republic,* New York, 1945, pp. 317–380.

responsibilities are different from legislators', as are the pressures to which they are exposed and even the kinds of decisions which they are called upon to make. While the evidence on M.P.'s and Senators, combined with the material cited in Chapters 6 through 8, strongly suggests a correlation between ties and responsiveness generally, it certainly does not prove it.

Devising a proof is not easy, for information about who did what in the making of a particular decision is difficult to find. The most promising field is perhaps that of the Cabinet in both countries, for Cabinet members are likely to have written memoirs or autobiographies, or to have had biographies written about them. Official documentation on decision-making in recent years is scanty, but for the earlier periods State Department and Foreign Office archives are open and can provide a very substantial amount of material.

Another area worth exploring is that of structural similarity. In the chapter on military relations, we found that the American Joint Chiefs of Staff first met as a body because of the need for a group capable of negotiating with the British Joint Chiefs. It would be illuminating to know what other structures — not only military but such branches of the executive as the State Department, Treasury, Commerce Department, Foreign Office, and Board of Trade — have tended to become alike in both countries. Similarity, by facilitating the synchronization of policy machinery, should be an important capability. It also should be a useful indicator of expectations. The sequence and timing of steps in the process should be made clear. A tentative hypothesis would be that one tends to imitate the machinery of one's friends, from whom one expects rewards, rather than one's enemies.

Yet another kind of internal change is in the size of the government sector in each country. In 1890 the budget of the federal government made up about 3 per cent of the United States national income, but in the fifties it accounted for over 20 per cent of all income. The change in exchequer expenditures in Britain, from 5 per cent to 35 per cent, is even sharper.[3] One possible result is that both governments have more flexibility and greater capacities for attention to each other, on the theory that they can most effectively control, and most rapidly

---

[3] Budget figures from *Historical Statistics of the United States, Colonial Times to 1957*, Washington, 1960, p. 718; *Statistical Abstract of the United Kingdom, 1890–1904*, p. 10; and *Annual Abstract of Statistics, 1960*, p. 251. Income data from Robert F. Martin, *National Income in the United States, 1799–1938*, New York, 1939, pp. 6–7; A. R. Prest, "National Income of the United Kingdom, 1870–1946," *Economic Journal*, LVIII, 229 (March 1948), p. 58; and *United Nations Monthly Bulletin of Statistics*, November 1960, p. 159.

receive intelligence from, agencies within the government sector. Quite the opposite hypothesis is that the expansion of government activities has overloaded the capacities of the top decision-makers, so that they have less time to devote to the other country and less flexibility. Neither of these hypotheses has been tested at all satisfactorily.

A number of changes in the international arena are also highly relevant. For one thing, we ought to know the relationship between each member of the Anglo-American partnership and a number of other countries taken separately. Data on changes in the two countries' relations with each other and with the rest of the world in general must be supplemented by information which breaks the rest of the world into its constituent national units. For instance, we know that Anglo-American trade has declined sharply relative to the partners' trade with the rest of the world. We also found that American exports to other industrialized countries had not fallen nearly as much; in fact, relative to the null-model "expectations" exports to the European "Six" had actually risen slightly since World War II. The British have changed sources of raw materials, so that they now import from Africa or India much of what once came from the United States, especially cotton, wheat, and tobacco.[4] Thus the decline in Anglo-American economic links is not simply the result of forces weakening ties throughout the North Atlantic area but is a special case requiring additional explanations. Further analysis of the commodity structure of trade among a great many pairs of countries is required here; and, in fact, all the information given in Chapter 3 and Chapters 6 through 8 should be reproduced in the form of matrices including many nations. The benefits of such inquiry would be far-reaching.

Although this procedure would give us more insight into the *explanation* of change, it would not add so much to our *description* of Anglo-American relations. The fact is that various kinds of mutual capabilities have declined. If we discover that they also have declined vis-à-vis other members of the Atlantic Community, this does not make the particular Anglo-American problem less real or less serious. It does, however, contribute something to the *explanation,* and this insight may make it easier consciously to reverse the trend.

Another trend in world politics promotes what might be called the "contrast effect." With the rise to power of Russia, China, and the newly independent states, both the world culture and the world power constellation have become more alien (i.e., more Afro-Asian). This development, one might hypothesize, would tend to highlight the common elements of Anglo-American culture and promote greater responsiveness. If this is examined, it would be particularly important

[4] See Chapter 3.

to check with other pairs of countries. There might not be greater emphasis on Anglo-American similarities, but rather on those things which each holds in common with Western Europe. Content analysis might be useful on this point, as would more recent responses to the Buchanan and Cantril type of question ("What foreign country do you feel most friendly toward?") if they should become available.

Finally, the fact of *role reversal* may be highly relevant. In Chapter 10 it was noted that a major source of British desires to be militarily independent of the United States is an unwillingness to accept the relative decline of British power. From being the more powerful member of the partnership, Britain has fallen to a distinctly subordinate and dependent position. The Conservatives attempted to break the dependence by creating their own nuclear deterrent; when the attempt failed, they proved generally able to accept the consequences without trying some other radical means of terminating the dependence. But many members of the Labour party have adopted just such a radical position — withdrawal from NATO if the alliance continues to rely on nuclear weapons. Unilateral disarmament is expected to give Britain a new position of moral influence in the world. Not a few see her as the leader of a third force of neutral nations.[5]

Possibly the Conservatives, with their basically dominant position in British society, have enough adaptive tradition and basic ego strength to accept the role reversal. They can satisfy themselves that they are, in Prime Minister Macmillan's terms, playing the role of Greeks to America's Romans: civilizing, restraining, and guiding them.[6] The Labourites, on the other hand, have been out of power as a party for twelve years, and most of them have never had the kind of dominant roles in society which many Conservatives have achieved outside the government. Being less confident of their *individual* prestige, influence, and perhaps even worth, they find it harder to accept a decline in *national* power. Certainly, both Labour M.P.'s and Labour voters are more likely in some respects to be anti-American than are their Tory counterparts.[7] The sources and effects of these attitudes deserve careful analysis.

[5] Hedley Bull, "The Many Sides of British Unilateralism," *The Reporter*, March 16, 1961, pp. 35–37.

[6] Joseph C. Harsch, "Master Craftsman of Downing Street," *New York Times Magazine*, April 2, 1961, p. 41.

[7] One must be extremely careful to specify the content of the attitudes in question when using broad labels like "anti-American." Lloyd Free (*Six Allies and a Neutral*, Glencoe, Ill., 1959, pp. 57–84) found greater support for the Atlantic alliance among Conservatives than among Labour M.P.'s, and the analysis of this study (Chapter 9, Table 9.2) found Conservative M.P.'s to be more responsive, on a wide variety of issues, to American wishes. Morris

Thus this study makes no pretensions to being definitive either on Anglo-American relations or on international integration in general, but we hope that it has clarified a number of problems, answered a number of questions, and suggested fruitful areas for further research. By way of conclusion, let us use some of its findings to suggest possible conditions for the success of various kinds of integration. The exercise should be useful both as a means of clarifying a few points of theory and of adding to our understanding of Anglo-American relations.

Whatever the shortcomings of the Anglo-American relationship, the two countries obviously have achieved a *pluralistic security-community* as defined by Deutsch *et al.* — problems are handled, and are expected to be handled, without resort to violence. There have been no preparations for war between them since the end of naval rivalry in 1922, and no significant expectations of war since the Venezuelan crisis of 1896. In our lament over the failure to reach a higher level of responsiveness, this very substantial achievement must not be overlooked.

What are the conditions of this achievement? By examining the conditions present, we can suggest some of those which may be necessary. We cannot be sure that any given condition is essential, for the security-community under study might have been achieved without it, but we can at least know by their absence some of the conditions which are not essential. We assume, of course, that the actions of the two countries are relevant to each other, as those of Britain and America obviously are. The fact that two unrelated countries like Paraguay and Afghanistan do not prepare for war with each other is of no theoretical interest here.

One condition favorable to the pluralistic security-community is that throughout the last seventy years attention and communication between the two countries has been substantial. Transactions have been on the whole declining, and they have often been less than the null-model "expectations" on the basis of the countries' size; but *absolutely* they have been high compared with the absolute numbers for other countries. This is because both are "big" countries — big in their contribution to world trade, tourism, scholarly research, etc.

Davis and Sidney Verba ("Party Affiliation and International Opinions in Britain and France, 1947–56," *Public Opinion Quarterly*, XXIV, 4 [Winter 1960], p. 596) found that Labour voters much more frequently expressed attitudes favorable to the Soviet Union and unfavorable to the United States than did Conservative voters. William Buchanan and Hadley Cantril (*How Nations See Each Other*, Urbana, Ill., 1953, p. 140) found Conservatives more likely to give America as the country they felt most friendly toward.

Given this "bigness," it is almost unavoidable that a substantial proportion of their trade, tourism, and research attention should be directed toward each other. And this absolute size may be enough for the avoidance of war. Even if small relative to the "expected" volume, it is large enough to give many individuals in each country links of communication with the other nation, to transmit messages about their most urgent needs, and to give those individuals a personal physical or psychic stake in the maintenance of Anglo-American peace.

Another favorable condition is that elite and mass approval of the partner country has been high throughout the period. While mass approval has apparently declined in recent years, those with positive attitudes still substantially outnumber those with negative ones. Each remains the other's "favorite foreign country" among the populace. While we cannot prove that this is an essential condition, it may well be so if there are many serious issues which might potentially come between the two governments. Under certain political conditions it is possible that elite approval would be sufficient for the maintenance of peace regardless of mass attitudes. But where popular opinions carry as much weight as they do in Britain and America, elite approval alone would be insufficient. These two conditions — high absolute communication and approval — probably provide for the minimum level of responsiveness sufficient to avoid war.

In their study of a number of cases of integration, Deutsch *et al.* mentioned two other conditions, one of which they were sure was essential to a pluralistic security-community and one of which they thought might be necessary.[8] As theirs was in effect a "pilot" study, their conclusions are necessarily tentative, but they should be valuable here.

The necessary condition was compatibility of major values. To some extent, this condition may be the result of high communication, but it may also be a precondition, especially to high mutual approval. Clearly, it does and did exist for Britain and America, particularly with their common values of constitutionalism, democracy, non-Communist economics, and Christianity. There are differences of interpretation within each major class, especially on economics, but the differences have not been sufficient to cause serious trouble. The other condition, predictability, is likely to be a product of communication. Predictability from familiarity obviously requires communication. Though predictability from introspection does not necessarily demand communication, it must surely be an enormous advantage. In any

---

[8] K. W. Deutsch et al., *Political Community and the North Atlantic Area,* Princeton, 1957, pp. 66–67. Their findings as to the requirements for various types of integration are given on pp. 22–69.

case a compatibility of major values is essential. Perhaps in the Anglo-American case predictability around 1900 depended more on communication than it does now, for communication levels in many areas then were near or above the "expected" level. In more recent years, as relative communication has declined from the "expected" level, its place may have been taken by political acculturation, particularly the Americanizing and to some extent Anglicizing of more recent immigrants to the United States.

One other possible condition, the presence of only a small number of really serious divisive issues, is probably not essential. The tautology that there can be no war without a *casus belli* is of course true. But given the other conditions, there may be a large number of severe problems, as is witnessed by the Anglo-American *rapprochement* at the turn of the century, without conflict.

A second type of political community, also one which the United States and Britain have achieved, is an *alliance*. It would appear that only one condition need be added to those for the pluralistic security-community — the presence of an external threat. But note that the threat alone is not sufficient; it must be accompanied by some minimum of the conditions required for the absence of expectations of war. The level need not be so high (France and West Germany now have an alliance without a completely satisfactory security-community), but some of the elements must be present. Without them, the threat would not be perceived as common, and if the absence of those conditions was really severe, one member might see the "threat" actually as a potential ally against the other.

A third type is what we shall call, for want of a better term, a *highly responsive pluralistic security-community*. Depending of course on how high one sets the test of responsiveness, achievement of this objective is where Britain and America fall short. They are able to co-operate, respond to each other's needs, and pursue mutual goals in many areas, but there also have been a distressing number of serious lapses, even in recent years. Quite possibly responsiveness has, in some areas of common concern, declined over past decades. Tentatively we may impute this to trends we have identified and stressed throughout the study. High responsiveness certainly requires high mass approval. While net approval still is positive, it has fallen since World War II. Notable responsiveness also requires a high level of mass and of elite communication, almost certainly a level at least as high, and probably higher, than the "expected" one. In most areas, both elite and mass communication have declined and in recent years have usually been below the "expected" level. These trends probably can be reversed, at least speedily enough to satisfy us, only by conscious and deliberate effort. The recommendations at the end of the preceding chapter were directed to that end.

Finally, we may speak of an *amalgamated security-community*. If successful, it would almost certainly provide a higher degree of co-ordination than is possible under pluralism, and a number of writers have recommended it for this reason. But to be a success, such a community would require the conditions for a pluralistic community and also those for high responsiveness. Since all the conditions for the latter are not present, it is clear already that amalgamation would be a dangerous step. Another condition for successful amalgamation would probably be that, almost regardless of the current state of attention and communication, the trend be an upward one. While it is downward, amalgamation seems hazardous. There are in addition, according to Deutsch *et al.*, quite a few other conditions which also are essential to amalgamation. A few very obviously are present:

1. A distinctive way of life. Clearly this condition is met if any are. The Anglo-Saxon heritage makes America more similar to Britain than to any continental European state, and Britain probably, though less certainly, has more in common with America than with most European nations. The difference between the Anglo-Saxon tradition and that of the non-Western peoples needs no emphasis. And economically both states are great "have" powers in a world of increasingly vociferous "have-nots."

2. Increase in political and administrative capabilities. In this case too we need not labor the obvious. The figures cited earlier in this chapter illustrate the increasing weight of the national government in both economies. One should, however, express a caution, since the expansion of capabilities has certainly been accompanied by a vast increase in domestic demands upon government.

3. Broadening of the political elite. America is one of the world's most "open" societies. Even though it began the century with a very broadly based elite, the opening process has continued still further, thanks especially to the vastly higher education levels and opportunities of recent years. Britain is a somewhat more closed society, but the broadening *trend* has been more rapid and drastic than in the United States.

One condition which Deutsch *et al.* found probably but not certainly required for amalgamation was also met:

4. Balance of flows of communication and transaction. Though one party may be a net recipient of communications in one area, it

should send more than it receives in some other. Included here are also the balances of initiatives and of respect or symbols of respect. Looking only at the exchange of such mass cultural products as movies, television films, and magazines, and perhaps such financial transactions as the flow of American investment capital to Britain, one might worry that the process was dangerously one-sided. The British might be considered on the receiving end to an extent which might cause serious friction over their "Americanization." Yet this position overlooks the more subtle but highly influential processes by which great respect is accorded Britain as the bearer of the Anglo-Saxon cultural heritage, and the homage given important Britons of the recent and distant past. Hollywood produces films, and London the Coldstream Guards. One of the obvious carriers of this respect is the relatively greater attention given to Britain in American education than to America in the British educational system.

There are, however, a number of other necessary conditions about whose fulfillment we must be more doubtful:

5. Unbroken links of social communication between the political units concerned and between the relevant social strata within those units. Despite comments about the presence of "two nations" within Britain, the second part of this condition is fulfilled, but there is more question about the first part. Formal organizations of major domestic importance in both countries, like churches or political parties, show few links of any strength between the partners. Organizations like the Pilgrims and the English-Speaking Union lack influence, especially beyond the Eastern seaboard of the United States. Other links, such as student and other exchanges, and various personal ties of marriage and friendship, affect only a small fraction of the population; and the Anglo-American proportion of all international ties of this sort is declining.

6. Multiplicity of ranges of communication and transactions. If we had only a static image of present conditions we would say that, aided by the high state of economic development in both countries, this condition was undoubtedly present. But given our perspective on trends, one wonders.

7. Mobility of persons. Despite restrictions, more possibilities for free movement exist currently than actually are taken advantage of. High cost and lack of motivation limit transatlantic travel. At least two thirds of the British quota for immigrants to the United States has gone unfilled every year. Migration from the

United States to Britain is free of serious restrictions, but a yearly average of only about 3000 Americans took advantage of it during the 1950's. American tourists may enter the United Kingdom without a visa. While visas are necessary from Britain to America, recent steps promise greatly to simplify the procedure. Currency restrictions no longer inhibit any Briton from coming to the United States, though they did until only a few years ago. But one might hope for a higher volume of traffic, particularly east to west.

Individuals' attitudes towards free movement are favorable regarding *these particular countries.* Most Americans have been hostile to the admission of many European immigrants,[9] but the tremendous favoritism to British immigrants in the national-origins system suggests that many would welcome migration from that source. A survey in Britain indicates favorable attitudes toward Americans. When asked, "Would you favor common citizenship — that is, an American could come and live in England and an Englishman could go to the United States without regard to immigration laws?" 59 per cent answered yes, 35 per cent no, and 6 per cent did not reply. On "Do you think you would like to have an American family live next door to you?" the proportions were 55 per cent yes, 27 per cent no, and 18 per cent no answer.[10]

8. Superior economic growth. There is reason to question the presence of this condition. United States national income expanded by 71 per cent from 1950 to the end of 1960, and that of the United Kingdom by 90 per cent. But both these figures lagged well behind the 158 per cent for the economies of the "Six" of continental Europe. At constant prices this works out to an annual rate of only about 2.5 per cent for the United States and 3 per cent for Britain. These are hardly spectacular and might not give the flexibility and expansion of opportunity necessary to make amalgamation a success.

9. Expectation of economic gains. There is very substantial doubt as to the presence of this condition. A September 1945 survey asked Britishers what Britain had most to fear from the United States. In reply, 33 per cent mentioned trade competition, 30 per cent other actions, and 37 per cent said "nothing" or had no answer. When asked what Britain had most to gain from the

[9] Deutsch *et al.* (*ibid.*), p. 152, cite a January 1946 survey where only 5 per cent of an American nationwide sample favored admission of more immigrants than were then allowed to come.

[10] British Institute of Public Opinion (BIPO) Survey 148A; data obtained through courtesy of Social Surveys, Ltd., London.

United States, only 16 per cent mentioned long-term commercial benefits, while 53 per cent mentioned other gains (including emergency financial aid) and 31 per cent could think of nothing.[11] Britishers are more afraid of American competition than expectant of opportunities in the American market. A similar attitude is frequently manifested toward the Common Market. American political leaders have often hesitated to advocate the principle of freer trade as bringing economic benefits to the United States, though they might embrace "trade — not aid" for other reasons. Current balance-of-payments problems have not helped. Protectionist sentiment is still strong in America.

10. Compatibility of major values. This is the same condition that was necessary for the avoidance of war, but clearly it would have to be present to an appreciably greater degree than in the first instance. Attitudes toward the so-called "welfare state" seem the most likely causes of dissension. An amalgamated government would probably follow welfare-state policies much like those practiced if not preached by the current governments of both countries. These policies presumably would satisfy a majority of the populace and elites in both. Yet there is a sizable minority, perhaps 25 per cent of the electorate and half of one party in both countries, that would be seriously dissatisfied. In the United States it is of course the Republican conservatives, with some Southern Democrats, who would be disgruntled. In Britain the attack would come from the left, from those members of the Labour party who are still doctrinaire socialists. At present each of these groups can retain hope of someday reaching power and putting its plans into effect, but in an amalgamated government the middle way would be so strong as to condemn them both to permanent minority status. The disaffected groups would be large enough to provide serious cause for concern.

Two other conditions which were thought possibly to be essential, though the authors were not sure, appear to be present only to a dubious degree:

11. Mutual predictability. At first glance, one might give rather high marks to Britain and America, but second thoughts recall the Suez incident. Then, on a major issue of policy which was given great attention by both governments, each was astounded by the other's action. While predictability may be high enough for pluralism, it does not currently seem satisfactory for amalgamation.

12. Interchange of group roles, requiring especially that members of

[11] BIPO Survey; data provided by Social Surveys, Ltd., London.

one partner should not always be in a minority. Splits dividing almost all Britishers from almost all Americans seem unlikely, but some parts of both electorates might find themselves always outvoted. American conservatives are potentially such a group. On domestic issues the left wing of the Labour party would also be in such a position. On "colonial" issues this same group would probably become a majority with American support, though one doubts whether that would be adequate compensation. But this is a highly unpredictable area of concern.

Finally, the authors of *Political Community and the North Atlantic Area* found four other conditions to be helpful but not essential. Oddly enough, three of them are present:

13. Previous administrative or dynastic union.
14. Ethnic or linguistic assimilation.
15. A foreign military threat. (Note, however, that many Britons and some Americans believe that this is vanishing. Some others see only the kind of danger of nuclear annihilation that makes a military alliance seem a liability rather than an asset.)

One other helpful but nonessential condition is probably present but declining in strength:

16. Strong economic ties.

In sum, about half of the conditions deemed essential to amalgamation either are absent or are present only to a very dubious degree for Britain and America. Coupled with the declining strength of ties of communication and attention, any attempt to form a common government would seem foolhardy in the extreme. Many problems remain to be solved before the two countries will be sufficiently responsive to solve their mutual problems and pursue common goals through pluralism. It is hoped that this study has pointed out some of those problems and suggested some of the less obvious but vitally significant strengths and weaknesses of their relationship.

Appendix A

Chronology of Major Government Actions
Affecting Anglo-American Relations, 1890–1961

(*UNFRIENDLY* actions are recorded in capital letters and italicized.)

YEAR	MILITARY	ECONOMIC	POLITICAL
1890		U.S. *McKINLEY TARIFF*	Both: Extradition Treaty
			Both: Samoa Treaty
1891			U.S. Copyright Law
1892			Both: Bering Sea Convention
1893			
1894		U.S. tariff reduction	
1895			Both: *VENEZUELAN BOUNDARY*
1896			U.K. Venezuelan arbitration
1897		U.S. *DINGLEY TARIFF*	
1898			U.K. supports U.S. in Hawaii and against Spain
1899			Both: Samoa Treaty
			Both: Open Door note
1900			Both: 2nd Open Door note
			U.S. attitude on Boer War
1901			U.K. Hay-Pauncefote Treaty
1902			U.K. Venezuelan debt arbitration
1903			U.K. Alaska boundary settlement
1904			
1905			
1906			
1907			
1908			

YEAR	MILITARY	ECONOMIC	POLITICAL
1909		U.S. tariff reduction	Both: Newfoundland fisheries arbitration
1910			
1911			U.K. Anglo-Japanese Alliance exempts U.S.
1912			Both: Fisheries Treaty
1913		U.S. Underwood Tariff	
1914		U.S. Panama Canal tolls	Both: Bryan Conciliation Treaty U.K. agrees to U.S. Mexican policy
1915		U.K. *WAR TRADE RESTRICTIONS*	
1916		U.K. *WAR TRADE RESTRICTIONS*	
1917	Both: World War I		
1918	Both: World War I		
1919			
1920		U.S. *INSISTS ON DEBT PAY-MENTS*	U.S. *REJECTS LEAGUE*
1921			
1922	Both: Washington Naval Treaty	U.S. *FORDNEY-McCUMBER TARIFF*	U.K. gives up Japanese Alliance
1923			
1924			
1925			
1926			
1927	Both: *GENEVA NAVAL CONFERENCE FAILS*	U.S. gives up maritime claims	
1928			Both: Kellogg-Briand Pact
1929			
1930	Both: London Naval Conference	U.S. *SMOOT-HAWLEY TARIFF*	
1931		U.S. Hoover debt moratorium U.K. *IMPERIAL PREFERENCE*	
1932		U.K. *MORE IMPERIAL PREFERENCE*	U.K. *REFUSES STIMSON BID ON CHINA*

YEAR	MILITARY	ECONOMIC	POLITICAL
1933		Both: *LONDON ECONOMIC CONFERENCE FAILS*	U.K. *REJECTS USE OF 9-POWER TREATY*
1934		U.S. *JOHNSON ACT* U.K. *DEBT DEFAULT*	
1935			U.S. *NEUTRALITY ACT*
1936			U.S. *NEUTRALITY ACT RENEWAL*
1937			U.S. *NEUTRALITY ACT RENEWAL*
1938	U.K. agrees to big U.S. Navy	Both: reciprocal trade agreement	U.S. Roosevelt offer to Chamberlain U.K. *REFUSES OFFER*
1939			U.S. *NEUTRALITY ACT RENEWAL* U.S. Neutrality Act revision
1940	U.S. destroyers for bases U.S. frees sale of obsolete arms		
1941	U.S. convoying	U.S. Lend-Lease	Both: Atlantic Charter
1942	Both: World War II		
1943	Both: World War II		
1944	Both: World War II		Both: *GREECE AND ITALY*
1945	Both: World War II	U.S. *CUTS OFF LEND-LEASE*	
1946		U.S. British Loan	
1947		U.S. Marshall Plan U.S. Greece and Turkey aid	Both: *PALESTINE*
1948	U.K. grants air bases to U.S.		Both: Berlin
1949	Both: NATO ratified		
1950	U.K. joins U.S. in Korean War		U.K. *RECOGNIZES COMMUNIST CHINA*
1951		U.S. Mutual Security Act	
1952			
1953			
1954	U.K. agrees to German rearmament		U.S. *EGYPT AND IRAN* U.K. *REFUSES ACTION IN INDOCHINA*

Year	Military	Economic	Political
1955	U.K. *BUILDS OWN H-BOMB*		
1956			U.S. *SUEZ*
1957			
1958	U.S. revises Atomic Energy Act		
1959	U.K. abandons independent deterrent	U.K. relaxes import controls	
1960			
1961			

Appendix B

Table 2.1 U.S.: Number of Agreements Signed, Total Divided by Number of Countries in World (World Average), Number Signed with U.K., and Ratio of U.K. Total to World Average

Period (Annual Avg.)	Total Agreements	World Average	Total with U.K.	U.K. Total over World Average
1890-1913	13.3	.20	1.9	9.5
(1914-1918)	(12.2)	(.17)	(1.2)	(7.1)
1919-1929	19.1	.26	1.4	5.4
1930-1938	19.2	.27	1.1	4.1
(1939-1945)	(60.9)	(.86)	(4.3)	(5.0)
1946-1952	180.0	2.14	11.8	5.5
1953-1959	226.0	2.49	8.0	3.2

Sources: U.S. Department of State, List of Treaties Submitted to the Senate, 1789-1934, Washington, 1935; List of Treaties Submitted to the Senate, 1935-1944, Washington, 1945; Treaty Series, Washington, 1944-1946; Executive Agreement Series, Washington, 1929-1946; and Treaties and Other International Acts, Washington, 1946-1960. Number of countries applies to the final year of each period, as listed in the Statesman's Year Book. Since many treaties are multilateral, the world average above actually understates the number signed with any given country (since it merely divides the number of treaties by the number of countries), but this is irrelevant to the present task.

Note that we must use the relative number of treaties with any country, not merely the total, to indicate trends. Changes in technology and world politics have necessitated an absolute increase in the number of agreements reached between almost all states.

Table 2.2 U.K.: Number of Agreements Signed, Total Divided by Number of Countries in World (World Average), Number Signed with U.S., and Ratio of U.S. Total to World Average

Period (Annual Avg.)	Total Agreements	World Average	Total with U.S.	U. S. Total over World Average
1890-1913	30.9	.40	3.1	7.8
(1914-1918)	(16.6)	(.21)	(1.4)	(6.7)
1919-1929	33.3	.45	1.0	2.2
1930-1938	45.0	.59	3.3	5.6
(1939-1945)	(22.1)	(.26)	(3.7)	(14.2)
1946-1952	87.4	.92	10.0	10.8
1953-1959	67.4	.66	7.6	11.5

Sources: Edward Hertslet, Hertslet's Commercial Treaties, London, 1890-1918, and Foreign Office , Treaty Series, London, 1919-1960. Because of definitional differences the totals are not the same as in the American series. Although the Hertslet series is entitled "commercial," it encompasses practically all agreements, including those for territorial cessions and boundary settlements.

Table 2.3 Diplomatic Representatives in Partner Country as a Percentage of All Foreign Service and of Total National Government Civilian Employment

	1890	1913	1928	1938	1954	1958
U.S. Total Foreign Service	88	254	1230	1230	3160	3580
No. in Great Britain	5	10	69	68	149	144
Total National Government Civil Employment (000's)	157	396	561	882	2408	2382
U.K. Total Foreign Service	930	1400	1470	1480	1900	1820
No. in United States	47	87	110	84	152	158
Total National Government Civil Employment (000's)	n.a.	n.a.	474	579	1090	1016

Sources: U.K.--G.E.P. Hertslet, Editor, Foreign Office List, 1884, London, 1884; Foreign Office List, 1914, London, 1914; Foreign Office List, 1931, London, 1931; Foreign Office List, 1939, London, 1939; Foreign Office List, 1955, London, 1955; and Foreign Office List, 1959, London, 1959. Data for 1890 were not available, so I substituted figures for 1883. Government employment from Central Statistical Office, Annual Abstract of Statistics, 1935-46, London, 1948, p. 110; and Annual Abstract of Statistics, 1960, London, 1961, p. 112. No fully comparable data were available for 1928, so 1936 figures were used. U.S.--State Department, Diplomatic and Consular Service of the United States, Washington, 1894; Foreign Service List, 1913, Washington, 1914; Foreign Service List, 1928, Washington, 1929; Foreign Service List, 1938, Washington, 1939; Foreign Service List, 1954, Washington, 1955; and Foreign Service List, 1958, Washington, 1959. Government Employment figures from Bureau of the Census, Historical Statistics of the United States, Colonial Times to 1957, Washington, 1960, p. 710, and Statistical Abstract of the United States, 1960, Washington, 1960, p. 393.

Table 3.1 Exports and National Income (in Million $)

Exports	1890	1913	1928	1938	1954	1959
U.K. to U.S.	154	143	336	141	451	1,076
U.K. to World	822	2,556	4,085	2,603	7,766	9,677
U.S. to U.K.	445	591	848	521	693	884
U.S. to World	845	2,484	5,127	3,094	15,106	17,566
National Income						
United States	11,100	31,500	81,700	67,600	300,300	399,600
United Kingdom	6,800	11,500	20,200	25,100	40,800	53,600

Sources: Income data, U.S., 1890, 1913--Robert F. Martin, National Income in the United States, 1799-1938, New York, 1939, pp. 6-7. U.K., 1890, 1913--A. R. Prest, "National Income of the United Kingdom, 1870-1946", Economic Journal, LVIII, 229 (March 1948), p. 58. Both countries, 1928, 1938--United Nations, Statistical Papers, Series H., No. 8, Statistics of National Income and Expenditure, New York, 1955, Tables 1, 7. Both countries, 1954, 1959--United Nations Monthly Bulletin of Statistics, November 1961, p. 149.
       Trade, 1890--U.K., Accounts and Papers (35), XCV, Trade (Foreign Countries and British Possessions), London, 1895, c. 7759, p. 5, and Accounts and Papers (45), No. 21, Statistical Abstract for the Principal and Other Foreign Countries, 1883 to 1892-93, London, 1895, p. 181. 1913--League of Nations, Memorandum on the Balance of Payments and Foreign Trade Balances, 1911-1925, Geneva, 1926, I. 1928--League of Nations, Memorandum on the Balance of Payments and Foreign Trade Balances, 1926-1928, Geneva, 1929, I. 1938 and 1954--United Nations, Statistical Papers, Series T, Vol. VIII, No. 7, Direction of International Trade, New York, 1957, pp. 51-52. 1959--United Nations, Statistical Papers, Series T, Vol. XI, No. 9, Direction of International Trade, New York, 1961.

Table 3.2 Holdings of British Investors in the United States and American Investors in the United Kingdom as a Proportion of Their Holdings in All Foreign Countries

British Investment (Million Dollars)

	(1) Total Foreign	(2) In U.S.	(3) (2) as % of (1)
1890	8,000	2,000	25.0
1913	18,200	3,650	20.1
1928	18,100	980	5.4
1938	17,400	1,310	7.5
1954	6,200	504	8.1
1957	5,900	480	8.1

United States Investment (Million Dollars)

	(1) Total Foreign	(2) In U.K.	(3) (2) as % of (1)
1890	n.a.	n.a.	--
1913	2,605	200	7.7
1928	15,170	641	4.2
1938	11,491	631	5.5
1954	24,365	1,257	5.2
1958	37,516	2,147	5.7

Sources: U.K. Investment in U.S., 1890, from A.K. Cairncross, Home and Foreign Investment, Cambridge, 1953, pp. 183-84. U.S. Investment in U.K. in 1913 a rough estimate from personal correspondence with Professor Albert H. Imlah of The Fletcher School of Law and Diplomacy. U.S. in U.K., 1958, from Survey of Current Business, XXXX, 9 (September 1960), pp. 20-24. U.K. in U.S., 1957, from Annual Abstract of Statistics, 1959, p. 236. 1957 figures are the latest available. For all other sources see Tables 4.1-4.4.

Table 3.3 Vessel Entrances, in Thousand Net Tons, of British and American Ships in U.S. and U.K. Ports

Tonnage of British Ships Entering

	(1) U.K.Ports	(2) U.S.Ports	(3) (2) as % of (1)
1890	26,778	9,698	36.1
1913	46,603	24,532	52.7
1928	56,562	28,543	50.4
1938	49,976	24,307	48.8
1954	49,884	9,933	19.9
1958	51,836	9,880	19.0

Tonnage of American Ships Entering

	(1) U.S.Ports	(2) U.K.Ports	(3) (2) as % of (1)
1890	4,381	147	3.4
1913	13,073	818	6.2
1928	31,284	3,409	10.9
1938	19,020	3,145	16.5
1954	33,860	3,219	9.5
1958	26,842	3,780	14.1

Sources: For British ports--Board of Trade, Statistical Abstract for the United Kingdom, 1902, London, 1902, p. 174; Statistical Abstract for the United Kingdom, 1931, London, 1931, pp. 292-93; Statistical Abstract for the United Kingdom, 1957, London, 1957, p. 212; and Statistical Abstract for the United Kingdom, 1959, London, 1959, p. 206. For U.S. ports--Treasury Department, Annual Report and Statements of the Chief of the Bureau of Statistics on the Foreign Commerce and Navigation, Immigration, and Tonnage of the United States for the Year Ending June 30, 1890, Washington, 1890; Foreign Commerce and Navigation of the United States, 1914, Washington, 1914, p. 875; Foreign Commerce and Navigation of the United States, 1928, Washington, 1929, p. 579; Foreign Commerce and Navigation of the United States, 1938, Washington, 1940, p. 962; United States Foreign Trade Summary Report, 1954, FT 975, Washington, 1955, p. 2; United States Foreign Trade Summary Report, 1958, FT 975, Washington, 1959, p. 2; and personal communication from Department of Commerce. Data are for vessels both in ballast and in cargo.

Table 3.4 Tourists Admitted (in Thousands)

	(1) To U.S. from World	(2). To U.S. from U.K.	(3) (2) as % of (1)	(4) To World from U. S.
1913	229	29	12.6	348
1928	194	19	9.8	430
1938	184	24	13.0	398
1954	566	54	9.5	1412
1958	848	69	8.2	1484
	(1) To U.K. from World	(2) To U.K. from U.S.	(3) (2) as % of (1)	(4) To World from U.K.
1913	480	100	20.8	842
1928	316	113	35.7	1228
1938	357	77	21.5	1566
1954	686	194	28.3	1853
1958	962	310	32.2	2876

Sources: For U.K. to U.S., U.S. to World, and World to U.S., letter from Department of Justice, Immigration and Naturalization Service. Data exclude travelers to and from Canada and Mexico.

Totals for U.K. to World were obtained as follows: The number of all British subjects leaving the U.K. are in Board of Trade Journal, March 6, 1929; March 9, 1939; May 12, 1956; and May 6, 1960. Totals for 1913 were provided by the Board of Trade. From those were subtracted U.K. emigrants to countries other than Europe, as given by Brinley Thomas, Migration and Economic Growth, Cambridge, 1954, p. 294; Whitaker's Almanac, 1956, London, 1955, p. 592; and Whitaker's Almanac, 1960, London, 1960, p. 590. For 1954 and 1958, however, it was necessary to use Board of Trade totals for all passengers from the U.K. From those were subtracted both the number of U.K. emigrants and the number of all foreign passengers, obtained from Statistics of Foreigners Entered and Leaving the United Kingdom, 1954, Cmd. 9590, London, 1955, pp. 4-5, and Statistics of Foreigners Entered and Leaving the United Kingdom, 1958, Cmnd. 701, London, 1959, pp. 4-5.

Data on tourists to the U.K. are from the above Statistics of Foreigners, and Aliens Order 1920, Statistics in Regard to Alien Passengers Who Entered and Left the United Kingdom in 1928, Cmd. 3332, London, 1929, pp. 10-11, and Aliens Order 1920, Statistics in Regard to Alien Passengers Who Entered and Left the United Kingdom in 1938, Cmd. 6036, London, 1939, pp. 8-9. Data from U.K. sources exclude Commonwealth citizens from World total, and data on U.K. citizens include all British subjects, as well as those from the Commonwealth.

The estimate of World visitors to U.K. in 1913 is based on figures supplied by the Aliens Department, Home Office. The estimate of U.S. visitors to the U.K. is based on figures in Bureau of Immigration, Annual Report of the Commissioner General of Immigration, Fiscal Year Ended June 30, 1914, Washington, 1915, pp. 116-29, and a comparison of the U.S. data on citizens departed given in the letter cited above with the U.K. admission figures for later years.

Table 3.5   Total Earnings from Foreign Investment, Shipping, and Travel

U.K. Earnings (Mil. £)	1913	1928	1938	1954	1958
Investment	194	n.a.	205	315	338
Shipping	105	n.a.	100	402	510
Travel	35	n.a.	28	95	137
Total	334	n.a.	333	812	985
U.S. Earnings (Mil. $)					
Investment	137	922	583	1955	2922
Shipping	29	372	267	1171	1672
Travel	50	121	130	595	825
Total	216	1415	980	3721	5419

Sources: U.S. Earnings--Historical Statistics of the United States, p. 562; and Statistical Abstract of the United States, 1960, p. 867. U.K. Earnings--Cairncross, Home and Foreign Investment, p. 180 (1913 travel earnings, my estimate); Statistical Abstract of the United Kingdom, 1938-48, London, 1949, p. 275; and Annual Abstract of Statistics, 1959, London, 1960, p. 229.

Table 4.1   Anglo-American Investment Competition by Country, 1913 -- in Million Dollars

Countries Where G.B. Dominant				Countries Where G.B.--U.S. Compete				Countries Where U.S. Dominant			
Borrower	Lender	Amount	%	Borrower	Lender	Amount	%	Borrower	Lender	Amount	%
British Empire *,**	G.B.	5850	100	Mexico	U.S.	1050	68	Philippines	U.S.	75	100
	U.S.	--	--		G.B.	485	32		G.B.	--	--
Egypt and Turkey	G.B.	335	100	Cuba	U.S.	100	38	Puerto Rico	U.S.	30	100
	U.S.	--	--		G.B.	160	62		G.B.	--	--
South America **	G.B.	2900	97	Central America	U.S.	50	29				
	U.S.	100	3		G.B.	125	71				
China and Japan	G.B.	515	84								
	U.S.	100	16								
Canada and Newf'land	G.B.	2490	77								
	U.S.	750	23								
Europe ***	G.B.	1060	75								
	U.S.	350	25								
Total	G.B.	13150	91	Total	U.S.	1200	61	Total	U.S.	105	100
	U.S.	1300	9		G.B.	770	39		G.B.	--	--

*Excluding countries listed separately

**In following tables these categories are further broken down.

***Includes U.S. investment in Britain

Sources: The Problem of International Investment, pp. 121, 128.   These estimates include over 98% of American investment by area and over 97% of that of Britain (excluding funds invested in the U.S. by Britishers).

Table 4.2 Anglo-American Investment Competition by Country, 1928 -- in Million Dollars

Countries Where G.B. Dominant

Borrower	Lender	Amount	%
Br. Empire**	G.B.	233	100
	U.S.	--	--
India	G.B.	2625	99
	U.S.	39	1
Malaya	G.B.	525	95
	U.S.	27	5
Br. Africa**	G.B.	1510	94
	U.S.	90	6
Australia and N.Z.	G.B.	2995	88
	U.S.	419	12
Non-Br. Africa**	G.B.	165	86
	U.S.	28	14
Br. West Indies	G.B.	196	82
	U.S.	40	18
Total	G.B.	8249	93
	U.S.	643	7

Countries Where G.B.--U.S. Compete

Borrower	Lender	Amount	%
Chile	U.S.	701	75
	G.B.	238	25
South America*	U.S.	976	71
	G.B.	408	29
Canada and Newf'land	U.S.	3942	61
	G.B.	2550	39
Japan	U.S.	445	55
	G.B.	360	45
Europe	U.S.	976	50
	G.B.	968	50
Brazil	U.S.	557	38
	G.B.	890	62
China	U.S.	130	36
	G.B.	229	64
Argentina	U.S.	808	27
	G.B.	2190	73
Total	U.S.	8535	52
	G.B.	7833	48

Countries Where U.S. Dominant

Borrower	Lender	Amount	%
Philippines	U.S.	167	100
	G.B.	--	--
Mexico, Central America, and West Indies	U.S.	969	77
	G.B.	287	23
Germany	U.S.	1421	76
	G.B.	461	24
Total	U.S.	2557	77
	G.B.	749	23

*Excluding countries listed separately

**In following tables these categories are further broken down.

Sources: Ibid., pp. 16, 142, 186-7. Totals include over 98% of all holdings (excluding British investment in the U.S. and American investment in the U.K.). Estimates are for the beginning of 1930, as no figures for 1928 were available.

Table 4.3 Anglo-American Investment Competition by Country, 1938--in Million Dollars

Countries Where G.B. Dominant

Borrower	Lender	Amount	%
India, Burma, & Ceylon	G.B.	2130	98
	U.S.	49	2
Br. Africa**	G.B.	1800	96
	U.S.	78	4
Eire	G.B.	78	96
	U.S.	3	4
Australia & N.Z.	G.B.	3200	93
	U.S.	218	7
Malaya	G.B.	328	93
	U.S.	24	7
Br. West Indies	G.B.	103	91
	U.S.	10	9
Greece	G.B.	127	86
	U.S.	21	14
Austria	G.B.	54	77
	U.S.	16	23
Argentina	G.B.	1800	76
	U.S.	582	24

Countries Where G.B.--U.S. Compete

Borrower	Lender	Amount	%
France	U.S.	132	71
	G.B.	54	29
Mexico	U.S.	659	67
	G.B.	323	33
Chile	U.S.	612	66
	G.B.	308	34
Norway	U.S.	100	65
	G.B.	54	35
Canada & Newf'land	U.S.	3795	65
	G.B.	2060	35
Denmark	U.S.	111	62
	G.B.	69	38
China	U.S.	230	56
	G.B.	181	44
Peru	U.S.	136	53
	G.B.	122	47
Europe*	U.S.	305	49
	G.B.	313	51
Hungary	U.S.	57	42
	G.B.	78	58
Brazil	U.S.	538	40
	G.B.	804	60
Japan	U.S.	155	39
	G.B.	245	61

Countries Where U.S. Dominant

Borrower	Lender	Amount	%
Italy	U.S.	157	100
	G.B.	--	--
Philippines	U.S.	134	100
	G.B.	--	--
Cent. Am. & West Indies	U.S.	863	86
	G.B.	137	14
Germany	U.S.	697	76
	G.B.	220	24
South America**	U.S.	602	77
	G.B.	181	23

Table 4.3 (Continued)

	Countries Where G.B. Dominant				Countries Where G.B.–U.S. Compete				Countries Where U.S. Dominant		
Borrower	Lender	Amount	%	Borrower	Lender	Amount	%	Borrower	Lender	Amount	%
				Neth. East Indies	U.S.	71	38				
					G.B.	117	62				
				Egypt	U.S.	23	32				
					G.B.	49	68				
				Uruguay	U.S.	47	29				
					G.B.	113	71				
				Persia	U.S.	57	25				
					G.B.	167	75				
Total	G.B.	9620	91	Total	U.S.	7081	59	Total	U.S.	2453	18
	U.S.	1001	9		G.B.	4957	41		G.B.	538	82

*Excluding countries listed separately

**In following table this category is further broken down.

Sources: Lewis, The United States and Foreign Investment Problems, pp. 232-38, and Bank of England, United Kingdom Overseas Investments, 1938-1948, London, 1950, p. 14. The totals include over 98% of both countries' long-term foreign lending that is classifiable by area (excluding British investments in the U.S. and American holdings in Britain). Lewis provides an estimate of British investments which is appreciably higher than that of the Bank, which includes only investments in securities listed on the London Stock Exchange. While Lewis' data are undoubtedly more complete, we shall use the Bank's because they were designed specifically to be comparable with the data used in Tables 4.2 and 4.4. Lewis' estimates of American investment, however, are quite comparable to those in the other tables.

Sources for Table 4.4 (following page): Survey of Current Business, August, 1956, pp. 18-19; and Bank of England, United Kingdom Overseas Investment, 1954, London, 1956, p. 4. Estimates include over 97% of U.S. and U.K. investments classifiable by area (excluding British holdings in the U.S. and American investment in the U.K.).

Table 4.4   Anglo-American Investment Competition by Country, 1954- in Million Dollars

Countries Where G.B. Dominant				Countries Where G.B.--U.S. Compete				Countries Where U.S. Dominant			
Borrower	Lender	Amount	%	Borrower	Lender	Amount	%	Borrower	Lender	Amount	%
Ceylon, Burma, and Pakistan	G.B. U.S.	132 --	100 --	Norway	U.S. G.B.	40 14	74 26	Liberia	U.S. G.B.	230 --	100 --
Greece	G.B. U.S.	132 --	100 --	Austria	U.S. G.B.	24 11	69 31	Philippines	U.S. G.B.	217 --	100 --
Eire	G.B. U.S.	101 --	100 --	Egypt	U.S. G.B.	54 28	66 34	Canada	U.S. G.B.	9513 468	95 5
China Mainland	G.B. U.S.	98 --	100 --	Br. West Indies	U.S. G.B.	172 102	63 37	France	U.S. G.B.	334 17	95 5
Hungary	G.B. U.S.	39 --	100 --	Br. Empire*	U.S. G.B.	272 216	56 44	Latin America	U.S. G.B.	6732 518	93 7
Romania	G.B. U.S.	39 --	100 --	Indonesia	U.S. G.B.	65 51	56 44	Europe*	U.S. G.B.	663 132	80 20
Br. Africa*	G.B. U.S.	608 85	88 12	Japan	U.S. G.B.	105 106	50 50	Germany	U.S. G.B.	283 81	78 22
New Zealand	G.B. U.S.	277 40	85 15	India	U.S. G.B.	92 171	35 65	Denmark	U.S. G.B.	39 11	78 22
				Union of S. Africa	U.S. G.B.	216 454	32 68				
				Australia	U.S. G.B.	393 945	29 71				
Total	G.B. U.S.	1376 125	83 17	Total**	U.S. G.B.	3539 2099	63 37	Total	U.S. G.B.	18021 1227	94 6

*Excluding countries listed separately

**$2105 million of U.S. portfolio investment in areas other than Canada and Latin America has arbitrarily been assigned to the "G.B.--U.S. Compete" column because no geographical breakdown is available. Such a practice understates the amount of U.S. capital lent to areas where the U.S. is dominant.

Table 7.2 First-Class Letters Exchanged (in Thousands of Pieces)

	1890*	1913**	1928	1938	1954	1958
U.K. to U.S.	10.1	818	20.5	16.8	44.1	34.4
U.K. to World	49.3	5440	169.8	154.0	280.0	268.0
U.K. from World	49.1	3910	172.9	156.0	269.0	278.0
U.S. to U.K.	10.0	866	23.6	19.4	33.3	44.5
U.S. to World	50.1	3150	114.9	118.0	286.0	322.0
U.S. from World	48.8	3240	111.8	115.0	297.0	312.0

*Includes postcards, but postcards were no more than 2% of all U.S. and U.K. foreign first-class mail.

**Thousands of pounds, not pieces

Sources: Forty-First Report of the Postmaster General on the Post Office, c. 7852, London, 1895, p. 123 (data are for year ending March 31, 1895); Report of the Postmaster General on the Post Office, 1913-14; cd. 7573, London, 1914, p. 41; Union Postale Universelle, Bureau International, Relevé des tableaux statistiques du service postal international (Expédition), 1928, Berne, 1930; Union Postale Universelle, Statistiques des expéditions dans le service international, 1937, Berne, 1939; Union Postale Universelle, Statistiques des expéditions dans le service international, 1955, Berne, 1957; and Statistique des expéditions dans le service international, 1958, Berne, 1960.
U.S. to and from World, and U.S. to U.K. after 1913, are from personal communication from U.S. Post Office Department. U.S. figures do not include mail exchanged with Canada and Mexico, and British figures do not include Canadian mail. From 1928 onward U.S. and U.K. did not have comparable data on total receipts, so it was assumed that receipts from other than the partner country were equal to the number of letters sent.

Table 7.3   Telegrams Exchanged (in Thousands)

	1938	1954	1958
U.K. to U.S.	2,066	1,686	1,742
U.K. to World	5,570	8,290	7,910
U.K. from World	5,570	8,420	7,700
U.S. to U.K.	2,066	1,521	1,702
U.S. to World	8,510	9,920	11,200
U.S. from World	8,510	10,710	11,330

Sources: U.K. to and from World estimated from statistics provided by the U.K. General Post Office. U.S. to and from World and U.K.--1938: letter from Federal Communications Commission.   1954: Federal Communications Commission, Statistics of the Communications of the United States, 1954, Washington, 1956, pp. 118-20.   1958: Federal Communications Commission, Statistics of Communications Common Carriers, 1958, Washington, 1960, pp. 136-38.

Table 7.4   Telephone Calls (in Thousands)

	1928	1938	1954	1958
U.K. to U.S.	3	10	45	138
U.K. to World	455	1004	1908	2680
U.K. from World	455	1004	1767	2590
U.S. to U.K.	3	10	45	129
U.S. to World	302	544	4550	7110
U.S. from World	302	544	4550	7030

Sources: U.S. to and from U.K. and to and from World: For 1928 and 1938, from letter from Federal Communications Commission. For 1954 and 1958, from Federal Communications Commission, Statistics of the Communications Industry in the United States, 1954, p. 27, and Federal Communications Commission, Statistics of Communications Common Carriers, 1958, p. 27. For 1928 to 1954 separate totals were not given for the number of messages sent to and from the United States, so it was necessary to assume an equality between incoming and outgoing traffic. Data for calls to and from Canada and Mexico were given in a letter from the American Telephone and Telegraph Company and added to the F.C.C. totals.
U.K. to and from World: Statistics provided by the U.K. General Post Office.

Table 8.1 Percentage of Students in High Schools Taking Various Social Studies Courses

Course	1922	1928	1934	1949
English History	3	1	--	--
World History	--	6	12	16
Medieval and Modern History	15	11	6 ⎫	
Ancient History	17	10	7 ⎬	4
American History	15	18	17	23
Problems of Democracy	--	1	3	5
Geography	6	7	3	6
Civics, Sociology, or Economics	26	28	23	16
Total	82	82	71	70

Sources: U.S. Office of Education, Offerings and Registrations in High-School Subjects, Bulletin No. 6, Washington, 1938, pp. 28-29; U.S. Office of Education, Biennial Survey of Education in the United States, 1948-50, Washington, 1951, ch. 5, pp. 100-01. No more recent data are available.
Note that the table is only for students currently taking a particular course. If, for example, the American History course were required of all students, only about 25% would take it in a particular year, though everyone would be exposed to it at some time during his four-year stay in high school. Thus to find the total proportion of students who at some time had a course, the proportion in the above table should be multiplied by four.

Table 5.1   Import Licensing and Government Imports--Percentage of Total Imports by Commodity Classes at June 30, 1954

Private Imports Permitted from:	Food	Raw Materials	Fuels	Manu-factures	All Goods
World (incl. Dollar)	16.6	61.0	--	13.5	28.1
All Non-Dollar	17.6	18.2	--	3.2	13.1
"Relaxation Area"*	22.1	7.7	94.9	58.4	32.1
Sterling Area	6.5	11.1	--	10.7	8.0
Specific Licenses Required from All Sources	13.2	.5	--	13.5	8.1
Government Import**	24.0	1.5	5.1	.7	10.6
TOTAL	100.0	100.0	100.0	100.0	100.0

*"Relaxation Area" was a result of the establishment of OEEC. It included almost all the non-dollar world except Japan and the Soviet Bloc (but included Communist China).

**Government agencies consciously discriminated against dollar goods.

Source: Adapted from Hemming, Miles, and Ray, "Statistical Summary," pp. 104-07.

Table 6.1 Percentage of References in British Scientific Journals to British, American, and Other Foreign Journals, with Nobel Science Prizes Won by Each Country and References in Physics Abstracts as Controls

	1901-07	1908-17	1918-27	1928-35	1936-42	1943-49	1950-57
% of References to Articles in Journals Published in:							
Britain	55	55	47	50	46	44	46
U. S.	11	10	18	19	19	28	35
Rest of World	34	35	35	31	35	28	19
Attention Ratio--% of References over % of Nobel Prizes Won in Each Period							
Britain	3.2	5.0	3.4	2.0	2.4	2.4	2.9
U. S.	2.8	1.4	2.6	.9	1.0	.7	.7
Rest of World	.4	.4	.4	.6	.7	.7	.7
Attention Ratio--% of References over % of Articles in Physics Abstracts in Each Period.							
Britain	1.8	1.8	1.3	2.9	--	2.6	3.8
U. S.	.8	.7	.4	.8	--	.6	.7
Rest of World	.6	.6	1.5	.5	--	.8	.5

Source: K. W. Deutsch, R. D. Enzmann, B. Lippel, et al., Is European Attention to American Research Results Declining?, Cambridge, Mass., 1954, offprint; data on Nobel Prizes from Harry Hansen, Ed., The World Almanac and Book of Facts for 1958, New York, 1958, pp. 531-32. The examination of footnotes is not, of course, a perfect indicator of scientists' attention. As the authors indicate, all that is read may not be cited, nor all that is cited, read.

Table 6.2 Percentage of References in American Scientific Journals to American, British, and Other Foreign Journals, with Nobel Science Prizes Won by Each Country and References in Chemical Abstracts as Controls

	1901-07	1908-17	1918-27	1928-35	1936-42	1943-49	1950-57
% of References to Articles in Journals Published in:							
U. S.	41	47	52	57	62	69	66
Other English	15	13	16	12	14	10	11
Rest of World	44	40	32	31	24	21	23
Attention Ratio--% of References over % of Nobel Prizes Won in Each Period							
U. S.	9.1	6.7	7.4	2.7	3.3	1.7	1.2
Other English	.9	1.2	1.9	.4	.7	.6	.7
Rest of World	.6	.5	.4	.6	.4	.5	.7
Attention Ratio--% of References over % of Articles in Chemical Abstracts in Each Period							
U. S.	2.1	2.2	1.6	2.2	2.2	1.8	1.9
Other English	1.1	.9	1.1	.9	.9	.7	.7
Rest of World	.7	.6	.6	.5	.4	.4	.5

Source: K. W. Deutsch, G. E. Klein, J. J. Baker, et al., Is Attention to Foreign Research Results Declining?, Cambridge, Mass., 1954, offprint; data on Nobel Prizes from World Almanac, pp. 531-32. References to all non-American, English-language periodicals were given because the authors did not list British journals separately. For this reason it was necessary to follow the authors' use of Chemical Abstracts in this monograph rather than Physics Abstracts (which did not list the English journals by themselves) as in the previous study.

Table 7.1. Emigration from Britain and Immigration to the United States

Year	Total Emigration from Britain	Immigration to U. S.	
		From Britain	From All Countries
1890	218,000	123,000	455,000
1913	389,000	88,000	1,198,000
1928	137,000	20,000	307,000
1938	34,000	2,000	68,000
1954	145,000	19,000	208,000
1958	111,000	28,000	253,000

Sources: Migration to U.S. from Historical Statistics, pp. 56-57, and U.S. Bureau of the Census, Statistical Abstract of the United States, 1959, Washington, 1959, p. 94. Total U. K. Emigration from Thomas, Migration and Economic Growth, pp. 276, 294; Whitaker's Almanac, 1956, p. 592; and Whitaker's Almanac, 1960, p. 590.

Formally, the matrix analysis should include data on U. S. emigration and immigration to Britain. This is not possible because before World War I the U. K. kept no adequate records of foreigners entering the country, and the authorities have never distinguished between immigrants and other arrivals from the Commonwealth. Yet because U. S. emigration to Britain is so small (in 1954 only 31,000 Americans emigrated, less than 10% of them to Britain) it does not constitute a major link of communication. For the matrix analysis I assumed that migration in these three classes (U. S. to U. K., U. S. to World, and World to U. K.) was zero. The effects of this simplification are not important enough to distort seriously the trends shown above. A similar pattern would be shown if one assumed low but higher-than-zero estimates for these classes.

it was necessary to project those data backward to 1890, where possible, with help from studies of particular industries.

Accounts and Papers (31), LXXVII (1890–91), *Minerals* (*Output 1860–90*), London, 1891

—— (31), LXVII (1903), c. 1761, London, 1903

—— (35), LXXXII, c. 6342, London, 1891

Board of Trade, *Statistical Abstract of the United Kingdom, 1876 to 1890*, XXX, London, 1891

——, Fifth Census of Production, 1935, I–IV, London, 1938–1944

——, *Report of the Census of Production for 1954*, London, 1958

Burnham, T. H., and Hoskins, G. O., *Iron and Steel in Britain, 1870–1930*, London, 1943, p. 331

Customs and Excise Department, *The Trade of the United Kingdom with British Countries and Foreign Countries, 1938*, III, London, 1939

——, *The Trade of the United Kingdom with Commonwealth Countries and Foreign Countries, 1954*, III, IV, London, 1956

Ellison, Thomas, *The Cotton Trade of Great Britain*, London, 1886, p. 126

Final Report on the First Census of Production of the United Kingdom (*1907*), c. 6320, London, 1912

A concentration on corporate officeholders has one drawback: It often ignores stockholders or corporation lawyers who may have close ties to a particular firm. In fact, it was occasionally mentioned that an individual had been legal counsel to a firm, and ties of that sort were noted. Stockholders were not likely to be as closely tied to the firms as were those with offices. They would be less involved in the day-to-day operation of the businesses, and their fates less closely connected with the fate of one or two particular corporations. In short, their exposure to international communications, to American interests through the interests of their firms, would be less direct and less strong.

It is practically impossible to identify directly those companies which export a substantial proportion of their production to the United States, so they were tentatively identified this way: First I made a list of British exports to the United States in each of the three years, taking care to use commodity definitions which were comparable over the whole period. Then I compared the value of the exports in each classification with a list of domestic production in the United Kingdom and identified those industries which sent 5 per cent or more of their production to the United States. Directors and officers of firms in those industries were then assumed to have an economic tie to the United States. The whole procedure is of course imperfect; it undoubtedly catches some firms which do not in fact export anything to America, and loses a few which do a substantial American trade. Nevertheless, I show in Chapter 9 that

Appendix C

I. SOURCES FOR TABLES 6.6 AND 6.7

Data on the personal and business connections of members came from:

Dod's Parliamentary Companion, London, 1890–1955
Price, E. D., ed., *Hazell's Annual, 1891,* London, 1891
Skinner, T., *Directory of Directors,* London, 1885–1954
The Times, House of Commons, London, 1935–1955
Who's Who, London, 1897–1954

Because members of the government are required to divest themselves of their corporate offices (but not holdings), it was necessary to look at the *Directory of Directors* in the last year before the government came to power. Use of the *Directory of Directors* enables us to eliminate most of the bias that would be caused by members who did not, in their biographical sketches, report all their industrial and commercial connections. Directorships are reported by the firms themselves. Only ties from family connections, or from partnerships, would escape this check.

Information on the products and business activities of various firms came from these sources:

Bankers' Almanac and Yearbook, 1890–91, London, 1890
———, *1938–39,* London, 1938
Banking Almanac and Directory, 1954–55, London, 1955
Clegg's International Directory of the World's Book Trade, 1950, London, 1950
F.B.I. Register of British Manufacturers, 1937–38, London, 1938
———, *1954,* London, 1954
Hurd, Sir Archibald, ed., *Shipping World Yearbook and Who's Who, 1958–59,* London, 1958
The Shipping World, V, 57 — IX, 104 (1888–91)
Skinner, T., ed., *The Stock Exchange Yearbook, 1891,* London, 1891
The Stock Exchange Official Yearbook, 1938, London 1938
———, *1954,* London, 1954

Data on exports and production came from the works listed below. Because the first United Kingdom Census of Production was in 1907, it really is able to identify a great many legislators who are responsive to the wishes of the other country.

II. SOURCES FOR TABLE 6.9

Data on the personal and business connections of Senators came from:

Congressional Directory, Washington, 1890–1955
National Cyclopedia of American Biography, Vols. I–XXVIII, C–H, New York, 1898–1958
Who's Who in America, Vols. 1–29, Chicago, 1899–1956

In order to discover whether a Senator had divested himself of any commercial interest before the year under study, I also checked *Who's Who* for the last year before he was elected or appointed to Congress.

Information on the products and business activities of various firms came from:

Bankers' Almanac and Yearbook, 1890–91, London, 1891
Financial News Association, *Manual of Statistics,* New York, 1884
Investor's Publishing Company, *Manual of Statistics,* New York, 1891
Moody, John, ed., *Moody's Manual of Industrial and Miscellaneous Securities,* New York, 1900
Porter, J. S., ed., *Moody's Bank and Finance Annual,* New York, 1943–55
———, *Moody's Industrial Manual,* New York, 1944–55
Skinner, Thomas, ed., *The Stock Exchange Yearbook, 1891,* London, 1891

Data on exports and production came from the following:

Bureau of the Census, *United States Census of Agriculture: 1954,* Vol. II, General Report, Washington, 1956
———, *United States Census of Manufactures: 1954,* Vol. II, Industry Statistics, Washington, 1957
———, *United States Census of Mineral Industries: 1954,* Vols. I, II, Washington, 1958
———, *Report No. FT410, United States Exports of Domestic and Foreign Merchandise,* Washington, 1955
Census Office, *Report on Manufacturing Industries in the United States at the Eleventh Census: 1890,* Parts I, III, Washington, 1895
———, *Report on Mineral Industries in the United States at the Eleventh Census: 1890,* Washington, 1895
———, *Report on the Statistics of Agriculture in the United States at the Eleventh Census: 1890,* Washington, 1895
Easterlin, Richard A., "State Income Estimates," in Simon Kuznets and Dorothy S. Thomas, *Population Redistribution and Economic Growth, United States, 1870–1950,* Philadelphia, 1957, p. 753

Office of Business Economics, *Personal Income by States, since 1929,* Washington, 1956

Treasury Department, Bureau of Statistics, *Summary Statement of the Imports and Exports of the United States,* Document No. 1284, No. 6, December 1890–91, Washington, 1891

There were no estimates for income by states for 1890, so figures were obtained by interpolation between estimates for 1880 and 1900, adjusting for the *national* income in 1890 relative to 1880 and 1900 and individual states' variations in population increase over the same period.

III. The following is a list of issues in Anglo-American relations on which sampled members of the House of Commons made public statements, with the number of members speaking on each.

1890
1. The American tariff (3)
2. British restrictions on import of American cattle (3)
3. American adherence to International Sugar Convention (1)
4. The American copyright law (1)
5. American import restrictions other than the tariff (1)

1938
1. The Anglo-American Trade Agreement (9)
2. Calls for co-operation with America in specific areas (5)
3. General calls for co-operation with America (3)
4. Settlement of British debt to U.S. (2)
5. Imperial Preference (2)
6. U.S. gold policy (1)
7. Restrictions on the import of U.S. films (1)
8. Dismissals of British nationals by American firms (1)
9. U.S. disarmament proposals (1)
10. Visa requirements for travel between Britain and U.S. (1)
11. Exchange of aircraft landing rights in the Pacific (1)

1954
1. German rearmament (30)
2. Withdrawal from British military base at Suez Canal (20)
3. Trade with Communist countries (19)
4. Alleged U.S. intervention in Guatemala (14)
5. SEATO (12)
6. Policy toward Communist China (10)
7. Actions of U.S. servicemen in Britain (9)
8. Commonwealth Preference and trade with America (8)
9. British defense spending and length of national service (8)
10. Possible intervention in Indochina (7)
11. Friendship and co-operation with U.S., general (6)
12. Civil liberties in the U.S. (6)
13. Adoption of standard NATO Belgian-designed rifle (5)

14. U.S. military bases in Britain (5)
15. Anglo-Iranian oil agreement (5)
16. Amount of consultation and information from U.S. (5)
17. NATO (4)
18. American foreign policy, general (3)
19. U.S. activities in British Honduras and British Guiana (2)
20. Call for summit meeting without U.S. (1)
21. American aid to Spain (1)
22. American shipping subsidies (1)

The 1890 statements include only those in Parliament; those in later years, especially 1954, include many statements outside Parliament reported by newspapers.

IV. Below is a list of roll-call votes used to form Responsiveness to Britain scale in 1890, in the order in which they appear in the scale (high responsiveness votes first). Numbers are page references to *Congressional Record*, Vol. 29, Washington, 1890. When a vote for the measure is considered responsive, the symbol (+) follows, where responsiveness indicates a vote against the measure, the symbol (−) follows.

1. Naval appropriation bill. Amendment to strike out appropriation for three long-range battleships. During the debate fears of antagonizing Britain were expressed. (p. 5297) (+)
2. Revenue bill (tariff). Conference report. (p. 10740) (−)
3. Bill to classify worsted cloths as woolens, pay higher duty. (p. 4300) (−)
4. Customs administration bill. Evarts amendment regarding importers' rights of appeal on decisions of Customs. (p. 4128) (+)
5. Revenue bill. Amendment to reduce duty on tin plate. (p. 4128) (+)
6. Revenue bill. Amendment to reduce duty on band and hoop iron. (p. 8393) (+)
7. Revenue bill. Plumb amendment to allow free import where domestic supply is controlled by a monopoly. (p. 9911) (+)
8. Customs administration bill. Vest amendment regarding importers' rights of appeal. (p. 4121) (+)
9. Customs administration bill. Evarts amendment regarding importers' rights of appeal. (p. 4121) (+)
10. Revenue bill. Amendment to reduce duty on band and hoop iron. (p. 8370) (+)
11. Revenue bill. Final vote. (p. 9943) (−)
12. Merchant marine subsidy bill. (p. 7188) (−)
13. Customs administration bill. Final vote. (p. 4132) (−)

Coefficient of Reproducibility of scale = .962. Where a Senator was absent but either paired or put his opinion on record, that expression of opinion was counted as a vote. Complete absences were counted neither as errors nor as item responses in calculating the Coefficient of Reproducibility.

At least a score of other roll-call votes, mostly on the revenue bill, scaled with these items and could have been included, but since they added no information (the voting pattern, except for absences, was the same as on one of the votes included), there was no point in adding them.

Note that although most of these votes were on tariff questions, a wider range is covered, including the maritime subsidy bill (an ocean mail bill showed exactly the same pattern and so was not included) and the naval appropriation bill. A number of other tariff votes might have been included, but in the interest of keeping to votes which would most seriously affect British manufacturers I decided to include votes only on measures which *The Times* of London listed as likely to injure British producers. The goods affected by these bills were linen, hoops and hoop iron, cutlery, tin plate, and woolens. See *The Times*, June 2, 1890 (11:2); June 23, 1890 (11:7); and September 29, 1890 (9:1).

V. Votes in Responsiveness to Britain scale for 1954 are listed below in the order in which they appear in the scale. Numbers refer to *Congressional Record*, Vol. 100, Washington, 1954.

1. International Sugar Agreement ratification. (p. 5662) (+)
2. Mutual Security authorization (p. 13052) (+)
3. Mutual Security authorization. Long amendment to reduce authorization by $1 billion. (p. 13038) (−)
4. Mutual Security authorization. Long amendment to reduce authorization by $500 million (p. 13039) (−)
5. Bricker amendment. George amendment providing that nontreaty agreements may not take effect as internal law unless implemented by Congressional action. (p. 2358) (−)
6. Bricker amendment. Final vote. (p. 2374) (−)
7. Bricker amendment. Ferguson amendment that any provision of an international agreement which conflicts with the Constitution shall not take effect. (p. 1740) (−)
8. Bricker amendment. Morse motion to recommit. (p. 2267) (+)
9. Atomic Energy Act. Lehman amendment to delete provision that the AEC give maximum effect to policies contained in international agreements made after enactment of the bill. Lehman said the provision implied that the United States would treat "less seriously" agreements (i.e., with Britain) previously entered into. (p. 11954) (+)
10. Bricker amendment. Knowland amendment to require the Senate to ratify treaties by roll-call vote. (p. 1782) (−)

Coefficient of Reproducibility = .952.

Although many of these votes are on the Bricker amendment, a wide range of other matters is also covered. The vote on the Lehman amendment is particularly related to policy toward Britain. There were no other foreign-affairs votes that would have scaled with these items, but there were five other votes that met the criteria set up in the main body of the article. One of these, however, was on reconsideration of the Universal Copyright Convention (p. 9133), which was of little interest to the British government but of great importance to American printers. A number of liberal and otherwise responsive Senators voted to reconsider this measure because of its effect on labor. The other four votes — one on Mutual Security appropriations (p. 14507), two on the Bricker amendment (pp. 1916, 2262), and one on extension of the Reciprocal Trade Act (p. 8886) — showed just too many errors (slightly over 10 per cent) to allow their inclusion, indicating that some other variable or variables affected voting behavior. One of the major values of scale analysis is just this — it enables us to identify and concentrate on those votes where the variable of interest (responsiveness) is of overwhelming importance.

The Senators located at the two extremes of responsiveness are largely those whom the "common-sense" observer would put near the same extremes from an independent knowledge of their opinions. The four highest-scoring Senators were "internationalist-liberals": Hayden, Hennings, Lehman, and Morse. At the bottom of the range were "isolationist-conservatives": Bricker, Butler (Nebraska), Frear, Malone, McCarthy, and Russell.

Index

For data see also Appendix B